Worldbridger

Juliet Carter

DEDICATION

For Malia
For all the children

CONTENTS

ACKNOWLEDGMENTS

Physical reality manifests through a complex pattern of interlocking waveforms. This book has evolved through an equivalent dynamic; the abundance of support, both practical and inspirational, creating ripples of good intent, concentric waves that collide and coalesce into matter. In offering our thanks for the support we have received we cannot separate 'Worldbridger' from 'The Template', the Template model of transcendence being the core message that 'Worldbridger' delivers.

The path of a visionary covers shaky ground as mysteries take shape from the mists of the future. It has been our challenge to present to others that which we have barely incorporated as part of our own reality and yet the visionary process requires that we maintain the integrity of the information without the censorship of our own limitations. Every letter, email and word of support has been an invaluable source of encouragement, especially when there have been those - some very close to us - who consider us as mad as hatters.

The uncompromising nature of the Template information has meant that for the core members of the Template family, allegiance has sometimes been exacting. The Template's mandate is to return Earth and Her people to the holistic space-time continuum. Its precept swims against the tides of mortality, claims that by anyone's standard are astonishing, and, for many, preposterous. At times it has certainly seemed so to all of us involved. And yet, encoded into the harmonic of the numinous intelligence that defines the Template model, is a resonance that envelops heart and mind. However, it is the phenomenon of the undeniable transformations in the lives of those that have experienced the reconnections that continues to elicit fidelity and passion from even the most cynical. We thank these bold individuals who have, against the currents of resistance, held their ground and continued to offer their support, love and friendship.

First and foremost, our thanks go to Jennifer and Nick. Their roles in the crystallization of 'Worldbridger' exceed those of editors. Apart from their exceptional skills in this department, in researching and cross-referencing the diversity of the Template range of information, they have drawn upon the deep wells of their life experience and are together conversant and accomplished in sacred geometry, astrology, psychology, esoteric teachings and the calendrical systems of the Maya. Their ability to fully 'grok' the Template has been invaluable. Seers in their own right, they are treasured as Template ambassadors and even more so as friends. Fortunately, they are inclined toward tolerance, patience and humour, qualities that are essential when editing the work of a dyslexic.

I must again acknowledge Jennifer, this time as part of the team that includes her husband Cosmos and his mother Teresa. Cosmos is the classic 'behind the scenes' contributor, often unacknowledged, yet always indispensable. For both he, Jennifer and Teresa, much has been surrendered and sacrificed in order to give the support that has required a great deal of their time.

Our thanks go to Teresa for her unconditional commitment to the endless laborious work on mail-outs, emails and the computerization of the editing process.

We are fortunate and thankful to have Margo in the USA who has attended to the wearisome details of administration for many years and, through thick and thin - mostly thin - held on to the dream.

Our heartfelt appreciation goes to the Template ambassadors. Their ability and commitment to holding Template ceremonies is vital. Our thanks to Claudie, Jennifer, Jeremy, Lynne, Nick and Rhian for their patience, understanding and unfailing faith in the Template.

Thank you, Tantra, for your unwavering alliance from the beginning and for the car, which, like yourself, just goes on giving.

A heartfelt thank you to Jacqueline for her support at a crucial time and her generous donation that helped to sustain us while we wrote this book. The recollection of our magical days spent together in Kapoho, weaving visions of the future, will be with us always.

There have been times when the altruism of others has been crucial to the sustaining of the Template and the creation of 'Worldbridger'. Our gratitude for their generosity goes to Anita, Cosmos, Beth, Gita Govinda, Jaqueline, Jennifer, Margo, Russell,

Suzy, and Teresa.

Further appreciation goes to Lawrence, Kent and Victoria, Gabriella, Joie, Dawn and Victor, Catherine, Agneta and Kira, Randy, Jan, Gordon and Mosen, Shawn and Michelle, Lindsey and Chris, Zak-Kai-Ran, Cynthia, Marsha, Jane and Bobby, Patricia, Suzanne, Dan, Mary and Dave, Mark, Janice, Sam and La Fleur, David, Greg, Richard and Denise, Tara Grace, Lois, Nina, Jade … and all those who graced the Template ceremonies.

You will notice that although my partner Jiva is credited as author, it was I who took pen to paper: a mere detail. To have simply acknowledged Jiva here as my 'inspiration' or 'unfailing support' would have been unjust in the light of his contribution. We have lived 'Worldbridger' together, and it has come as much from his heart and soul as it has from mine. In this, and in many ways, we are indivisible. Besides which, I am informed that I could get into a bit of trouble over the contents of this book and I feel it's only fair that Jiva takes some of the heat.

Juliet Carter
Bali, October 2007

PREFACE

Over the years that we have experienced the Template Ceremonies as they emerged we have come to know Juliet and Jiva Carter as unassuming, private people who have entered the public arena due to the necessity of the job they have pledged to undertake. The decision to write 'Worldbridger' was not made lightly. It became clear that a personal account of their journey of discovery was necessary to explain and contextualize the Template. The living of this story, and the telling of it, has required almost inconceivable resilience and courage. As editors, we have come to honour and respect the fierce integrity of the hard-won Hawk Medicine carried by Juliet Carter. This vision and focus have been essential to deliver the Template message.

In the spring of 2007, the sixth Template Ceremony took place in Glastonbury, England, signalling a milestone in the 'download' process to which Juliet and Jiva have been dedicated for nearly two decades and the beginning of the next phase heralded by the publication of this book.

In receiving and integrating the Template mandate the authors have been challenged to think the unthinkable and express the near-inexpressible. The Template model of transcendence is radical and unprecedented, but so are the times in which we live. Our planet is in crisis and Humanity is called to awaken from the collective amnesia of ages.

The apocalypse, a term usually synonymous with destruction, means, in fact, 'uncovering'. In this time of prophecy many mysteries, secrets and lies are now being exposed. Our history has been 'spun', falsified and scrambled by those who have ruled from the shadows, but the masks are starting to slip. As we approach the portal of 2012, disturbing revelations of an alien agenda on Earth are coming to light, with far-reaching implications for Humanity.

The choices we make at this fulcrum point are crucial. The Template's holonomic model of transcendence provides an alchemical system of integration that allows for the understanding, acceptance and transformation of Humanity's eons of suffering and betrayal. It is not intended for a spiritual elite, but for all Human beings of any age, race or creed who wonder what is happening to our planet and our people - who feel, however dimly, the stirring of the remembrance of their quintessential identity.

The Human Soul Covenant contains a holonomic symbiotic code in which the Human design is the sensory organ for planetary ascension as Earth is the sensory organ for Human ascension. The codes of the Template Ceremonies resurrect our ability to translate and utilize, through our physical bodies, the language of light - to achieve, literally, en-light-enment.

The shamanic initiations that were necessary to retrieve the codes which reactivate, through resonance, dormant genetic material within the original Human 'blueprint' were exacting. However, the alchemy of the Template ceremonies ensures that the instigation of individual and collective transmutation is accomplished safely, holistically and with grace. Such is the gift offered by those who have bridged the worlds.

As more and more people accelerate their personal frequency through the reconnection of bio-circuitry, the feedback we receive on the transformations in their perceptions and their lives confirms and reinforces our appreciation of the Template as an empowering model of transcendence which honours the Human as a sovereign, sentient entity.

The Template acknowledges the body as the pinnacle of the manifestation of our spiritual identity. As conscious conduits of light and life eternal we are the sacred enclosure for the sacred marriage of the Sun and the Earth. The core message that 'Worldbridger' delivers is that it is through the reinstatement of our electromagnetic integrity that we and our Earth will be re-embraced into the divine immortal continuum. We are not only worldbridgers - we are the bridge.

Jennifer Carmen

PROLOGUE

To my Mayan community I am a shaman king.

When I catch a glimpse of my eyes
reflected in the bowl of water brought to me each morning
to wet my face and hands, I see an imposter.
The fearless leader
who thrusts himself into the uncharted mystery of the skies
to journey for the information
that never slakes the thirst of his people —
that is not me.
He has power...real power.
He joins with me
when the animation of the vision-plant
is almost more than I can contain.
When it feels as though this ingested consciousness
will burst the seams of my self,
he makes a mockery of the pathetic confines of my identity.
I can hear him laugh,
see him shake his head with pity
before he casually annihilates my sense of self,
sweeping aside my point of conscious reference,
and, with a great blinding radiance,
replaces it with his own knowing.
When I am sure I will visibly shrink with terror
and betray my cowardly heart,
when I am convinced of my imminent failure,
he comes to me...he becomes me.

He is the Navigator.

The journey ahead is no challenge to him.
It is he that tears me from the shore of all I know,

PROLOGUE

to chart and divine the ocean of darkness
till we find entry through the spiralling tunnels of light.
Central to the existence of the tribe
into which I was born twenty-two years ago,
is the Sun.
The hub of all our considerations is the great golden orb of light
that brings the day,
that brings life itself,
the point of divine reference
that is factored into every decision.
We do not see sunrise as a certainty,
but a gift.

My stone throne is the portal through which
my ability to draw down knowledge of the Sun and the stars
and the mysteries of Hunab Ku, the Galactic Centre,
defines my political power.

My people are driven
to the acquisition of cosmic knowledge
from a simultaneously primal and complex instinctual need
that embraces every spectrum of the definition of their existence,
just as a bee must make honey.

Was it because we came from the skies?
Was it because we had some inherent knowing
stirring in the cerebral cortex, the temple of remembrance,
that, written in the empirical language of the stars,
was a code through which we, and the people of the future,
would understand the higher physics of creation,
and by so doing
track to a distant point in time
when we could re-tune the discordance
disturbing the harmony of the heavens?

Everything comes from the Sun.

WORLDBRIDGER

The Sun, epigenesist of creation,
pulsating ripples of primal data...
Who or what informs the Sun?
It is this question and its answer
that defines the worth of a Mayan shaman king.
It is this question that I held before me
as I took my place upon the throne of stone
on which my journey to the heart of the mystery,
to the heart of creation,
to the centre of the galaxy, to Hunab Ku,
began.
On this occasion it was an altogether different question
that was answered.
I was not to learn from whence came the source of life,
but the source of death.

My journey was to be taken in the light of day.
Attended by my advisor and the tribal council,
I spent the night in ritual and meditative preparation
that culminated in the ingestion of the vision-medicine
in the manner I had been trained to bear.
The break of dawn found me melding with the stone
on which I sat.

As the assimilated consciousness took hold,
familiar points of reference seemed juvenile and superficial.
Rather than hold on,
I breathed myself free
and surrendered to the transcendence.
Soon I would have no choice in the matter.
The momentum built in syncopated waves of rushing energy
rippling through my heart, body and mind.

I rode this wave through the various bardos of my ego.
The paling blue horizon was touched
with a hint of yellow that quickly turned to amber
and then to fiery and ever-deepening shades of orange.

PROLOGUE

The molten white gold core of this, the Earth's star lover,
rose above the horizon.
I kept my eyes open,
the effects of the plant-elixir allowing my pupils to remain dilated,
to swallow the ever-intensifying fields of light into my pineal.
My pineal absorbed and distributed this light intelligence
through my central nervous system into every cell
where my DNA code drank thirstily
of the activating life elixir.

As the full sentient presence of the orb left the horizon
and seared its geometry into my pineal,
I experienced an orgasmic rush within my conscious perception.
The resonant receptors
within my electromagnetic field of awareness
acknowledged and honoured this living sentient sphere
as the ultimate monadic form of Source Consciousness;
not only an emissary for the Benevolence of Creation
but a transubstantiation of its Prime Presence.

The sphere …
the form on which we live,
the eye with which we see,
the form that brings life, light and warmth,
the form that fills the heavens
and transmits day and night,
the Stellar Radiance that animates our divine blueprint,
the geometry that holds within its matrix
the dawn of the Universe,
the Primary Seed of Creation,
the beginning and the end
that begins and ends again…
and begins.

As my self moved forward to fully embrace this divine Presence,
I searched through the labyrinth of my own awareness
for total morphic resonance with this energetic body of light

and found to my shock
that I was not the resonant mandala
that this union required.
Scanning further, I found
that where there was belief in my mortality,
there was discrepancy between my self
and the measure of the Sun's nurture.

The infrastructure of the circuitry meridians
that would enmesh me
into the holography of the Sun's immortal embrace,
although present etherically,
was not activated or integrated
into the manifestation of my incarnate presence.
Because of this disconnection,
I, all of Humanity and its Mother planet
were tied into a cycle of degeneration
with the passing of each year, each turn,
as the Earth circles the Sun.

The Sun, the giver of life,
instead,
counts off these increments of 'time'
that define not only our journey to the grave,
but also the suffering and disease
that are the milestones of our mortal degeneration.

The Sun has become the hourglass of our death.

Moisture streamed from my eyes;
not only due to the sting of light,
but also to the swell of pain in my heart.

It was then that the Navigator slipped gently into my self.
This time he did not mock me,
but instead gave me knowledge of a future time
when light would be newly and fully comprehended

through the reconnection of electromagnetic circuitry,
and I would once more become the sacred crucible
that would hold this light code.
Every ray of sunlight would become the definition of endlessness,
sealing, within my Human matrix, life eternal.

This future Human race was from the distant past,
our original root race,
whose genetics were given
by many sentient sovereign star-beings
from many far-flung star systems,
in a time of peace that was sealed by the symbol of the bird.
The very existence and organic technology of this race
was based upon its ability to translate light,
and so maintain the integrity of its primordial soul-resonance
with the Sun's Consciousness, and
with the supreme organizing principle
of the Galactic Core, Hunab Ku.

The heat of the Sun warmed my skin
and sank into my muscles and bones.
As the fiery pulsations of light radiated from the star,
I harmonized my breath, my entire existence, with its rhythm,
which drew me into its furnace of cosmic comprehension.
When there was no differentiation
between the limits of my body-mind
and the radiant matrices of solar light,
I entered its labyrinth of lens-like crystalline chambers
and returned to that from which I came.
Quenched in this reunion,
I moved beyond the Sun
and found the container of my consciousness
floating above it in a silence that was absolute.
I drifted in a sea of potentiality.
There was neither the passage of time
nor the absence of its passage.

WORLDBRIDGER

A starry display before me,
I beheld the courtship of creation
between the Sun and Earth.
Liquid gold fractals of geometric energy
formed an unremitting and endless transmission
of light-code Intelligence
pulsing in orgasmic spherical waves from the Sun,
generating the photonic matrix of creation,
cascades of primal data rippling out to Earth's bio-spheric aura.
A responsive shiver of energy emanated from Earth,
an egg-like receptive embrace
which integrated the electric seed impulse of the Sun's attentions,
a womb from which all cosmological solar transmissions
were birthed into time and space.
This sacred communion
formed interference patterns of geometries
that nested seamlessly,
morphing, birthing ever more dense fields of manifestation.
The life mandate,
entering the bio-spheric membrane of Earth,
descended into the crystallization of matter,
translating light's subtle impulse as life forms
that walk, fly and swim,
clothed in fur, feather and skin...
trees, flowers and shimmering wings;
Earth interpreting the love from her Sun
as the living poetry of form and feeling,
colour and sound.
Into the ratio of this symbiotic relationship
was the peripheral but essential influence of other planets
through whose presence within this solar system
the symbiosis of evolution was coded.

It was then that I felt the discordance.

It reminded me of every negative response, thought or feeling
that I had ever experienced

within the scope of my life as a Human.
I felt from behind me in the shadows of space,
a transmission;
a contorted mutant influence.
Its invasive presence permeated the sacred communion
I had witnessed,
downgrading the resonant tantric harmonic
created by the two potencies of creation
transmitted and received by Earth and Sun
to that of a lesser frequency,
disrupting the sacred order of evolutionary embryogenesis,
and instead,
birthing a deformed foetal paradigm,
creating a field of diffracted frequency around the planet
in which all living units of circuitry collectively transmitted
the electromagnetic consensus of a mortal realm,
a cocoon of belief in which the dormant immortality of Humanity
never finds its wings,
but dies over and over again.
I understood that this imposter within our solar system
has brought death to Earth,
showing only one face,
keeping its dark side in the shadows.
Its ultra-magnetic field instigates
the dualistic infrastructure of conflict
that has, in the living memory of Humanity,
torn the world apart.
It stabilizes the genetic mutation
of the divine blueprint of all life forms on Earth,
perpetuating the disconnection of core circuitry that would allow
for the reciprocal communion of life with the Source of its Creation.
This congenital disconnection has spawned
a devastating spiritual chasm
to be filled with innumerable erroneous concepts of God,
creating a deeply rooted mycelium of deception
in the Human psyche.
The transmission of this synthetic and heartless presence

never misses a beat,
but transmits its mutant message
relentlessly and remorselessly in the disease, suffering and death,
it has catalysed
since it was placed within Earth's orbit.
It is the grand deceiver in the sky.
It is our moon.

I wait for the shock of this new knowledge,
only to find it is not truly new to me.
I am flooded instead with relief:
a relief that speaks and spreads
through every level of my being
as my sensorium factors in this realization.
I know nothing will be the same again.

I sense my journey drawing to a close and realize
that the Navigator has been speaking within my mind
in a language that was not from my time,
and yet I have understood it perfectly.
It was a language
he had gleaned from the future
from which he had been returning to me
time and again throughout my life.
He was another myself,
surfing time,
distilling knowledge,
creating a shamanic groove of recapitulation
through the illuminating pathway of a psychedelic continuum.
I feel the lies of time that have separated us, dissolve.
I realize…

I am the Navigator.

I am the worldbridger.

I am the invincible radiance of life eternal.

PROLOGUE

I feel the weightlessness of space replaced by cold hard stone.
Realizations crystallize.

We have been removed electromagnetically
from the holography of the divine continuum.

We are a solar race locked in a lunar asylum,
an immortal race locked in a mortal prison,
a stolen race on a stolen planet.

1

SACRED DEATH DANCE

THERE WAS NO ANGEL standing in a luminous pool of light to wake me at the dawn of that Hawaiian morning, no loving celestial presence to gently inform me of a forgotten mission for which I had, apparently, volunteered. Instead, I awoke from a dream to find, less than an inch from my nose, a .44 Magnum. An unnecessarily large and shiny gun, I thought, as I struggled to remember my role in this scenario. My mind became a hyper-data processing machine as I frantically searched for a past point of reference on which I could base my present behaviour in this exotic scene. After all, I had on some level expected this; I was soon to realize I had actually created it.

I did not yet understand that I had entered the sacred enclosure of an initiation that would transform the lives of myself and my family and would usher in a completely new model of existence, a model that would reach to the very infrastructure of our genetic makeup. I had, however, begun to itemize the many aspects of my life that were no longer under my control.

Without the tribal structure of enforced and planned initiatory experiences, gradually taking a child through an exponentially intensifying series of small ego deaths into the responsibility of a shamanic existence, I had instead collaborated unknowingly in the complete annihilation of my reality-tunnel in one fell swoop.

The gun that now aligned with my third eye was a fitting instrument for my initiation into the work that was soon to take over my life. In its economic, cold and deadly construct was the definitive tool of modern destruction perfectly suited to the mutant parasitic consciousness which, I was to learn, had invaded the very structure of the Human genetic code. More intimate than a bomb, yet sufficiently disassociated from the deed to avoid any corporeal contact, the gun allows just enough proximity to grant the user a near spectacle of the suffering and destruction it wreaks. A most cowardly invention: its smooth, flawlessly mirrored surface a perfect extension of the ruthless consciousness that was capable of annihilating, with one gentle squeeze, a masterpiece of divine design; the index finger casually beckoning life to cross the threshold into death. This was the consciousness which the initiation of that morning was preparing me to confront.

Right from the start there would be no holds barred. The Consciousness with which I would soon begin to collaborate had begun as it meant to continue. There would be no New Age axioms to lull me into thinking that all I needed was a positive attitude and the power of prayer. Both the tool and the manner of its use in this wakeup call echoed the reality that has Earth and its people in the grip of innumerable wars, a world in which genocide is relentlessly carried out, thousands of people die of starvation every hour, mothers sell their children into slavery, women are stoned to death for exposing more than their eyes and a petrochemical addiction overrides all other allegiances and agendas. The yellow brick road is riddled with land mines. A nuclear warhead is trained on the Land of Oz. No benevolent extra-terrestrial race is going to turn up in the playground and save us from the bullies.

Poised symmetrically above the firearm that pinned me to my bed were beady black eyes holding the expression of a gundog focused on and proud of its kill, eyes that told me their owner was savouring the moment and registering every nuance of my reaction, to be filed away and relished at his leisure. Everything extraneous that defined my existence ripped away in a moment: I entered the enclosure of initiation.

"Are you Juliet?" he asked.

"Yes." My answer reverberated in the emptied space that was my mind. The sacred death dance had begun.

20

He withdrew his weapon a few inches and I slowly came to a sitting position. A wave of nausea entered my stomach as pain clutched my heart. I tracked these feelings to their origin and found that they welled up from the inevitable loss of all that I held familiar, safe and comfortable. My head spinning, I began to breathe deeply and rhythmically, allowing each breath to bring me into my body, into the moment, accepting, without censorship, responsibility for what I had created. Through my breath I surrendered, surrendered to the pain, the fear, the moment. Releasing, releasing, releasing … shattered fragments of my former self scattered around the tiny wooden room. Each breath drew in points of reference that existed beyond the logic of the situation, bringing with them a quintessential core identity. These two selves - the domestic and the magical - battled to dominate my consciousness.

Wordlessly and at gun-point I was led out of the one-room annex to cover the ten feet to the back door of the main house which led into the kitchen. Before entering my home, I glanced over my shoulder at the shed that stood a couple of yards from the annex which held seventy pounds of premium Hawaiian marijuana. As I walked into the living room, I saw at once my partner in crime and love, Jiva, my other self, my beloved. He was handcuffed and surrounded by five armed men. A woman, also armed, moved towards me with a pair of cuffs in her hand and ordered,

"Hands behind your back!"

I locked into Jiva's eyes. In that moment my magical self

won the battle for heart, mind, body and soul and I would never again walk this Earth in the same way. My peripheral vision began to kaleidoscope around Jiva, creating between us a tunnel of transmission. His eyes were full of tears and it was with some surprise that I realized they were tears of bliss as he said to me,

"We've done it. We've finally done it." His meaning and my comprehension ignited instantly. Our identities which existed beyond the 'Jiva' and the 'Juliet' of this, our Earth drama, rose up to greet each other. What a liberation it was to experience consciously such a sense of wholeness. We had, as Jiva conveyed to me, finally created the shamanic portal of potential through which we would cross the threshold into a new model of existence; an existence that would, over time, through the reconnection of more and more vital circuits of electromagnetic Source Consciousness, gradually realize the full spectrum of our cosmic identities.

It was through Jiva's sublime and unswerving love, through his total recognition and acceptance that I was able to take this journey. It is only because of this love that I sit here today to share it with you. Since the sacred day that I met him, nothing in this dualistic fear-based reality has been that difficult. Beneath the struggle and the sacrifice, Jiva's devoted presence in my life has made all things possible, the formidable made not only bearable but always to some degree enjoyable… simply because, in this insane reality, we had found each other.

Scattered around our feet were two large suitcases filled with several thousand 'Thai sticks', six oil-making machines, three black bags full of 'shake leaves' and several smaller bags of 'wheelchair weed'. Everything swirled around us in a mandala of initiatory meaning and rendered our living room a crucible of ceremonial initiation. Nine of us gathered around the paraphernalia that formed the catalytic component within the alchemy of this occasion. In those few slow-motion moments out of time, Jiva and I paused in full recognition of the event and all the parts played within it. The Sun, barely risen, peered curiously through the wall of glass that constituted one side of the living room. In magnetizing this event we had chosen a house that was eighty percent glass on top of a well populated hill. We surveyed the faces around us and knew without doubt that these seven Drug Enforcement Agents were the ambassadors of the orthodox society, one of whose roles, as Joseph Campbell was to point out to us several days later, was to give the mystic his desire. We silently expressed our love and gratitude for their co-operation before they hustled us out of the door and into two of the six police cars waiting in the long driveway.

The driveway was a shared easement with our neighbours. Several days later we would learn that these neighbours had filed a petition to win control over the easement. For many months, to build a case in their favour, they had been videotaping our home and all that went on behind its glass walls. It was they who had alerted the authorities to tap our phones, filter our mail and generally keep us under constant surveillance. In the process of making hash oil we would grind the leaves of the marijuana plants to make a fine powder which we would then weigh in scales that hung in full view of the kitchen's huge glass picture window. We would then combine this powder with alcohol and extract the cannabis oil through a process of distillation. Because we were dealing with a powdered substance it appeared to the neighbours and anyone else who was watching that we were weighing large amounts of cocaine, hence the level of drug enforcement backup and the heavy artillery.

As we left the living room, my arrest and inevitable incarceration took on a more frightening tone. Jiva, my bridge to the transcendent, was in another car and out of sight. As I leaned against the backrest in the police car, the sharp edges of my handcuffs bit into my wrists and reminded me, as did the beefy and sweating officer sitting next to me, that this day and many others to follow would be spent away from my home and my family. The most painful aspect of this was that it would be some time before I would be reunited with my five-year-old son who, fortunately, was staying with friends. We slowly descended the spiraling mountain road to be greeted by the morning Sun which, having cleared the horizon, was busy warming the white Hawaiian sand for the beach lovers to enjoy another day in paradise.

From an early age I had trained myself to gaze directly into the white-gold core of the Sun and embrace its spherical geometry, breathing in its life-affirming Intelligence. Never more than on that morning would its illumination soothe my fears and bring me to the zero point of my identity, reinforcing the true definition of abundance. As the rays of Earth's star lover melted the bands of steel around my heart, I regained my equipoise within the centre of the storm that raged around me. Had I not already been familiar with the Consciousness with which I was undoubtedly collaborating, this time of termination would not have led so quickly to the rebirth that was already taking place. I felt this Presence in the radiance of the Sun. There was no blame, no guilt, no regret... love was my protection. Even so, I was afraid. I was in the grip of a very Human terror. It belonged, however, for the most part, to another aspect of me whose cries were fainter with every passing moment. We had both been thrown, she and I, into the fast and dangerous waters of perpetual renewal. I had crawled up the slippery bank; she was floating down-stream.

By the time we had reached the straight coast road, the Sun was dancing diamonds across the surface of the water and I, though still in shock, had begun to resonate with the rhythm of this initiation. My heartbeat slowed to the cadence of its cosmic coherence. The cavalcade of police cars was a rumbling hum beneath the surface of my awareness, a funeral procession that celebrated the welcome death of denial and the birth of a new and older innocence. What seemed, upon the surface, to be an absolute disempowerment was the exact opposite: its true architecture was a magnificent gateway offering passage from victimhood to creatorship. The way ahead was an avenue of opportunity, each passing palm tree a milestone in this journey of liberation that would ultimately lead to the transcendence of the life-death-rebirth cycle. We reached the darkness at the end of this tunnel of light; the holding cells for the Hawaii County Correctional Centre. Six cars decanted the seven government agents in our cosmic employ.

Having shed the first layer of my mortality, I felt lighter as I entered the ugly brick building and underwent the various humiliating procedures that would render me searched, numbered and deposited into my cell.

2

WHO DO YOU THINK YOU ARE

MY SMALL CELL WAS WINDOWLESS with a cement slab in one corner on which was a folded grey blanket. A rudimentary toilet graced another corner. The harsh austerity of this environment was designed to heighten the sense of deprivation and powerlessness of its occupant. It worked. Jiva's cell was in the same block around the corner and although I could not see him, I could hear him. Intermittently he would call out to me in a voice that was calm, confident and strong, to tell me that everything would turn out okay and that I must trust in and celebrate this experience. I conjured up his face from that morning, remembering the ecstasy in which he had been enveloped and had transmitted to me. His words, for the most part, held me in the embrace of the initiatory energy that had permeated our experience thus far.

For the eighty hours allotted to a prisoner in a holding cell prior to being officially charged, several of the officers who had participated in our arrest did their utmost to derange my equanimity and erode my reason. It was their job and they loved it. They were disappointed to have caught two marijuana minnows in their net instead of the huge cocaine sharks they had patiently looked forward to entrapping. No doubt they had invested a considerable amount of time and funding to the months of covert surveillance and needed to justify this expenditure to their superiors. There were two main officers involved in my interrogation; we would learn later that the Japanese man in the black leather jacket and 'shades' was the head agent and his much nastier companion was an ex-grower who had sold out to the other side. During my interrogations both of these men would put much stress upon the fact that I was being charged with far more than marijuana and I was assured, time and time again, that I was looking at three Class A convictions that carried twenty-five years each and that I would do at least twenty-five years behind bars.

My mother had died of breast cancer seven months earlier. As a qualified nurse I had cared for her at home. She did not spend one day in hospital and she passed from this life in my arms. Rousing briefly from her coma to meet my eyes for the last time she whispered, 'Beautiful child', and slipped away. The cancer had metastasized into her bones and her brain and spine were riddled with tumours. It was an incredibly painful form of cancer and she was prescribed various heavy pain-killers derived from morphine and heroin. The unused remnants of this medication were still in my bathroom cabinet, in their properly marked child-proof prescription bottles. These were not only listed on my charge sheet but were also included in a front-page newspaper article that listed the 'drugs' found at our home. No mention was made of the prescription bottles or that they had indeed been traced to the legitimate dispensary.

During my many interrogations I would be told again and again that the presence of these drugs would make things go very badly for me; that if I were to co-operate with the DEA some charges would be dropped, other steps would be taken to lessen the charges against me and there would be fewer years that I would spend away from my son. They were looking for information that would lead to further arrests. I knew of many other growers and distributors of marijuana. After all, Hawaii's economy was hugely bolstered by this booming island industry. I said nothing except to ask for a phone call and a lawyer. I had watched enough TV to understand the drill.

The only information I gave them was that I was a vegetarian and yet every meal brought to me was meat with vegetables swimming in its gravy. I ate nothing for the eighty hours of my stay in the holding cells. Neither did I get much sleep, as every couple of hours throughout the night the sliding bars of my cell door would clang violently open and bright lights come on, as another hour or so of intimidation and threats would begin. With no food and little sleep my already altered state was amplified. I passed through many layers of fear and simultaneously experienced an undiluted ecstasy that had no rational foundation under the circumstances. Each passing hour strengthened my conviction that this event was unfolding on many levels. I knew that this expanded sense of reality was not merely a knee-jerk reaction to assist me in dealing with my predicament, a biological overdrive that would disappear with the dissipation of the intense adrenalin coursing through my veins. This was another self that had lain dormant, to be awakened by a combination code that would appeal to the sophistication of a contemporary aboriginal mind. Having no sentimental regard for my comfort zones, it had been drawn out of the hypnosis of my past conditioning and was here to remind me how to bridge the worlds.

The friction of the bliss and fear I was experiencing simultaneously was creating a portal into the moment in which I felt exquisitely present - for it was only in the moment that I could harvest the alchemical component for the transmutation of the poisons of my predicament. When my breath would bring me to the epicentre of my awareness, the sound and fury swirling around me seemed driven by some clockwork mockery. As I went deeper into the alternate reality of my situation, the strained and surreal faces which woke me from sleep seemed as masks that could hardly be kept from slipping. I know that the transformation of my perception was affecting the levels of animation my interrogators were able to sustain and they were running out of threatening scenarios to throw at me. It became obvious that they could not fathom the source of my equipoise and although at first this simply drove them to ramp up their endeavours to break my composure, they eventually gave up on gaining any information at all.

In the silent intervals between inquisitions I began to understand the extent to which I had arranged this drama and the far-reaching benefits it offered. In our society there is no conscious structure of deep initiation carried out by Elders. We must instead create our own. In a tribal community a youth displaying signs of shamanic abilities might be taken one moonless night into the heart of the jungle, buried up to his neck and left to face his fears. Every swaying shadow, every creaking branch might be the beast that will devour him. He is trapped: the fight-or-flight impulse that galvanizes every muscle of his body is prohibited. And so, denying, at least on the physical level, his ability to respond to the manifestation of his fear, he is driven deep within the hidden recesses of his identity to discover alternative keys to his liberation, tapping into the wellspring of courage and strength in which he must now abide, not only for that one night, but within every breath. This is the non-negotiable pact he makes with the forces of creation; everything else is fickle, mutable. All sense of self which is reliant upon the ordering of the world to meet his extraneous needs is the mutant self-created by those needs. He learns to trust, not because he is 'safe', but because he has remembered his invincible self that exists beyond the mortal lie.

It was the second night, as a rare silence descended on our cell block and my windowless cell was cave-dark, that I suppressed a need to call out to Jiva, who I knew had found some valuable sleep. Instead, I entered the stillness and became my breath, relaxing my awareness into the night. Dismantling any sense of differentiation between myself and the promise of possibilities that gathered around me, I was not alone.

I had no formal training for this kind of meditation, but when I was almost thirteen my idea of entertainment was to sit perfectly still and silent in our garden with my right hand extended and filled with bird-seed. I would do this for hours on end and did, in fact, lure sparrows to eat from my hand. Eventually my mother had me see a child psychiatrist. He was not able to find anything 'wrong' with me; however, I stopped this activity, realizing it was somehow inappropriate and worried those I loved.

That night, as I found my way down that familiar path to stillness, my cell became the blank rune of potential. Within its confines were the end and the beginning, pregnant and empty, filled with the power of the unknown. I relinquished the final residue of control and merged with a Consciousness that was to become, in the years ahead, Jiva's and my constant companion.

"Now who do you think you are?" it asked of me, lovingly, yet sternly. I was not unduly surprised by this communication, as it seemed I had waited all my life for this Presence to finally speak.

The answer to the question it presented to me rushed through my body and into my awareness. I felt my identity expand beyond the limits set in place by the confines of this life and all its memories: this incarnation was a fractal of a much more universal identity that was not constrained by the petty and unholy laws that brought me to this cell and yet there was a supreme perfection in my incarceration. I had individualized from the quantum field of Source Consciousness to be fully present in this moment, to unify, to remember the divine embrace from which I had emerged to incarnate as its autonomous, sentient instrument. To find such freedom in this prison was beyond any common measure of irony. The cement and steel prison in which I found myself was feeble in comparison to the fortress of belief and perception from which I was, moment by moment, being liberated.

"Remain in total trust and you shall pass into a state of grace," I was assured by the soundless voice. Another layer of mortality shed, I fell into a blissful sleep from a place of inexplicable joy.

I awoke a few hours later in a state of extreme disorientation and could sense Jiva awake also. I called out to him softly in case I was wrong. He was awake and had been marvelling at the bizarreness of the dichotomy we inhabited. He had been worried about me and had been surrounding me with light and filling my cell with Sanskrit chants that held ancient sound vibrations designed to dismantle delusion.

Jiva was born in the early 1950s and grew up in Texas. His family was a wild mixture of Cajuns and hard-shell Baptists. His childhood desire was to become a minister of the church. It was not long before he realized the deep and dangerous deceptions inherent in the religions that shaped, modified and controlled the spiritual lives of his family and community. The deep-seated prejudice that was a way of life in the American south was against the grain of his elemental perception. Something not quite formed awakened at the crux of his blossoming youth and he drew back more and more from the traditional rites of manhood that were exacted from him by his father. Eventually he could no longer accompany him on the 'fishin' n' huntin' bonding expeditions and when his pet rooster was served up on the dinner table, Jiva surveyed his family, their mouths filled with the murdered flesh of his friend, and an irrevocable realization settled into the matrix of his being, awakening further the sensitivities of his immortal self.

His father, like my own, had served in the Second World War; his father a tank commander, mine a bombardier. 'Generation gap' comes nowhere close to describing the chasm of discrepancy between the children of the sixties and their parents. However, Jiva was blessed with a mother who, although scarred by her own deep emotional wounds and the subservience created by the brutally patriarchal environment of her immediate and extended family and community, recognized in her son a potential to bring forth into this world his quintessential divine identity. Even when it was very difficult to do so she shielded him from the cruel and violent influences to which he was frequently exposed, not by coddling him but by nurturing his own inherent discernment. Many years later she was to become the Reverend Billy of the Aquarian Foundation in Portland, Oregon.

Rather than growing into a bitter and angry man who would repeat the dysfunctional patterns of his male role models, instead Jiva chose, like many of his generation of fatherless young men, to surrender his formative juvenile years to an alternative eastern philosophy. The non-negotiable dissonance between his world view and the American dream drove him to renounce his inherited culture in favour of the discipline and austerity of the Krishna movement. This spiritual sect was comparatively new to the United States and Jiva was among its first initiates. He was vastly fortunate to be numbered among those who enjoyed a close relationship with the founder of the American branch of this spiritual body, his eminence Bhaktivedanta Swami Prabhupada. Jiva spent most of his time in the movement in private tutelage with Prabhupada who taught him to play the murdunga, a double-headed clay-bodied drum. He spent many, many hours with Prabhupada absorbed in debate and the intricacies of ancient Hindu philosophies. Spending two years in India, he learned Ayurvedic massage and on his return to Dallas, Texas, as a self-contained young man, he expanded his healing arts through the teachings of another man he was to grow to greatly respect. This was Virgil Crane, from whom he learned Alphabiotics, a neurological alignment through physical manipulation that fires synapses which have been disconnected due to emotional, physical and chemical trauma. During this time under Virgil's tutelage Jiva witnessed a paraplegic treated using this method begin to walk within six months. The years were filled with new knowledge as he fervently studied the Bhagavad Gita and the Vedas - and of course he learned the Sanskrit chants he was to teach me that night in our prison cells.

We spent the rest of the night filling the air with sacred and ancient sound vibrations that not only lifted our spirits but transformed the space around us and, we were soon to discover, the consciousness of our jailors. I was enthralled by the effect of these words and their lilting familiar melodies. The guards would yell at us to be quiet: we would stop for a few minutes and then begin again. Eventually they gave up and we could sense that not only were they enjoying the chanting, but it was activating something forgotten deep within them.

The next day their treatment of us had changed remarkably. Due to lack of food I had an excruciating headache and asked one of the jailors for some aspirin. He said it was against the law to give prisoners any form of medication without signed permission from a doctor. A few minutes later he appeared with two pain killers and a can of Coca-Cola. He had stolen the drink from his boss and asked me not to tell anyone. He returned several minutes later to remove the incriminating can and asked with real concern if I was feeling better. Sugar, caffeine and paracetamol were racing round my bloodstream - I was feeling better.

Miraculously, our bail of fifty thousand dollars each was being posted by a couple who lived close by but who we barely knew. They were putting up their home as collateral, a process which was to take some time. We would wait out this time at the main prison in Hilo on the other side of the island.

On the night of our transfer we were taken from our cells to a waiting area to be restrained for the journey. I watched, waiting for my turn, as Jiva was being fitted with his leg restraints. For some reason three officers were involved in this chore and they were all joking around with him. As one attached the high-density plastic leg braces to his ankles they commented laughingly that he might be a secret martial artist who would at any moment pull some fancy footwork and knock them all out. Playing along, Jiva's retort was that he would simply melt the braces with his chi. In that second the brace fell from his ankles to the floor. No one was more surprised than Jiva, but he immediately covered his shock with a casual shrug of his shoulders as if to say, 'I did warn you!' Any attempt on my part to describe the myriad of emotions that passed across the faces of the three security officers would fall short of the reality. Suffice to say that neither Jiva nor I were restrained that night. To this day we can only imagine the magic involved in that event. Not before nor since has Jiva ever melted anything with his chi!

We were not familiar with the two officers who transported us that night, as they were from the Hilo Correctional Centre to which we were on our way. Their massive 'moke' forms filled the windscreen and they took some pleasure in taunting us and doing their best to fill us with fear on our journey to what they assured us was 'a real bad place'; a place we deserved to be, as we were 'hippie dopers' responsible for the degeneration of the youth of Hawaii. Jiva's fearless and cocky response was that the government they worked for was the real criminal factor responsible for the importation of truly detrimental 'drugs', the undermining of the Hawaiian way of life and the distressing of the tradition of Ohana (family), driving the children to the streets, away from the art of their ancestral lineage and into the sprawling concrete malls. It was their employer that had sanctioned the buying up of sacred Hawaiian land for the building of the luxury hotels which barred the public from enjoying its beaches. He finished by accusing them of growing the herb with which we were involved in their own backyards. There was no argument and after a long ponderous silence, the rest of the journey was spent in mutually respectful conversation. In the back seat, Jiva and I enjoyed our closeness, soaking it up, knowing it would soon end.

We parted company on our arrival at the prison and after hours of humiliating procedures collectively termed 'prisoner processing' I was delivered to my cell at around 3am. Exhausted, I climbed to the top of the bunk that almost filled the tiny cell, noticing a sleeping figure on the lower bunk, and quickly fell asleep.

3

THE MYSTIC'S DESIRE

I AWOKE THE NEXT MORNING to the sound of running water as the Sun reached through the bars of the one small window in the wall adjacent to my top bunk. Peering over the edge of the mattress I saw a thick-set, muscular, dark-haired woman washing her face at a tiny sink attached to the wall. She was naked and tattooed on her rear was a large black gun.

"Oh great!" I thought; from this angle it appeared that I had a formidable and, if her tattoo was anything to go by, aggressive cell mate with whom to pass the long days. The woman felt my gaze on her and slowly turned to face me. She was younger than I first thought, and her face broke into a huge innocent smile as she welcomed me to her cell. She had remained asleep through my arrival in the night and was surprised and delighted to have a cell mate.

I learned from her that Hawaii County Correctional Centre was a male facility and that the cell we were in, and one other, were the only ones to house females before they were transported to the women's prison on the island of Oahu. She informed me that all the jailors were male, that one of them would soon be coming to 'see' her and not to worry or take any notice of him. In a couple of hours, he arrived. Sitting on her bunk, he shared a cigarette and chatted with her: I stayed still and quiet on the top bunk. Nora seemed to be enjoying his company and was by no means non-consensual to the sex in which they eventually engaged. After he left, Nora told me this was a daily occurrence. The jailor had promised to speed up her release and was planning to leave his wife for her.

"He has a huge fishing boat," she told me, wide-eyed with excitement. I congratulated her with as much sincerity as I could muster.

That morning, staring longingly at the bright Hawaiian sunshine that bathed the exercise court, it was impossible for me to deny the desperation and futility that permeated the prison. In the holding cells on the other side of the island I had only my own predicament to consider, but here I was faced with the suffering not only of my cell mate, but all the souls in the prison. This consideration was not separate from the overall significance of my initiation. It was as relevant to the nature of the work to which Jiva and I were to dedicate ourselves as the Magnum that had begun this adventure only a few days ago.

Later that afternoon I was taken from my cell and escorted to an office where I would meet with the bail bondsman to sign some papers. It was an incredible relief to leave my cell just for the short time it took to complete this task. Though my conversation with the bondsman was mundane, I relished every moment, especially as the practicalities we discussed were to lead to my release. I asked how long it would take to process the securing of bail: at least three more days; in fact, it was five.

On returning to my cell I was taken through the male indoor recreation room in which inmates were watching TV and playing board games. All eyes turned to me as I passed through their world. I had expected some jeering and withering looks but was surprised by their respectful attention. Some nodded their heads slightly in greeting. Of course, we have all seen movies and documentaries of prison life, but to be there in the midst of a room full of grown men whose liberty has been denied to them, who no longer own their lives, was heart-wrenching. Although the few days of my incarceration paled in comparison to the years many of these men were facing behind bars, their desolation was not beyond the range of my life experience. This initiation was not my first and I had long realized that treasures and joys often come by way of sorrow.

When I had awoken to the gun in my face, there was a part of me that was out of its reach and the range of power wielded by the man that held it; the part that was, and always had been, in this world but not of it. Our inability to acquiesce to the pathological mass obedience that oils the mechanism of the automated world order led to the self-imposed exclusion of many of my generation. In the 1960s and '70s the disassociation of the youth from the status quo of the previous generation was a phenomenon more pronounced due to the acceleration of dataflow present in the stream of photonic light Intelligence that had entered our solar system. It was the dawning of the Age of Aquarius, the galactic activation beam of this particular age of Ahau.

I was to learn that this accelerated frequency ray was stimulating and activating the frontal lobes of the Human brain, the cerebral cortex, which Jiva and I would come to identify as the temple of remembrance. This brain centre is specifically designed to receive and translate Source Intelligence or God-realization. The resulting bio-informational signals nurture the Human entity's quintessential identity as an instrument of Source Consciousness whose highest purpose is to function as a conduit of universal coherence…as an instrument of light and love. It is the cerebral cortex that holds the resonant field of memory that defines the true immortal identity of the original Human prior to genetic modification.

This photon beam is congruent with the original design of our evolutionary symbiotic relationship with light, with each other, our Earth and every other planet within the original design of the solar system. However, genetically, we are not on course with this transmission. We are not able to translate the full spectrum of evolutionary intelligence present in light, due to the disconnection of vital circuitry that has led to the atrophy of our endocrine systems. Genetic modification and the disturbance of the evolutionary ratios of planetary influence in our solar system have scrambled our evolutionary progress and have placed us in a dimension beyond the full spectrum of its potency. There is no doubt, however, that we have been and are under its considerable influence and, as we reach the maximum intensity of these core emissions in 2012 - if we have managed to resurrect our abilities to translate and utilize light - it is possible that we will collectively form a global resonant platform on which to retrieve and rebuild a future in resonance with the original divine Human blueprint.

An imploding cycle of energy increase quickened the intensity of light within the solar system in the '60s and '70s inspiring many to explore meditation, yoga, chanting, vegetarianism and experimentation with mind-expanding substances that triggered a disassociation from the predominating ideology of prejudice and separation, as their altered brain chemistry informed them that unity was the superlative Human state. Had they been able to fully integrate and synthesize this new frequency through electromagnetic circuitry, they would have crystallized its potency into manifestation within the overall culture as a shared perception. The stimulation of the cerebral cortex had, however, to some degree, diminished the over-activity of the reptilian brain and thus lessened the chronic state of survival stress that currently passes as normal Human existence. This altered chemistry intensified the manufacture of endorphins, opening portals of perception that activated a profound appreciation of the perfection of creation and stimulated a renewed yearning for communion with the natural world. The guilt and shame that was associated with the doctrine of original sin was rejected as a dawning sexual freedom celebrated the tantric secrets of the body.

We did not know then that we were transducing a photonic beam of Galactic Consciousness whose peripheral dataflow had entered our neighbourhood. This ray of Source Consciousness was awakening the dormant and divine immortal Human identity, stressing the seams of the mortal paradigm - but this stream of light was not yet able to overcome the disturbance and destabilization of the symbiotic evolutionary relationship that was encoded into the genesis of our solar system.

We did not understand that, although active resistance against prejudice would win us a degree of cultural tolerance, direct action would eventually tarnish our intention and that by fighting for freedom, we would embody the struggle within the dualistic consciousness we set out to overcome. Neither did we understand the deep roots of the cancerous tumour that gripped our planet, or the origin of the consciousness that built the nuclear weapons which are now trained on many cities on this, our Earth.

What lasting impact did this era have upon our conscious evolution? Without a resonant global infrastructure of shared perception there was no fertile field in which to sow the seeds of this newly perceived paradigm, but the morphogenetic field was forever altered: the way was prepared for a progressive disassociation from the fear-based paradigm and an inevitable recalibration in resonance with the divine immortal identity which is buried in the original Human blueprint. The predominant fear-based dualistic mechanism continued to direct our de-volution, for enlightenment is not simply a conceptual acquisition: it is a literal ability to become resonant with the evolutionary propensities of the geometries of light. We did not have the electromagnetic bio-circuitry to sustain, contain or make incarnate the implications of our transformational realizations. Having attempted to sever our associations with consensus reality, we returned from our journeys into bliss to a discordant world which we now perceived in shades of grey.

At the age of fourteen I had been unable to interact socially and found it very difficult to speak or even to leave the house. My mother once again put me under the care of a child psychologist who was unable to identify or honour the expansion of awareness that was incubating in the sacred enclosure of my inner sanctum. A year later my older brother, who was a student at the London School of Economics, took my mother on a tour of the beautiful Sussex countryside of England where we lived, having first given her some 'window-pane', a particularly strong and clean form of LSD. Life at home changed dramatically. My mother and brother would stay up late smoking joints, playing poker and listening to Bob Dylan and Leonard Cohen. This was an environment into which I could begin to relax, and I was soon initiated into the psychedelic experience. The confluence of dimensional perceptions and heightened sensitivities that I experienced supported my suspicions that things were not as they seemed.

Unfortunately, or fortunately, when I was almost sixteen, my mother and brother moved to California while I stayed on in Brighton to continue my studies at Davis' College of English Literature and at Sussex Art College. Just before my exams I dropped out. I felt I was not learning what I needed to know, and I followed my family to California. It was the early '70s and California was the epicentre of experimentation with consciousness and the myriad of alternative lifestyles to which it led. Even there, in the easy freedom of Sun-filled days, I felt I had fallen by mistake to Earth, drifting in and out of other people's lives, a stranger on a crash course, gathering some pretty amazing data as I wandered into some outrageous situations I will not go into now…that's a different book!

It was, I guess, time for another aspect of my 'street' education and events conspired to bring me back to England. I had lost touch with friends and had no family to turn to. I cannot entirely explain to you the painful disassociation I felt at that time: I suspect many of you will know it anyway. It drove me from the warm comfort of society and I spent the next four years living in derelict buildings around London and Brighton, spending most of my dole money on amphetamines and came to know the depths of addiction as I reached for the bliss that was my birth right. I walked the streets with the homeless and knew what it was to be desolate, hungry and cold. I loitered so close to the edge that on one occasion I stepped beyond it. I simply did not want to be here and made the choice to shuffle off this mortal coil, not yet realizing that this was impossible - the membrane of frequency control that encases the Earth would not allow any of its prisoners to escape the recycling of its slave race. Besides, although I didn't know it then, I had volunteered to infiltrate this dualistic, fear-based mutant paradigm and to infest its programs with a virus of holistic consciousness.

Instead of finding myself on the greener grass of the 'other side', I found myself corralled in the glass chamber of a psychiatric observation ward. Along with a number of other social casualties I was fully aware that my every move was being evaluated against some mysterious check-list of normality. I befriended one woman in particular, heavily tattooed and dressed in the leathers of a biker, her face swollen and bruised. She tried valiantly to belie the suffering in her eyes by smiling manically, hoping, as we all did, to convey a casually nonchalant air of sanity. By what measure did our observers evaluate that, in this glass bowl…this cuckoo's nest?

Much of my life had conspired to reveal to me the superficial nature of orthodox society but without providing an alternative. I was dying to the reality and yet could find no place in which to be reborn. What treasures did I find in this 'in-between' world? Many years later, when I read the words of Kahlil Gibran, 'Pain shatters the shell around our understanding', I understood. I treasured those days spent beyond the pale; the freedom to give up entirely, to quit the confines of acceptable behaviour, no pretence of adhering to the mediocre and compulsive obedience of 'society'. I recognized in the faces of my fellow inmates those who had grown weary of the fodder fed to them by the lords and masters of this reality, those searching for the quiet revolution that springs from internal evolution, for the redefinition of self that breaks the confines of socio-political and religious suppression.

Before my release I was to be interviewed by my case officer, Dr. Patel. Predictably, his first question was,

"Why did you take the pills?" Convinced that I was one of the sanest people he would ever meet, I looked deeply into his eyes and told him the truth;

"I wanted to get away from it all." This was not a viable answer to one in his profession, but something in his Hindu understanding of this world of Maya found resonance with my desire to escape what I perceived to be the true insanity. Between us, several minutes of transmission masqueraded as silence. He asked me no more questions, signed my release form and advised me that should I need a break in the future I should try Spain. I left Dr. Patel's office at the next stage of my metamorphosis. He had, wordlessly, without judgment, illuminated the stupidity and futility of my attempt at suicide. I decided to conform…to a degree.

Within that year, at the age of twenty-two, I entered the Wolfson School of Nursing in Westminster, London. I was one of thirty students in my class. It was a particularly disciplined and gruelling training program and no more than one third of the class usually survived its rigors. I was deemed to be one that would drop out quickly. Two years later I was awarded a State Enrolled Nurses license and began to work for the Department of National Health.

Westminster Hospital was strict in the Victorian sense of the word - skirts below the knees, no jewellery, no nail varnish, no makeup, no excuses. For a spaced-out hippie this discipline was so foreign it was in a surreal way an all-encompassing meditation whose hyper-structured rhythm took over my life and my mind. It was a challenge and I threw myself into it, cycling seven miles through London to be on the hospital floor by 7am. This was a whole new stage on which to observe the suffering and strengths of Humanity. At the Westminster Accident and Emergency Unit I observed the fragility of the Human body and would learn to detest motorbikes. At least once a day a young man would be brought in and then be taken away in a plastic bag. I observed, up-close, lungs caked in nicotine and legs amputated with electric saws. There was something surreal about finding myself in a windowless blood-splattered chamber at 7am, to spend eight hours within the sterile white world of bleeping machines, strip-lighting and the stainless-steel instruments of life and death. In the geriatric wards of St. Stephen's, I witnessed the degeneration of the sacred Human body-temple into the heart-breaking and frightening uselessness of old age and lonely death; that journey which is, in our culture, traditionally hidden from our refined sensibilities. At Great Ormond Street Children's Hospital, I comforted a young mother who's first born two-year-old son had an inoperable brain tumour and only days to live. An understanding of the Human condition and the compassion needed to deal with it was learned as much in those hospitals as it was on the streets. I have left out far more than I have shared.

For some of us, college is not an appropriate learning institution. For us, knowledge is to be gathered in a blood-spattered windowless chamber, in the unsharable silence of depression, in the dole queues, the wastelands of urban decay, the forests of fallen trees, on the banks of polluted rivers... and in prison, a place I had always known I would experience, not to stay, but to sample, that I might expand my compassion for Humanity and see even more clearly the futility of any shallow dream of happiness in this dualistic fear-based dimension, in this age of Kali.

This prison experience in which I was now immersed was only the beginning of a series of initiations of a specific flavour and intensity that were to prepare me and Jiva to understand that the de-evolution of Humanity went far deeper than socio-political decay, an understanding that included the knowledge of the modification of Human DNA and the resultant psycho-social, religious, chemical and electromagnetic manipulation of Human consciousness. There was no Human being in that prison who was there for any reason other than because of the modification of their genetic codes.

On the day of my release I was greeted at the gates by our neighbours who had posted our considerable bail and was driven home. I held close to my heart the light I had distilled from the darkness.

It was early evening and still light when I was delivered to my doorstep. As I opened the front door I was greeted by a scene of destruction: every drawer and closet were emptied; one cabinet door lay smashed beyond repair. Empty beer cans were littered around, accompanied by saucers from the kitchen overflowing with cigarette butts. Photographs of our family and other more intimate ones were strategically placed around the house. Instinctively, I knew some were missing. I found our camera and photographed the scene. Falling exhausted onto the living room sofa I reached for the remote control and, out of habit, turned on the TV. Joseph Campbell's wise countenance filled the frame as he spoke to me:

"The role of orthodox society is to give the mystic his desire."

4

OPPORTUNITY DISGUISED AS LOSS

I SPENT THE NEXT FIVE DAYS cleaning up the 'party' residue left by the members of the Drug Enforcement Agency and waited for Jiva's release. When he returned home we celebrated quietly, without fanfare, the dismantling of our former lives and the anticipation of what the future held. The geometry of synchronicity that had revealed itself as the true infrastructure of our initiation was still strong within us and we no longer saw the events of our lives as accidents of time and random congruence. We saw clearly that whatever lay ahead was to be significant and would reach to the far horizon of our purpose on Earth. We had no idea what this mission was. We only knew we had volunteered for it. There was, however, the shadow of the not insubstantial legal ramifications hanging over us; after all, we were 'dangerous criminals'.

A month or so later after our release, Nick, the jailor who had given me the Coca-Cola, called us and told us that he and his friend had resigned from their prison jobs. He said they felt strongly that we should never have been arrested or imprisoned and they could no longer work for a system they now felt was itself criminal.

Jiva assured me that the worst was over - and perhaps it was, but more likely it never really would be. Rather it was that we were to expand our thresholds of understanding and endurance and were able more swiftly to identify and integrate opportunity disguised as loss, to embrace the shockwaves of our initiations, careful not to modify our behaviour to conformity and reconcile ourselves to injustice, nor to allow our spirits to be beaten into submission to a paradigm whose mutant design has been arranged to do just that. We learned to transmute their apparent poisons into the mother's milk of our own conscious resurrection, honoring the divine plan that has brought us to this place in time, celebrating this incarnation; strengthening our trust in each moment... becoming the power of our presence.

In order to collaborate with the Consciousness introduced to us through our initiation it was essential that we unify with it, become it. This embodiment would require that we restore and fortify a resonant field of awareness that could contain it and throw off the discordance that would bar it from our consciousness. We needed healing.

We were to discover that to recalibrate the heart-body-mind

system with the frequencies of creation whose prime integrity will deliver you beyond the illusion of duality, you must embody them. We were not being called to take on a prefabricated system of belief, as this soon becomes an intellectual mimicking, an adopted philosophy, springing not from the heart but the mind. What was desired was an autonomous translation of the undiluted energetic nature of Source Consciousness before it is filtered and distilled through time and history, interpreted through hearts and minds themselves in need of restoration; not someone else's faith, structured by opinions and assurances built on foundations undermined by the modification of our DNA and by the imposition of genes alien to our symbiotic evolutionary relationship to light. What was required was an alchemical form of transformation, something that would honour and influence all levels of our sentient presence in equal measure, simultaneously; a coded event to liberate the pre-destined divine immortal identity waiting patiently beneath the dross of the mutant mortal self; an initiation distilled down to its essential form, free of the constrictions and impurities of 'suffering' that plague the dualistic realms; something easy, safe, aesthetic…beyond shame, guilt and repentance; something time saving, designed for a seed race of worldbridgers who have been inserted into this time zone in order to receive, stabilize and transmit the frequencies of creation that will burst the seams of the fear-based paradigm in which they have awakened; a solution spiraling above the problem, something not to be endured, but celebrated.

It would be a couple of years before we came to realize that the alchemical process we envisioned was ceremony. However, we were soon to be introduced to the infrastructure of its workings upon which we would later expand.

On our release we were contacted by family members and friends who were understandably concerned. We were offered fake identity papers and even a boat ride to the mainland by someone who provided this service for those in similar situations. We were also offered a great deal of sympathy. We did our best to assure everyone that this 'bust' was a meaningful gift. Some understood; most did not.

The transformative wheels and cogs were churning through the many visible and invisible energy systems of which we are comprised, stirring and unhinging memories, causing the necessary elemental disruption that comes before growth and realignment. It was me more than Jiva who suffered this process as I found myself in a chaos of conflicting emotions, struggling to reconcile the present with the past. My family needed me to stand firm and strong. I knew that only if I could hold fast to the self that had emerged in the darkness of my cell could I face without fear that looming beast, the trial.

The Juliet who had dragged her precious burden of pain through all the years was not going to meekly lay it down without a fight. And yet, there was no better time for this than now - and now it was to be. I simply had to find the path to it; the steps, the form of it, the stage on which to assign the parts and play this out. The sensitivity that was in my makeup, in the stars that imbued my matrix at birth, which would later serve me well in downloading information and receiving intricate and minutely specific codes, had not provided me with the immunity needed to escape unscathed the tribulations of my earlier life. I instinctively, categorically, rejected any form of psychotherapy…would not even discuss it. I would not now be thrust into the trauma-vortex of past events to identify and blame the usual suspects. I did not want to drag my sacred life through the post-mortem of therapy, to accept and adopt someone else's feel-good recipe of resolution, to use language to steer me further into the turbulent water of insane conflict. Enough, already.

Then, I did not consciously know that I anticipated a schematic that would simply return me to the magnificent masterpiece of my original Human design prior to my genetic modification, to resurrect my divine immortal blueprint…my Soul Covenant. My electromagnetic disconnection from Source was the cause of my wounds and those of all whose life-threads had woven with my own. I wanted not a return to the past, but a return to innocence.

A good friend, an amazing being, the single parent of seven beautiful children and who would later be the celebrant at our wedding, called to tell me of a very good psychic. Joyce strongly suggested I see him. His name was Rob Robb; he was very busy and expensive. I called and left a message with my phone number but gave no name. A couple of days later Rob returned my call to tell me he was booked up for several months and that I should give him all my details and he would 'be in touch'. Once again, I gave him my number and this time, my name in full. Silence...

"Are you the Juliet mentioned on the front page of yesterday's newspaper?" I confirmed this, reluctantly. He asked if I could come over immediately: he had some information for me - no charge.

There was no better person to visit after a strenuous initiation than this man who had no sympathy whatsoever and all the compassion in the world. Rob congratulated me on the scope and drama of our initiatory encounter, thinly disguised as arrest and incarceration. He was impressed. We talked of this event, its portents and its reasons. It was not long, however, before Rob took me into another room to gift me with that for which I had come: the mirror and the reflected truth it was to share with me.

It was a full-length mirror. Rob began the session he referred to as 'New Decision Mirror Work' by using kinesiology to test the life-force energy present in three meridians: the Thymus, Heart Alarm and CSX. They all tested weak. It was at this point that Rob directed my attention to the mirror and asked that I look at myself. It sounds simple - and it is and it isn't. I was to discover some time later that in this experience the mirror represented the sacred element of water which was functioning as a component in an alchemical rite of passage. The process I entered that day was already a ceremony, although Rob and the woman who had passed this on to him and the man (a scientist) who had passed it to her, were not aware of the shamanic nature of this rite and saw it within the context of therapy. It transcended therapy or any clinical form of treatment and functioned in accordance with sacred quantum laws of Creation.

I looked in the mirror and saw my 'self'. In all the years I had lived I had not seen my self before now. I had instead distinguished a semblance of that self, a composition of responses to the many sorrows and few joys that life had offered and frozen into the veneer of a projected persona; more a disposition of survival than a true self. I became my own witness and it was the power of my true presence that caused the façade of the years of social conditioning to slip, slide and shift, as I desperately held on to anger, guilt and regret. Beneath the many masks, strong and patient, was my self, beyond the reach of the dualistic definitions that shape us in this paradigm; beyond the yes-no, good-bad, light-dark, hot-cold, laugh-cry rollercoaster sensations we call life; the unremitting series of frequency transmissions and chemical response patterns of the dualistic mechanism. Locking into eyes that connected deep into the never-ending continuum I reached the fountainhead…the quantum. And here it was that I began to forgive.

Rob's presence behind me held the sacred space as he gave me the spoken codes of compassion, declarations that cut as swords of truth through the dross of negative emotions, sweeping aside the evidence I had gathered to uphold my victimhood. Moving my focus from eye to eye, I rooted out the various manifestations of the lie that convinced me I was not loved…never was, never would be. It had begun in the womb… but it does not matter where it begins; it begins for us all, somewhere.

In my case, it was moments after conception. At the time of this event my parents lived in Japan. My father was with the United Nations and, later, in cargo shipping. He had been away for six months, not an unusual occurrence. After several months of his absence my mother had an affair. On his return my parents joyously celebrated their reunion; I was conceived. Literally moments later my mother, in her open-hearted state, felt she must confess to her affair. Overwhelmed with her feeling of love for my father, she believed he would understand and have compassion. He never touched her again and the marriage quickly and loudly fell apart. My mother's pregnancy was filled with misery and, foreseeing a future as a single parent, she strongly considered terminating the life within her. It was this fulcrum point of misunderstood rejection within the womb that I tapped into in the mirror that day. It had manifested as my own death-wish, energetically blocking the flow of life-force in several major meridians.

I will not burden you with the details of my ensuing childhood: suffice to say that it was filled with heartache for all involved. I must say, however, in honoring the memory of my beloved mother, that she and I in the years beyond childhood became deep and devoted friends and my father, suffering only from the wounds of his own sad childhood, was a good and gentle man. All of that which happened to us individually and as a family is the common thread that I suspect runs through the lives of many of you who read this, as it is a part of the suffering that being Human has come to mean. Many of us have been there, on the therapeutic journey into childhood, to the point that we have become almost over-exposed to the concept of the wounded inner child. And yet there are no more powerful words on our planet than mother, father.

A beautiful example of this was shown to me one late afternoon in Hawaii when my son Zak was two years old. I had taken him to the top of a mountain to watch the Sun set into the ocean. He sat in perfect silent stillness until the great golden orb disappeared completely. Turning to me with wonder in his eyes, he said,

"Do that again, mum." In that moment I saw the magnitude of the trust and faith he had in me and the deep iconic position that every parent holds within the psyche of their children and the power of that position. We are, as universal progenitors of life, as men and women, as mothers and fathers, the incarnate emissaries of the Benevolence of Creation - gods and goddesses. The impact we have on our children is incalculable.

I was to understand that it is not only about healing the relationship with mother and father in this incarnation: it is also the return of ancestral integrity and the deep reunion between the self and the first manifestation of the divided aspects of the divine androgynous tantric potency, the first female and the first male ambassadors of god-goddess. This reunion establishes a strong and stable platform of identity on which to assemble an expanded sense of self, a self that breaks the confines of identities fashioned by the prevailing social, economic and religious institutions of this patriarchal, dualistic paradigm. Ultimately, the healing of this divine relationship results in the resurrection of dormant genetic codes that spell out the magnificence of the original Human masterpiece.

As an individualized fractal of Prime Consciousness moves out from the omnipotent Heart of Creation to experience the conceptual world of Earth, it enters matter through the stargate created by the union of the male and female, the sacred gateway that allows for Source Intelligence to embody a sentient instrument of consciousness. At birth, this divine infant takes its first independent breath upon planet Earth and instantly all its centres of computational awareness open in a state of extreme vulnerability to receive its cosmic signature, as the prevailing celestial and earthly influences imprint upon its soul-matrix the unique gift it brings to the global community; its astrological propensity. In this ultra-sensitive and receptive state, it is not difficult to negatively impact the emotional body. There are certain circuits of electromagnetic energy that provide, for every infant, a cosmic umbilical cord to the monadic Source of Creation. During conception, gestation, birth and childhood, these circuits come under the guardianship of mother and father.

Circuitry delivers the electromagnetic life-force that is the foundation of the Human hologram. Each set of circuits delivers the intelligence data that defines a fractal of the quintessential

Human. The major circuits that provide the strata of identity intrinsic to conception, gestation, birth and childhood are almost always disturbed during one or all of these stages. These circuits are the lifeline that keeps intact the Human aspect which is simultaneously a connection to Source and the manifestation of that relationship in all earthly communications. To reconnect these circuits and heal this primary relationship it is no longer necessary or ultimately effective to engage in lengthy post-mortems of childhood, regurgitating past tragedies and injustices, reinforcing identities anchored in disempowering scenarios. Our personal histories can no longer be considered in isolation from the global Human predicament. The scientifically validated fact that out of three billion base-pair chemicals only sixty million are active must be considered in the evaluation of any part of the Human experience.

The emotional and spiritual retardation of our evolutionary process, blatantly evident in the war and genocide, starvation, disease and rampant paedophilia that ceaselessly plague this planet, make it painfully obvious that, as a race, we are disconnected from the Benevolent Source of Creation, a connection that would nurture our ability to act as conduits of light and love. This retardation and disconnection can be traced to the genetic manipulation of our DNA and is also the fundamental cause of our inability to engage unconditionally in all our relationships, relationships that stem from our primal resonant integrity with the divided aspect of the divine androgyny...mother, father.

OPPORTUNITY DISGUISED AS LOSS

We are Earth orphans lost in a false spatial-timing frequency. As a result of the manipulation of our genetics and the insertion of an erroneous definition of God perpetrated by religious indoctrination, we do not know who we are, where we are from or why we are here. When we have integrated this aspect of the Human predicament into our past and present relationships we cease to be overwhelmed by their personal implications and become empowered by this deeper level of understanding to heal them. Equipped with the knowledge of Humanity's true history and the present limitations of its genetic capabilities we begin to apprehend the core deviation that leads to destructive behaviour. From this empowered standpoint we can begin to affect the waters of life by altering the fountainhead from which they spring.

In this state of grace, we can embrace that forgiveness which activates transformative healing and goes beyond the acknowledgment of transgression or the intellectual evocation of compassionate understanding in order to excuse offending behaviour. This forgiveness acknowledges that there is nothing to forgive; it transcends blame, guilt and shame as we take full responsibility for our decision to incarnate. By so doing, we understand that we are the source generating all experiences that we have… that all experience adds to the perfection of who we are.

Forgiveness propels us into a sense of ourselves as creators rather than victims. Life is not happening to us but because of us - we stand in the centre, generating, orchestrating and choreographing every movement. From this divine perspective we begin to resurrect our original identity as it was prior to the genetic modification of our DNA. Forgiveness is the most fundamental forward movement towards the integration of light and shadow within. Without it, we run aground in the quagmire of judgment and denial. It is the foundation of the shamanic journey which requires that we immerse ourselves in the waters of perpetual renewal. Shamanic forgiveness instigates a dynamic that employs not only the emotions and intellect but reaches the very fountainhead of behaviour, the DNA, setting up new neural pathways and changing the chemical balance within the Human brain. In this way, the electromagnetic field then holds a resonant support system for forgiveness, creating an inner dialogue of compassion. When we forgive, we embrace absolutely our response-ability within the interconnectedness of all creation. The gateway to the path that leads to the transmutation of the life-death-rebirth cycle is opened through forgiveness and is the shedding of the first layer of mortality, initiating the journey from victimhood to creatorship.

On that day with Rob, who gave me the sonic code word for word, I alchemically catalysed powerful forces of change at the deepest bedrock of my being, demanding radical discontinuity from constricting identification with erroneous definitions of self, not the cajoling request of the supplicant but the invocation of the exacting warrior within, demanding growth, now. Terminations and new beginnings tumbled one upon the other as my core self arose free from the entanglement of past points of reference. As a steel blade emerges, honed and strengthened from the blacksmith's hammer and fire, the events of the past, no longer the limiting shackles of regret, became the many milestones on the journey toward liberation, every event precious. I stood before my mirrored self and saw again the pain that had brought understanding not only of my own circumstances but for all Humanity.

Through my eyes, the windows of the soul, my message of forgiveness was transmitted and received into the fulcrum level of my DNA. The eye: that most incomprehensible organ that gives sight, its opalescent and shimmering watery surface a mirror in itself, upon whose surface the never ending or beginning continuum of reflections delve into the infinite 'in' and the infinite 'out', my identity residing on the fulcrum border between the two; in this mutant paradigm, between the divine self and the mortal lie. On this threshold, inner realization meets its manifest reflection. Witnessed, honoured and understood, the injured child left me, leaving behind her gift of compassion.

I had noticed that Rob had placed several large crystals on the table between us by his mirror. When I reached home that afternoon I moved the massive hand-mined, milky quartz, self-healing Arkansas crystal that Jiva had given me from its post as a door-stop and set it more reverently on its own little table. Perhaps there was something to this New Age stuff after all. I did not then imagine that this crystal would become a beloved member of our family, present at every sacred ceremony and carried at some expense all over the world. In fact, as I sit here now in the mountains of Bali writing this, it is here with me, inspiring me. Neither did I imagine that there were to be thirty more meridians (or circuits as we came to name them) to reconnect. At that time, it seemed to me that all that was needed was the emotional resolution of personal suffering and the world would be all right.

Jiva and I did not yet realize that we were posing as members of a stolen race on a stolen planet, inhabiting a false time-space continuum; nor were we aware that the electromagnetic energy flow of a circuit was the delivery system for the energetic nature of Source Consciousness that defined our divine immortal identities prior to our genetic modification. When the entire system of Human circuitry was re-established, it would transmit the frequencies of creation. A critical mass of fully reconnected units of Human circuitry would collectively form a global resonant field of Source Consciousness on which to establish the future paradigm. It all began with the self in the mirror.

5

FORESTS IN AN ACORN

ADDICTIONS COME IN MANY GUISES. When a deep-seated pattern of behaviour is disowned it clings to the rut where it has been stuck for so long, more often than not re-establishing its dominance over emotional and mental intentions. When an overriding behavioural reference is established tangibly in the body as an electromagnetic field of holistic intelligence, the transformation of emotional, mental and chemical addictions is not only facilitated and accelerated but rendered sustainable. Resonant support for the desired change is constantly available. This is what occurs when a circuit is reconnected.

The holistic data delivered by the circuitry system is initially a density of undifferentiated potential of Source Consciousness. It is translated in accordance with the optimum requirements of the emotional, mental and physical functions of the specific centres it feeds, using as its template the original Human blueprint prior to its genetic modification. The full spectrum of its potency is not immediately realized but is integrated and synthesized according to individual capability.

The circuits do not begin and end around and through the body. Each reconnected circuit joins with the never-ending, never-beginning spheres of an interactive, co-creative holonomic system of shared cognizant potential. This is the infrastructure of all manifestation. As the Human energy field is reintegrated into this matrix, its dataflow imbues all levels of awareness, overriding past perceptions founded on a dualistic platform of understanding; cleansing, harmonizing, recalibrating. The sacred temple of the Human system integrates and synthesizes this acceleration of divine life-force, translating its influence into a user-friendly program through which the everyday and mundane is newly perceived as an extraordinary portal of opportunity.

The first three circuits Jiva and I had reconnected fed the centres that correlated to mother and father, man and woman, conception and birth. With the reconnection of these circuits, our responses to the dynamics of relationship were realigned with the sacred laws of tantric creation rather than the present prevailing logic of the patriarchal paradigm. When all the storms of emotional resolution were spent during this period of readjustment, our relationship realized a deep strength and a new dynamic that was based not on our past patterns of trigger and response, but on one that greeted each interaction as a new dawn. Each day shared blossomed forth from the crux of our devotion. It was not a relationship of negotiated request and compliance, but a seamless unification that came into being as a result of organic alignments radiating out from the core of our being.

The vibrational recalibration instigated by the acceleration of electromagnetic input of reinstated circuitry translated into everyday adjustments of perception. In my case this included an altered resonance with music, literature and colour. One day, Jiva returned home to find me dyeing almost my entire wardrobe violet and, a few weeks later, indigo. We discussed this with Rob and he explained that according to what he had learned from his friend Pam Osley, who had documented her discoveries in a book called 'Life Colours', the auric colours that surrounded my body were rearranging their bands of intensity and dominance as a result of the emotional cleansing set in motion by the circuits we had reconnected. These colours had been liberated by the removal of the 'red overlay' that I had sustained as a result of the unexpressed anger, frustration, and pain of abandonment in my early childhood.

Once again it was the impingement of orthodox society that was to propel us into an event that would reveal another aspect of our mission. We had both consciously decided that we did not need to and would not marry, feeling that this was a patriarchal arrangement based on an archaic foundation that shackled rather than unified. It was the legal necessity imposed by our arrest and the threat of deportation that drove us to our first ceremony…our wedding.

We had been financially wiped out by our bust and so this event was to be very low key. My dress was a simple white cotton shift that I had picked up in India many years previously. I sewed fresh gardenias all over it, transforming it into a stunning pre-Raphaelite garment. This I wore with a deep green open-ended lei of leaves that hung to the ground, brushing my bare feet.

The night before, we had gathered together all the old and broken gold, accumulated from our combined pasts, which Jiva then took to a friend's home to melt down to make our wedding rings. On our rings Jiva engraved a secret code of runes that have now, through eighteen years together, worn away to the naked eye, but in time and memory remain. These magical rings united the past with the potential of the future and, through the transmutation of fire, married both into the present. The ceremony had begun. On the morning of the wedding I awoke and prepared for the event, expecting it to be a formality I was resigned to going through as a necessity dictated by my circumstances. I was so very mistaken.

Joyce Taylor, a licensed celebrant, had composed a beautiful ceremony, and was to preside at our wedding at sunrise on the beach. Making the same journey down the winding mountain road to the ocean that I had made just over a month ago, handcuffed, in a police car, I marvelled at the power in the passage of time. The blessing of the Sun was not yet upon the waters as we arrived at the white sand beach to be greeted by family and friends. My beautiful son Zak held our two rings proudly and reverently on a small velvet cushion. Busy smiling for the camera as usual, he was to lose these rings in the sand in the midst of our ceremony, eventually to be retrieved after the entire congregation had frantically searched for them.

The brightening of the horizon heralded the soon-rising of the Sun and all present gathered together in silence. Sensations heightened; the coolness of the soft sand between my toes, the crisp dawn air around me, the water lapping gently on the shore. I turned to Jiva and felt his love encircle me. The Sun climbed out of its watery bed and touched us all with its 'good morning'. Our vows that day set in motion a never-ending wave of commitment that would find no shore on which to break, but would instead gather in strength, linking us together throughout eternity.

Just as a thousand forests are held in one acorn, an alchemical ceremony is a seed of limitless potential. It bridges all worlds, a fourth dimensional tapestry of time and space. All ceremonies are weddings; an alchemical merging of elements that conspire to synchronize in a burst of conception, surpassing collectively what they can achieve individually, but without the loss of autonomy. Portals opened, and ever-expanding circles of ancestral presence moved out in all directions, holding us, their children of time, in the heart of their embrace. Rings, retrieved from the clutch of sand, slipped on fingers forever. Sand, now kissed warm by the Sun, warm lips kissed. Knots tied deep, never to be undone.

The ceremony over, we went in search of the pastries we had brought to share with our guests, only to find little mongoose footprints where the food had been. The champagne they left for us and, drinking this, we shed our clothes and jumped in the ocean to swim with the dolphins that had gathered.

For many reasons it was time to move from the glass house on the hill. Our neighbours were only a few yards away and we could feel their discomfort. We were informed by our lawyer that they had approached the police and requested that we be evicted as they were in fear of their lives! We were dangerous drug-crazed criminals who should not be at liberty, and certainly should not be living next door to them. The newspapers reporting on our case told half the tale and a fraction of the truth. Small towns being what they are, the fiction soon spread that we had been dealing 'crack' to school children and that we had a cache of dangerous weapons in our home.

However, there were many members of the small community of Waimea who knew us and rallied to support us. We were offered a thirteen-room mansion on two acres just down the road from our old house. It was usually rented for a couple of thousand dollars a month, but it was ours for two hundred and our services in taking care of a ninety-year-old Zen master who lived five minutes away. His name was Paul Reps, author of the famous 'Zen Flesh, Zen Bones'. We moved in and awaited our trial. Our neighbours who posted bail for us gave Jiva the job of selling a shipment of Buddha and goddess figures they had bought in Thailand. Some of the Buddhas were reclining and seven feet long. Jiva sold them to private collectors and hotels along the Kona coast.

One day we were summoned by our lawyer and told that we had been subpoenaed by the owner of our old home to testify in the court case instigated by our neighbours over the easement of our shared driveway. The case was heard in the main town of Hilo in a boardroom-type setting. We sat on one side of the long table, our neighbours across from us. They were visibly distressed. At one point everyone left the room except for the four of us. They could not look at us. Finally, Jiva broke the thick silence,

"Thank you," he said with great feeling and sincerity. The woman jumped in her seat and looked as though she was going to bolt from the room, away from this crazed madman.

"You helped us transform our lives. We are incredibly grateful," he continued. A variety of emotions played across their faces; shock, confusion, fear. They could not put it together.

"We understand, we forgive you," Jiva offered. Their immediate response was silent outrage as they both turned a deep red, holding back their indignation. We held our space, our hearts open. For us this was happening on many magical levels. Portals of opportunity were opening for these people, offering liberation from their fears. We knew the pain and suffering that had sculpted their faces - not the details, but the general condition of disconnection that separated them from Source, from each other, from their children, from their true selves; the baffling pain that breaks all Human hearts. We felt, without reservation, so much compassion: silently and energetically we reached across the great divide of consciousness that stretched between us and beckoned them to make the leap, to meet us part way, to break free of the shackles that were restraining them. They could not deny, try as they might, the frequency of integrity and total cosmic logic that pulsed in waves of pure love from us to them; we were the same, the same race on the same planet with the same wounds. For a brief moment, light came into their eyes and the true implications of the situation dawned on them, trying for a foothold in their hearts: they wanted it so much, and yet not quite enough. Some part, however, did surrender its fear, their shoulders sank, and in some small degree they gave up the battle to hold on to the hate. The lawyers returned... it was over.

A year or so before I met Jiva he had bought forty-five acres of prime property on the Hamakua coast. With seven waterfalls, the land backed on to the forest reserve and had an almost 360° view of the ocean. Often we would see triple rainbows when we went to swim in the waterfalls and walk around the property in bliss. It was Jiva's dream come true. It was sold to pay our legal fees.

Our lawyer was very good. Ira Lytel (yes, this was his real name!) was from New York and exuded an air of 'nobody-messes-with-me', which was comforting. Ira knew the ropes and had the connections. We did not resent the loss of our land: we had not come to this planet to buy the package deal. We were the invincible light of life eternal. Abundance was not to be defined by the loss and gain within a culture that created puppets of need and desperation. Having found each other, we had already won the lottery. Everything else was icing on the cake.

The circumstances of our arrest were such that Ira felt we had a good case for 'suppression of evidence'. This was mostly due to the fact that all the evidence provided by the neighbours was inadmissible as they were already in a legal battle with the owner of our house for the shared easement. Added to this was the wreckage of our home and the theft of some of our photographs. As a result of the latter, a member of the DEA team had resigned - the ex-grower who had taken part in my interrogation in the holding cells. Ira explained to us that had we been on Mainland USA the whole case would have been thrown out, but because it was Hawaii, we would have to spend a little time behind bars. I was never sure what this all meant. There were secret deals and wheels churning in the private chambers of law. It was all corruption. Greed oiled the machine. We accepted this, knew the all-pervading fraud and decay that riddled the 'system'. Anyone who has witnessed the ebb and flow of sacred law expressed in the living natural world knows the sham that is the 'justice system'.

What I could be sure of was that I would not spend one more day behind bars...period. I had been assured of this by the flow of Intelligence that I had not yet identified. I only knew we were collaborating with some well-informed source of information that was to be emphatically trusted. More than that I could not say and was not driven to. It was enough that I felt held in the embrace of a loving guidance whose instruction, during the ordeal of arrest and incarceration, was impeccable.

My dogged insistence that I would not go to jail infuriated Ira. At times he would shout and bang his fist on his office table: everything on it would jump an inch. I would stay cool and calm in my conviction.

"You're living in a fantasy," he would scream at me. Sometimes, at his wits' end, because he was worried that I was not preparing myself for what lay ahead, he would quietly implore me to 'be realistic'. According to Ira, Jiva would spend two years and myself a year in prison.

As the trial drew near, we consulted a brilliant Vedic astrologer, an old friend of Jiva's, who had trained in India. He advised that we should do all that we could to ensure that the trial took place after Jiva's birthday: May 1st. At this time Jiva would be entering a more auspicious 'Dasa' that would align the celestial influences in his favour to a considerable degree. Soon after our reading we were informed that the trial was set on May 1st. We consulted Shambu hoping that the date was close enough to the shift in Jiva's chart. Shambu was adamant that it was not. Even one day of postponement would make all the difference.

The prosecuting attorney for our case seemed to have a personal vendetta against us. She displayed extraordinary emotional viciousness and lacked the professional objectivity and decorum you would expect from someone in her position. A week before the trial date, she was given a long-awaited promotion and was replaced by a young man. He needed some time to familiarize himself with the details of our case. The trial was postponed to May 2nd. Ira assured us that, even with the suppression of evidence and the 'oiling of the machine', the downgrade of twenty years each to two years for Jiva and one for me was an incredible deal and the very best he could pull off.

As the date of the trial drew close our confidence in its outcome did not wane but grew even stronger. On the morning of May 2nd, we left our home having made no preparation for our threatened incarceration. It was a beautiful sunny day, the like of which is unique to Hawaii, the deep taut blue sky a back-drop for the riot of colours that made you wish your eyes had taste buds.

The moment we set foot in the courtroom the frequency hit us, dreamlike and mellow. Inexplicably, the prosecutor turned and smiled at us with an unmistakable air of reassurance. We had decided to make a plea of mitigation. Jiva, knowing that the judge was Japanese, had written his speech with a samurai flavour, mentioning his family obligations and lost honour. Our mitigating speeches over, Ira did his bit and it was time for the prosecutor. Even in our confidence, Jiva and I were not prepared for his opening statement.

"Your Honour, the State feels these people have suffered enough." I looked across to Ira: on his face was a mixture of bafflement and shock. After the prosecutor finished his delivery the court convened to Chambers to discuss and come to a conclusion. The courtroom was cold, sombre and dark. One small window hung like a Hawaiian holiday poster of oblivious brilliance.

Jiva and I, the only people remaining in the room, did not speak, but in unison crossed our legs in full lotus and, instantly and effortlessly, entered deep meditation. At some point we were drawn from this state of grace as the Chamber's door opened quietly and the Head of Probation stepped silently into the courtroom to retrieve a file on his desk. Our eyes met, and we could see him take in the implications of our meditative bearing. He was also Asian, and without doubt, a Buddhist. He stood still in his tracks and bowed his head in our direction: we responded in kind. A connection of consciousness flowed between us and we felt his recognition and respect. Another coded prearranged event slipped cunningly into the drama. He turned and left. Jiva and I held hands, our bodies flushed with a strange ecstasy. A soundless voice inside informed me, "The time of travail is over."

The court members re-entered the room and sentencing began. I was sentenced to four hundred hours of community service and two months of house arrest...no jail time. Jiva was sentenced to a month in prison, a month of house arrest and a two thousand dollar fine. As we got up to leave the courtroom, the Head of Probation caught up with the prosecutor, and looking in our direction exchanged a few words. The prosecutor then approached us and let us know that if we could give them just one name of someone involved in the growth or sale of marijuana or in the distribution of cocaine or heroin our sentences would be further reduced. Without pause we answered in unison in the negative. Looking down at his shoes, he sighed deeply. He then informed us that they had decided that Jiva's prison and house arrest time was to be served only at night as they were concerned about his need to work and provide for his family. We met Ira outside the courthouse. He was pale and shaking his head as he kept repeating that he had never seen anything like it in all his years in the legal system.

In a state of elation, we left for our favourite lookout point on the Hamakua coast. Standing on the edge of the cliff overlooking the ocean we watched a small waterfall pouring its rainwater back into the source. We could feel the magic of our future together gather around us and knew we were not celebrating alone. The Presence that had been there at our arrest, in the darkness of our cells, at our wedding and in the courtroom was with us and always would be - and most probably always had been.

6

MAYAN ALLIANCE

THE DAYS FOLLOWING THE TRIAL were a gentler rebirth.

We woke every morning before dawn, our very first thoughts a celebration of being free of the spectre of incarceration which, regardless of our optimism, had thrown its shadow over our days and our dreams.

My two months of house arrest began. A plastic cuff was placed around my wrist and I was supplied with a phone that was its security counterpart. I was called by a computer at random intervals through the day and night. To this computer I would give my details and fit the small box that protruded from my cuff into the receptive port situated on the body of my phone, thus proving I was still at home. This was inconvenient, especially at three in the morning and again at a quarter past. The phone might ring again at four. This pattern obviously made a good night's sleep impossible, but I did have a beautiful mansion in Hawaii to be sleepy in, a dream house where many would pay a lot to stay. I placed the monitoring device in the meditation room and dragged a mattress in, so we could sleep there and answer it in the dead of night. Jiva, a heavy sleeper, did not mind.

The meditation room was a sky-blue, clear space, three sides of which were glass. The room opened up onto a deep circular deck that looked over the acre and a half of beautiful manicured lawn embracing a pond and waterfall, beyond which was an expansive view of the ocean. We had a gym room, a laundry room and a refrigerator you could have lived in. Zak spread himself out over the four rooms on the third floor. We rattled around in this huge house and often had trouble finding each other. Soon Jiva no longer had to deal with the late-night wakeup calls as his nights in the Hilo jail began. As was Jiva's nature, he found a way to turn this time into something valuable and on his first night offered Chiropractic and Alphabiotic alignments to the inmates and officers. Within a few days there was a line outside his cell waiting for 'the Doc' to arrive every evening. He was soon to begin counselling in health matters including diet, as one of the jailors had bowel cancer.

The end of my house arrest coincided with the return of the owners of our temporary home. It was time to leave the house at Waimea and make a new start. My son's teacher from his

Montessori school offered us his meditation retreat in a small beach community on the south side of Hilo called Kapoho. He warned us that it was only two very humble rooms; basically, a wooden shack. From thirteen rooms to two!

Moving often takes longer than you think it should and it was late in the day when we finally left Waimea for the coast road that would take us through Hilo and Puna to the volcano side of the island and to Kapoho. Exhausted, we arrived well after dark, the headlights of our pickup truck illuminating the ramshackle front of our new home. Zak, fast asleep, was laid down on a small foam mattress in the corner of the completely empty, bare-boarded room and we set about unloading our few boxes of belongings. Speechless at the austerity of this tiny space, apart from raising our eyebrows, we did not communicate much to each other and lay down our own bedding to follow Zak into deep sleep.

We awoke the next morning to a blast of sunlight illuminating the fine white curtains that covered the sliding doors which constituted two sides of our shack. Half-heartedly, I drew them aside expecting a garden to match the austerity of the shack. The doors opened on to an uncovered wooden porch extending on stilts over a clear deep wide pond into which I could have dived from where I stood. Before me I beheld a little paradise. The left side of the pond was spanned by a small wooden bridge. The water in the pond was half ocean and half rainwater, fed in through a series of lava tubes. The neighbourhood was dotted with these ponds that were not only a perfect temperature, they were also effervescent and thus called 'champagne ponds'. Dotted around the garden were dwarf papaya and coconut trees, offering their fruits at only an arm's length. The trees rose up from a mossy lawn of a type which never needed mowing. On the far side of the pond, and jutting a couple of feet over it, was a large wooden sundeck. A few feet away there was a metal bathtub, sitting up on bricks above a fire pit. The whole of the garden was surrounded by deep thick foliage beyond which could be heard the waves crashing on the lava fields that formed the shores of Kapoho. It was glorious. I woke Zak and tugged him, sleepy eyed, onto the porch. His jaw fell open and he shook his head in disbelief, already envisioning the days of joy to come in his own natural swimming pool. He let out a whoop, rushed down the side steps of the porch to dance around the garden and was soon sampling the waters.

This was to be one of our family's favourite homes. In its warm and watery embrace, we integrated the deep and wide implications of our past initiation and prepared ourselves for an even more dramatic one that, unbeknownst to us, loomed ahead.

Jiva's nights in jail continued for a couple of weeks. When they ended, he began his nights of house arrest that began at eight in the evening. We settled into a stretch of hot and sunny days that caught us up in a blanket of nurture. With us was another member of the family, Monkey. She had been dropped off near the house where we had been arrested, one of a litter of three abandoned kittens. We had decided to keep her when, having turned on the vacuum cleaner, we saw the other kittens fly off in a panic to hide, but Monkey jumped on it for a ride. One morning Monkey slipped off the railing around the porch and fell headlong into the pond. Swimming to the edge she climbed out, half the size of her normal self. A short while later she jumped in again of her own volition, having decided that this Human pastime was quite enjoyable. Soon she took to taking hot baths with us in the outdoor tub, lying on her back with just her face showing, her eyes opening and closing in drowsy bliss. Jiva and I liked to lie on the mossy grass in the gentle warm drizzly rain and Monkey joined in this also, covered in little pearls of water that clung to the tips of her fur, the pearls fattening until they formed a solid layer of water soaking her to the skin. She would beg for pieces of papaya and coconut that we harvested from the garden and soon rejected her normal cat food, becoming vegetarian.

One evening I took off for the beach in front of our house to view the sunset alone. Lost in my own world of introspection, I suddenly became aware of a pickup truck making its way along the pitted road towards me, its bed packed with a group of enormous, muscle-bound, raucous young men who seemed to be excited about something. As they got closer it was evident that I was the focus of their attention. The closer they got the more animated they became, and I began to feel afraid. Looking around in a panic for someone, anyone, to appeal to, I realized the isolation of my surroundings and the adrenalin began to pump though me. They were now only a few feet away and although they seemed aggressively animated I noticed they were grinning, waving, giving me the 'thumbs up' and calling out to me,

"Nice one, sista!" Although they had slowed a fraction, they did not stop and as they rolled past me one of them asked,

"What you in for?" It took me a few seconds to figure it out. Looking down at my T-shirt I saw the letters H.C.C.C., standing for Hawaii County Correctional Centre. It all fell into place and I waved proudly back at the new found fellow members of our exclusive club.

Exploring Kapoho one day, Jiva and I came across a chain-link fence that enclosed a huge piece of land on which rose a large hill and what appeared to be a jungle-encrusted crater. A sign on the gate read: 'Kapu!' Beware! Another read: 'Private Property. Keep out!' Sometime later we learned from friends that what we had seen from afar was indeed a crater, a water-filled volcanic crater. This body of water, called Green Lake, had no banks and dropped off into a wide stretch of enticing clear water that was a deep emerald green. The volcanic lake was surrounded by thick vegetation that included some of the best avocado and papaya trees on the island. Although the signs clearly stated this land to be off-limits it was known to be used for swimming and gathering fruit. The Hawaiians, however, never went near it as they believed that monsters lived in its unfathomable depths.

With some trepidation, we decided to visit the lake and were well rewarded by an experience that was the ultimate tropical paradise fantasy. Lying on our backs on a bamboo raft that drifted aimlessly across the wide lake, our field of vision was filled only with the endless blue sky surrounded on all sides by a circular wall of rampant jungle. The world disappeared into a silence broken only by the calling of tropical birds and insects humming in the heat of the day. We languished in the lap of tantric exuberance and profusion, the water, the foliage, the pillowy white clouds that now and again slipped over the rim of the crater, all the expression of the goddess Earth's enchantment with Her star lover, the Sun, telling through Her creation a living story of love. Wrapped in light's embrace, Her desire blossomed through leaf and tree, through butterfly, flower, moss and fruit. How do I love thee? Like this and like this and like this...

The atmosphere here was so vibrant as to make you feel that the lake and the land around it had become dislodged from the rest of civilization and was floating far and away, beyond the criteria that govern the rest of Earth and Her inhabitants, a portal between dimensions, creating a convergence of earthy and cosmic influences that together conspire to bridge the worlds.

The fecundity of the male and female potencies of creation welled up from the crystalline heart of Earth, creating a portal of intense magic that swam in the very air we breathed. This frequency was penetrating our waking awareness and our dreamtime. The Consciousness that first came to us in our jail cell now imbued cells of a different nature, as more and more we engaged with, and inhabited, a reality that supported a different way of being and seeing.

One morning, as we lingered on our bed in the soft light of morning, not quite ready to admit the day had begun, Zak wandered in and sat formal and serious at the end of our bed. With a distant look in his eyes and a sombre tone in his voice, he told us,

"The new world has not yet begun. At a time in the not-too -distant future the Earth will stop spinning and in that moment of non-time the world will be born." This said, Zak sat very still. His words somehow came as no surprise; the air around us was charged with our collective acknowledgment and comprehension. We had known of the time of which Zak spoke before we took one breath upon this planet: it was the reason for our coming here. The alliance between the three of us was remembered from beyond this life, this dimension; the difference in years between us and Zak non-existent, as was the illusion of any parental position. I knew before his birth that I was only his guardian.

Jiva and I had fully integrated Zak's coded call across time; its meaning had seeped into all levels of our consciousness, triggering a new phase of the mission on which we had all agreed; and yet we wanted him to say it again, so we could hear again the reason for our being, to know with certainty that the opportunity for deliverance from the suffering of dualism was indeed ahead of us.

"What?" we asked him. The sunlight had been teasing the shadows in the room: having stilled with reverence for the occasion they now broke the spell with movement. Zak took a deep breath,

"What's for breakfast?" he asked and wandered off to find something to eat.

We had not yet heard of the 2012 'end date' of the Mayan calendar. It was, however, only a few days later that we were called to look into the world of the Maya. Infinite numbers of stars graced a moonless onyx night, charged with an energy that had kept us from sleep. The hour slipped past midnight as I lay on a thick Native American rug, pillows piled around me, enjoying the simple yet exotic beauty of our humble home. A four-foot white pillar stood in the corner, a voluptuous banana flower springing out of the crystal pineapple vase that sat upon it. The flat surface of a pirate trunk held a collection of scintillating crystals set aglow by the tea-lights nestling amongst them. Beyond the open glass doors palm trees beckoned.

I synchronized my breath with the ever-present sound of waves. The perfection of my surroundings bursting my heart with gratitude and wonder, I sat in the centre of it all in an effervescent lightness that lifted my being. We had just come in from a sublime swim in the starry pond and Jiva was taking a hot shower. Something made me turn to look at the bathroom door. Almost immediately, a being entirely etched in laser beams of blazing light stepped through the door, turned on his heel in a flourish of movement and looked directly at me, a confusion of manic feathered plumes on his headdress swaying as he did so. His angular, thick and proud features melted instantly into amused delight as he realized that I could see him! His attire, ornate and regal, was of a geometric armour-like design. All too soon, Jiva walked out of the bathroom and, merging perfectly with the Mayan light being, turned and faced me.

"What?" he asked, grinning obliviously.

The next day we made a rare visit to a close friend, Hanique, a surfer and an artist who lived about twenty minutes from Kapoho. She had not been able to sleep the night before and was excited to show us the strange painting she had been working on all night which she had just completed. I stared at it wordlessly for a few moments before carefully turning it upside down. There he was, my Mayan friend who had stepped out from and back into Jiva's body the night before. Hanique had done a beautiful job in painting his vivacious feathered headdress. Our explanation made perfect sense to Hanique who had felt the presence of this Mayan time-traveller as she unknowingly painted his portrait, his vibration an engaging mix of intelligence and humour.

The end of the school holidays signalled the closing of summer. We enrolled Zak into a laid-back Waldorf school a few miles away in Hawaiian Paradise Park. Jiva started to make day trips to Oahu to sell Buddhas and some antiques he had collected over many years and to find retail outlets for the jewellery we had started to create. We sold our pickup which left us with a rattling tin can of a car, a two-door ex-rental that complained, on the verge of collapsing, every time we drove on the pitted dirt road that led to our hideaway. Financially, we limped along.

I began to consider how I would honour my four hundred

hours of community service. There was no doubt in my mind about what it was I wanted to do. I called Rob and asked if it would be possible for me to facilitate the Re-decision Healing that he had taken me through. He felt sure that this was a good move and let me know that his sense was that it would be a platform on which I would develop something more encompassing. We invited him and his lovely wife Brook to come for lunch and to sample our champagne pond - but first we had to catch Biff, a nasty little fish that had taken a deep bite into Jiva's foot while he was floating in the water meditating. Biff was relocated to a lava pond just offshore.

Rob spent a little time explaining the process and ran me through a brief demonstration of the mirror work. He left a video that was incredibly helpful, and I watched it countless times. Jiva had learned kinesiology from Virgil Crane and he taught enough of it to me to allow me to apply it to the work I began to share with my community as my sentence stipulated. Everyone I worked with really appreciated this empowering testing procedure: it bypassed the opinions of others and even their own programmed beliefs, to tap into a cellular body-wisdom that exists beyond the guile of the mind. It showed an undisputable strengthening in the circuitry test points, offering tangible proof on a physical level of a transformation that was occurring within the Human hologram. The renewed level of strength was the physical manifestation of the shift that was taking place on the emotional, mental and spiritual levels.

Word soon spread that I was offering free healing and the chilled-out hippie community came in a steady stream. I took to this work like a fish to water. Before anyone faced the mirror, I would create a space for them to tell the story that had brought them to me. Shockingly, almost all these stories included considerable and sometimes overwhelming violent and sexual abuse in childhood. Some of the accounts I heard were close to unbelievable and, after sessions that lasted around four hours, I would climb into bed, exhausted and unable to communicate with anyone. Despite this, I was totally devoted to the work and, long after the four hundred hours of community service was completed, I continued to offer it.

From the reconnection of these circuits, I had personally experienced a deep and real liberation, my life had been transformed and I continued to benefit immeasurably. The feedback I received from the community was overwhelming and very satisfying. Through this work I was able to recognize the transformation that was taking place within Jiva and me. Our relationship had become totally honest, empowered and co-creative. Individually, we had not only healed the past, but also recognized the perfection of it.

It was also through this work that I found my relationship with the Consciousness with which we had been collaborating began to develop more dynamically. Zak was also aware of this energy that was tangibly present in our home, not as a nebulous lofty entity which looked down from on high on our Humanity, but as a heartfelt friend with as much respect for us as we had for 'it'. We realized that in order to truly integrate and interface with this presence as a member of our family we needed a name. My Celtic heritage drew me to the runes as a medium through which to listen to the unspoken and to see the invisible. Knowing that it was simply a way to refer to this Consciousness and that the name I gave it would only be a tag of reference in the stream of time, I picked a rune. I admit it may have been my imagination that this rune floated up into my fingers, but it certainly seemed to have happened that way. The rune was Sowelu.

It seemed fitting to us, as this is a rune that signifies a return to wholeness. Over time, its applicability to the Consciousness we collaborate with grew in all directions. The wholeness did not simply pertain to an ambiguous sense of well-being but would expand to encompass the resurrection of the divine immortal identity that is holographically embedded in the Human matrix. It was in the years to come that the fact that Sowelu is a rune signifying solar power took on more and more significance as we learnt that the original Human root race inhabited the entire solar system and was designed to evolve in symbiotic resonance with the intelligence data transmitted as light from our Sun. It was this morphic solar resonance that defined us and our connection to Source.

The first inkling that another initiatory adventure lay ahead came at sunset in the shape of an old Land Cruiser, its psychedelic paint job reminiscent of the Beatles' Rolls Royce. It was the chariot of a dear friend who would now and again drop into our lives out of the blue. That evening, Soma, as he was most appropriately named, had brought his new divining cards to show us, the Sacred Path deck. His sizable brood of children took off with Zak to terrorize the neighbourhood while we caught up with Soma's colourful tales. Eventually, the cards were brought out and reverently shared. Soma shuffled and offered them to Jiva. Feeling these to be just another prophesy tool, the like of which were flooding the New Age market and without placing much import on the event, Jiva played along and pulled out 'Sacred Mountain'. This card spoke of ascending the spiral path towards your destiny. Soma shuffled again and handed the cards to me. I pulled 'Sacred Mountain'.

These New Age props are not to be seen as holy objects that themselves exemplify some magical property - they simply provide a fulcrum point of focus upon which to stage your own empowerment. Offering a moment of stillness in the palaver of life's demands upon your time, they create a portal of opportunity to grasp the creative potency that is, in fact, always present. Scratch the surface of the dualistic distractions and object proliferation that parades as our everyday survival and you will find life conspiring to entertain you. There are, however, those that take these tools of focus too far, like the character in one of Douglas Adams' books, who got so hooked he threw the I Ching to figure out whether to clean out his refrigerator.

On this occasion the cards dealt had been a window through

which Sowelu was taking the opportunity to send a memo. I am purposely avoiding using the word 'warning' here, as I believe that the initiation that lay ahead was a prearranged event to which Jiva and I had agreed. I do know that if the details of it had been consciously realized by us we would have categorically declined to take part.

As I looked at the Sacred Mountain card, sensations like those of the morning I woke to find a gun in my face rippled through my body. My eyes met Jiva's above the card and the life-altering periphery of the coming initiation reached out and touched us both. The unmistakable tremors of elemental disruption, the epicentre of which was only hours ahead, destroyed the gentle ambience of the evening. I could no longer engage in the rare social encounter I had been enjoying and waited only for Soma and the gang to leave so that I might unburden this knowing to Jiva.

"For some strange reason," I told him, "we have to go to Green Lake tomorrow morning. Something very important is going to take place. I don't know what will happen… and I don't want to find out." We had visited the lake several times, but we had never even considered climbing the mountain.

7

ENCOUNTER ON GREEN MOUNTAIN

TWICE THAT MORNING we nearly backed out of the journey we knew we had to take and it was already past noon when we arrived at Green Lake. The lake, devoid of Human presence, was humming with life; the reflected clouds hurried across its surface. We did not descend the path down to the lake itself but sat above, in a canopied alcove that perched on the very edge of the crater rim. We centred ourselves with rhythmic breathing, intermittently playing Tibetan bells that echoed around the jungle walls and bounced off the water, our senses heightened by the adrenalin that flooded us. I admitted to Jiva that Green Mountain was the destination of the day's journey and reluctantly we crossed the lush valley that lay between lake and mountain. We found the vine-covered entrance that opened into the spiralling path which wound itself up the mountain and, wordlessly, began our ascent. Each time we spiralled to another level I felt I was reaching deeper into myself, releasing patterns of resistance in my body as slowly I surrendered to trusting the moment, whilst never completely losing a fear that hovered in the background.

As I paused to take a few deep breaths and appreciate the potent gusto in the countless forms of life that seethed in the jungle around me, my eyes caught the hurry of a bright red and black beetle making its journey across a patch of vibrant multi-hued moss that spanned the trunk of an ohia tree. Aware of exchanging molecular structures with this busy being, knowing the consciousness that binds us both together, I too continued on the journey. The dampness of the jungle floor enfolded my body, hot from the Sun I had absorbed by the lake. The earthy chill was trapped by the giant ferns and palms that bent and bowed over the seldom used path, creating a cool tunnel of deep green. The sound of our footfalls held the march of time and destiny within their rhythm, drawing us on to an event hidden in a mystery crafted by our own denial, a denial for which we are grateful, knowing that we were on a collision course with a hitherto hidden aspect of our quintessential identities; responding to an undeniable, non-negotiable coding set in place before our infant eyes beheld this stunning planet, each step triggering an awakening, a sensation similar to the pins and needles of a limb coming back to life. Upward and upward we spiralled the sacred mountain into a battlefield of consciousness that was to divide our lives into 'before' and 'after'.

At the summit we broke into a clearing that spanned half its space. The rest was hidden in a tight weave of jungle growth, in the centre of which was set what looked like a water tower. Spread below us was a 360° view of a classic tropical panorama. Lush rampant jungle cascaded recklessly down the mountain to meet the turquoise sea with a kiss of white sand. We settled ourselves on the edge, absorbing the waves of early afternoon heat into our bodies.

Within minutes of our arrival a large majestic hawk flew into view. She was only six feet away, level with us, as she floated, almost still, on a thermal rising off the side of the mountain. Our eyes met, and something shifted and unravelled. Remembrance loitered in the back of my mind…waiting. The hawk rode the thermal up and up towards the Sun until our eyes could no longer perceive her and then she would reappear, again making eye contact, spiralling in and out of view. Thus, she played with us for the next few hours.

There was something extraordinary about this hawk's insistence on connecting with us: eventually we realized that she was embodying a consciousness other than her own. In communications since then, we have come to understand the nature of the consciousness-grid created and maintained by the bird family and its covenant with the Planetary Evolutionary Guides, the Ahau Kines, The Solar Beings, The Bird Tribe… an agreement to transmit a certain integrity of frequency that maintains a link upon this planet with Humanity and its original seeding prior to genetic manipulation. The purity and ecstasy of bird song is the closest thing we know to the transcendental universal language of the Cosmos. The hawk was to us, that day, an encoded messenger, sending to us through her majesty and her eyes a message from her renegade heart, a message of faith and trust in the Benevolence that created us. I felt her kinship soothe my soul and prepare me for that which lay ahead.

It had been a couple of hours since we arrived at the summit when suddenly a young man sped into view on a mountain bike. He was the picture of health and strength and was barely out of breath. He stayed for a while and told us of his various rides around the island, of giant ohia trees and exotic orchids he had seen deep in the rain forest. Later, we realized that our interaction with him had lingered in our energy field and was tuned into and used by the beings we were soon to encounter.

As I peered over the edge of the clearing to glimpse the mountain biker on his way out of the property, my eye was caught by two magnificent horses gambolling in the swathe of short grass that cut a wide path through the valley between mountain and lake. Their frolicking was strange; it seemed they were responding to an unseen presence that was playing with them. I turned to call Jiva over to see the horses and, when I turned back again, not only did I see two children playing in and around them, I saw also that all three pathways that led on to the land were being converged upon by a mass of colourfully adorned people. Each group, of which there were three, was dressed in different colours; blue, red and yellow, and each person held aloft a banner of matching colour.

How did this happen so quickly? Where did they come from without us noticing? Jiva, now standing next to me, was as amazed as I was. The three groups were now converging in the centre of the valley and began a perfectly choreographed weave of colour in a ceremony of motion. Until now, everything was orchestrated in graceful silence; suddenly all assembled let out hoots and hollers as banners and flowing garments wove the mass of people together in rhythms of alternating reds, yellows and blues. From our high vantage point it seemed this weave of bodies played out a language of colour coding. We began to feel uncomfortable as it appeared that we had encroached upon some sacred Hawaiian ceremony, when the multitude of colourful beings began to fade away into nothing. Only the horses remained in our dimension and continued to play with the children we could no longer see. All was silent. Then again, we heard them, then again, they emerged from the very air and the marching, singing weave of celebration continued; then they seamlessly flowed back into their individual colours and withdrew like tides back into the ocean of time from which they had emerged. Only the memory of their raised voices echoed in the silence. Comprehension hovered out of reach.

At this point in our lives we were not yet familiar with the complex simplicities of the mechanics of creation. We had not been backstage to see how the show was put on: the interference patterns of magnetism and electricity, of wave and particle, the confluence which seals sequences of concordant impressions that decorate time with motion. The ceremony we had witnessed was an alchemical emulation of space playing with time performed by conscious beings. We may not have had the ability to itemize the various components of this experience, but we felt it just the same and knew that a portal had opened to us, giving us a tantalizing glimpse. We had stood in the doorway of time; soon we would step over its threshold.

Relieved by the mellowness of this initiation and pleased with ourselves, we decided to leave the property before any more crowds gathered to block our exit. The Sun had lost its intensity as it neared the horizon, but it was still warm, and we could feel the Earth currents begin a gentle descent into the early evening. Soft shades of lavender hinted at the coming sunset as we gathered our things together and set ourselves upon the path homeward. We had no idea of the courage it would take to reach that home.

We had gone only a couple of steps when we noticed a male figure coming toward us on the path. My first impression of him was of a middle-aged man dressed in tight Spandex sportswear. I could see that he was feigning interest in the view when, in truth, his interest was in us. As we drew closer, he turned to face us full on and in doing so, made it difficult to pass without an acknowledgment. We exchanged a brief greeting. By then we had entered his energy field and my computational awareness sent me a sudden and clear message of pure fear. I was frantic; my solar plexus was in spasm.

The fear was not my own. It pulsated off the 'man' in waves of intensity. And yet he was not afraid...he was fear. He was bulging out of his Spandex outfit in several places and his breathing was laboured, not from exertion but from an incompatibility with his environment. What I was seeing and what I was feeling did not compute and I was having trouble keeping up with all the warning signals my body was giving me. A silence followed our brief greeting and the stranger made no move to open the way for us. Jiva felt compelled to break the silence by commenting on the beautiful view and asked him where he was from. He hesitated before answering and it was then that I noticed a slim black slab of metal strapped to his waist. From it came wires that extended to his ears. I became aware of it when he tilted it in my direction when I addressed him.

"I live in Kapoho. Do you know where that is?" he asked. We were in Kapoho!

"Yes, we live in Kapoho, too," Jiva answered, a puzzled tone in his voice. The 'man' had tilted his hip device towards Jiva and adjusted his earphones.

"Oh yes, you live on Kapoho Kai Drive, in the fourth house on the left across from the white house." He said this exactly the way we gave directions, as though he had read Jiva's mind. I could tell that Jiva was feeling as uncomfortable as I was and yet I could also see he was not quite registering the information.

"Did you ride your bike up?" Jiva asked.

"Bike? Ahhhh… it was quicker to walk. Sometimes my bike is the same as walking only slower," the stranger answered haltingly. The last part was almost a question, as if he were not sure of the meaning of his own words. He had built his hologram according to the last Human we had encountered, the mountain biker, not really knowing what one was in Earth terms and having difficulty stabilizing the illusion. The residual impression of the biker was still in our computational awareness. I could see Jiva looking worried now.

At this point a female partner made her appearance, not from the path behind the male, but from behind a bush to our left. The menace and fear emanating from her were even more pronounced and obvious.

"These people live in Kapoho," the male told her as she approached us.

"Oh yes, I've seen them," she sneered. She wore a T-shirt with the words 'FRENZY BEACH' on the front. I could not tear my eyes away from these two words and began to feel dizzy. The conversation continued, as the male received and translated our electromagnetic thought pulsations with his hip device. Thus, a false conversation was constructed that gave the impression that these beings knew us, where we lived and even our future plans. I tore my eyes away from the words on the female's shirt and looked down to the ground, trying to make sense of what was happening to us. I realized later that I never once looked into their eyes. Fear was gripping my stomach and I felt great danger. It was then that Sowelu transmitted to me with great clarity,

"You are in the presence of reptilian humanoids." I could feel my panic rise and grip me.

"Stay calm; I have planned this for you. I am with you." Sowelu continued. "Invoke the light," he directed. Instantly I began to chant,

"I am the light. I hold the light; the light is with me always," the memory of these words old and from another time. Another aspect of me that stood on this deserted mountain top was not very impressed with Sowelu' s direction or the incantation it drew from me. It did not seem sufficient protection against what was in front of us. Never again will I doubt this chant or the power behind it.

Holograms, in order to hold their form, require both the conscious participation of and a degree of denial in the observer. With the knowledge in my conscious mind of what I was dealing with, the beings began to lose their holograms which began to disintegrate in patches, through which I saw bulbous limbs covered in a jelly-like translucent membrane. The female's hands were webbed with very long fingernails. Her hands were fibrillating against her chest. Although my faith in Sowelu' s support and my chant gave me courage, I was battling with tremendous fear and denial of what I was witnessing. I did not know then that I was under the influence of master hypnotists. It took everything I had to hide my panic. Notwithstanding the support that I had, I also knew that this was my initiation to win for myself the dignity and power that comes from knowing you are not a victim. Sowelu was not going to save me. He would support me in saving myself.

My warrior spirit was gaining ground and momentum, overriding my helplessness. I became aware of my breath, aware that my presence in this time and this space was a consequence of a series of my own choices. I blended with my chant, filling it with conviction and feeling. The tight bands across my chest loosened and my heart began to expand. I knew this event was an honour to which I could rise. Sowelu's energy blended with mine and I began to feel compassion for the strange beings in front of me. Now it was they who became confused.

"We must walk as we keep talking, we must talk as we keep walking," the male chanted in a monotone. His voice began to break up like a tape left out in the Sun.

"We must walk as we keep taaaalking." He took a step toward me and said,

"You are Juliet and Jiva and you live in Kapoho."

Why did these simple words seem like the most frightening threat against my very existence? Because beneath the sound of his voice was an extra-low frequency message designed to completely dis-empower. The full complexity of the technology used upon us that day we still have not fathomed. He knew he was losing us and gave everything he had to this last attempt at control through fear. I felt the full force of it and was flooded with an overwhelming despair, a temptation to lose consciousness. It was almost too much.

"I am the light. I hold the light; the light is with me always!" I came to myself. Reluctantly he stepped back. It was then I noticed that we had moved from our original spot - it seemed my legs did not belong to me as they marched forward. We were going with them!

"Tell Jiva to tell them you will not go with them," Sowelu suggested strongly. I turned to Jiva and wordlessly sent the message.

"We are not going with you," Jiva instantly said with a calm and quiet conviction.

This surprised and baffled them. It was clearly not what they were used to. They looked at each other and then nervously scanned the skies. With no more pretence at polite conversation, they turned and walked away from us. I watched them go in amazement. Not quite trusting my freedom, I made my way down a small pathway that led to the edge of the mountain. Jiva was not far behind. Reaching the end of the path, I turned to face him, searching his face for signs of comprehension. His expression was a mixture of alarm, disbelief and amazement. He had not trusted his knowing and yet he had known. Our eyes met.

"Do you realize who they were?" I asked. No sooner had the words left me when these words slipped through my lips, barely engaging my mind.

"Do you realize who we are?"

Realizations ripped through me. Reality's boundaries buckled beneath the weight of something it could not define, seams tearing to accommodate something potent, ancient and new that insisted upon its birth, stretching its arms to encompass and hold the past, present and future. It was dangerous and played a tune that woke the heart of a renegade, a time-bandit, to whom life was either a daring adventure, or nothing. The veil was lifted to reveal eternity in a moment. Its name was remembrance, a springboard into another realm of existence.

Memory sprang clear and away from this life lived here in duality, pulling free from the chaos and confusion of the past to become this moment that shed its light into the future from which we had travelled to be here. An awareness that allowed a greater understanding of our identities enveloped us, the implications of which impacted us on every level simultaneously, bombarding us with visions and information, the who, the where and the why answered as cellular codes were fired: codes that had maintained a denial of galactic heritage and identity until the time was ripe graciously gave way to reconnect the lineage of our souls. As we battled to keep pace with the speed of incoming data, words were caught in the net of our linear understanding: time-traveller, renegade, disguise, now do you remember? Now do you remember?

This had all been a shared experience between Jiva and me. Suddenly, his eyes left mine and his face drained of all colour as he looked over my shoulder.

"Don't turn around and please don't panic, Juliet." I did both. I heard it before I saw it. The military helicopter rose up the side of the mountain until it was level with us. I lost it!

"Quick, Jiva, jump!" I yelled as I prepared to dive into the jungle undergrowth that fell away down the mountainside.

"No, please!" said Jiva as he grabbed my arm. "Stay calm, don't panic. Put your arm around me. Act natural, as though there was nothing wrong," his eyes pleaded, as did his voice. I put my arm around his waist as he drew me to him. We clung to each other as we began to move down the path that spiralled down the mountain.

"We saw too much. They know," I said, as I thought of my son Zak and in my heart I sent him a message of love and farewell. The fear, the adrenalin, was indescribable.

The transcendental space we then moved into made the adventure to this point pale in comparison. How we found our way to this space I am not sure - perhaps through sheer shock, perhaps Sowelu aided us. By whatever means, we were consciously experiencing ourselves in another dimension simultaneous to this one. It is difficult to explain as there are few points of reference to measure the experience in a language that does not know it.

As we began to make our way down the path, I stole a glance at the helicopter that was circling around and around above us. The occupants, who were not dressed in military uniform, were straining their heads out of the sides as if looking for something. My fear lessened. Looking down at Jiva and myself I saw that we were at the centre of a sphere of light about twelve feet in diameter. It is only as I write this, eighteen years later, that we have come to realize what this sphere is and how it relates to circuitry and to worldbridging. However, at that time, we knew instinctively that its presence around us meant we could not be seen. My fear evaporated. My consciousness returned to the spot we had just left. I turned to find Jiva standing next to me. His smile reflected the joy and peace I was feeling. We both turned to the panorama that we had been looking at most of that day. Geographically it was the same view; however, its expression was very different.

We were gazing upon a planet whose beauty held no shadows, as every leaf and blade of grass radiated a light from within, emitting patterned fractal beams of violet, white and gold. Geometric symmetry danced beneath the surface of everything in a celebration of life, crystalline yet soft. Between all was conscious communion. The radiance of what we beheld was matched by our own radiant beings. Jiva stood just behind me, his hand resting on my shoulder. I felt his peace as I felt my own… we were one with all we surveyed, no separation between the observer and the observed. Harmony reigned as the recognition of our unity with and love for the Source of our Creation became the unspoken, ever celebrated thought behind each breath, pulsating rhythms fusing in a molecular dance in which art and physics were part of the same mystery. The same flow of expression that moved through each geometric structure of leaf, tree and stone was identical to that which flowed through Jiva's hand and the shoulder upon which it rested. The electromagnetic thought-emanations of creation flowed through the transducing component of my pineal, translating through the holographic prism of my conscious intent as visible, audible feedback from the world I beheld. I was a perfect conduit of the Consciousness that flowed through me to touch the heart of the planet and she responded in kind. We swam in the deep bliss of this union, simultaneously marvelling at the differentiation that allows us to experience relationship. Joy, peace, innocence and bliss awaits us all at the end of this arduous adventure.

I don't remember ever leaving this place. Perhaps I am there still. However, at some point my consciousness returned to where it had never left (if you get my drift) and I was walking down the mountain with Jiva. The helicopter had given up and gone on its way. We walked hand in hand through a spiralling forest much more enchanted than before. I felt that any minute a tree would speak to me. The trees seemed stylized to the point of animation, like some visionary art I have seen, but even more so. I saw shades of green with a vibrant blueness that defies description. The sphere of light still held us, and I noticed that we were dressed in robes of white light that, on closer inspection, were all the colours in the rainbow.

We were totally blown open by our experience and Sowelu was taking full advantage of this by bombarding us with information. We attempted to keep up with it by verbalizing it to each other, but soon collapsed with laughter. We absorbed much on a cellular level and to this day it is still resurfacing. The forest came to an abrupt end and it seemed as though we stepped out of it into a more mundane reality, but a reality that was beautiful all the same. The Sun was just touching the horizon as we walked into its warm glow. We turned to look at each other, our eyes wet with tears of gratitude for our adventure.

It was not only our encounter with the reptilian humanoids that divided our world into before and after - it was also the unveiling of our inter-dimensional identities, the far-reaching implications of which, in all the days to come, would provide us with a pivotal point of reference within this mutant realm. The precious memory of our incarnate presence within a fully manifest immortal paradigm, free of suffering, fear and death, was now an irrefutable realization recorded in our DNA.

It was a strategic move, putting us through this experience, as not only did we look into the face of primal darkness incarnate in living entities, but also felt the power of light and walked across the bridge to a realm created by the full spectrum of its intelligence. It was this experience that supported us through the many hardships and sacrifices that lay ahead in the eighteen years it would take to refine our ability to download and embody the holonomic model of transcendence that was to become the Template.

We became aware of an amalgamated presence of many beings surrounding us, holding us in loving embrace. Instinct took us, and I joined my palms against Jiva's, as it seemed we had done before in some other time. From deep within my soul came the words and we spoke them, a pledge of service which went beyond this world and may not be written.

Stars began to emerge in a pink and violet sky, hues that evoked the supernatural extravagance of the colours which made that other paradigm so aesthetically compelling. We felt so fortunate to have had this adventure and thanked Sowelu. To those beings we met we also extended our thanks, our understanding and our forgiveness. We loved and accepted them as we loved and accepted ourselves, recognizing our connectedness to all creation.

Once off the Green Lake property, reality regained its density and fear began to intrude. Jiva steered our disinclined car along the lonely pitted dirt road home, as darkness fell fast and gathered in our wake. At home, we sat for many hours going over and over all that had happened. We even considered leaving Hawaii that very night if possible! There was an all-pervading sense of helplessness. The memory of the authentic power we had wielded so beautifully with the chant of light had been subsumed by the density of our fear brought on by darkness and exhaustion and by a reality that equates power with force and the technology of control.

The beings we encountered obviously had a technology far superior to our own, devices designed to intrude into the very recesses of the mind, to instil fear and gain ultimate control. What had they wanted from us? We realized that we had escaped an attempted abduction. Did they really know where we lived? Were they watching us? Regardless of our prior positivity, this shadow side was inevitably going to surface. I was aware of being in shock. You can read about them and see the videos, but coming face to face with the impossibility of aliens in broad daylight sets a new point of reference which must be integrated into each and every day. Everything is then seen from a perspective that takes this event into consideration. It is impossible to describe these beings without it sounding like characters in a 'B' horror movie, for they so classically embody the stuff of nightmares; their presence instantly dredges up the most iconic fears, fears that are the fodder for all that drives this world of duality to murder and war. They are the embodiment of deceit, decay and the corruption of death itself. Standing in their presence affords no shade of reason with which to create an arena for diplomacy, no variable of emotion with which to negotiate. It is not part of their nature to have any concern or regard for anything other than their own agendas.

Neither time nor stars pause for the events we find so momentous and, finally, we could no longer keep at bay the sleep that would bring respite from the heady mixture of elation and trepidation.

8

KAHUNA CONNECTION

WE WOKE AS THE GENTLE MORNING SUN kissed the tips of the palm trees, filtering through them to dance a jungle motif across the wooden floor on which we slept. We felt better, but different - very, very different. Fear still lingered in the background, but the overwhelming feeling was of having awakened from a long dream, and beneath the fear was gratitude.

We viewed this experience as a gift beyond measure. However, for me it had brought to the surface fears I never knew I had. It was difficult to let Zak out of my sight for a moment. I never slept through the night, waking countless times to make sure that all was well.

Jiva had begged me not to mention the beings we met on Green Mountain to friends as he rightly anticipated their disbelief.

However, I did share this experience with a close friend who I knew to be very well informed about the various global deceptions that had begun to surface. Even though she tried hard not to show it, she was obviously concerned for our sanity.

In the years that followed we were to discover more and more information about the Annunaki (as we learned they were called) as it came forth from anthropological and archaeological sources. Some of this documentation had been around for quite some time but had not been able to break through the membrane of denial that our race maintains about the existence of extra-terrestrials on Earth.

But at this time, when Jiva and I discussed the Green Mountain meeting, it was mostly about the alternate reality we had experienced and that aspect of our identities it had revealed to us. We did not entirely comprehend certain aspects of the event. What dimension had we entered? How was it possible to be in two realities simultaneously? How was it that we looked different in that other place? As to the beings we met, we spoke of them to each other in order to integrate the impossible fact of their existence into our consciousness and to keep the story alive with the telling of it, as many had done before us. Up until this time our initiations, though jarring and arduous, had served to awaken us to a magical perception of life, to an expanded concept of reality, an opening of the heart and mind. Our experience of what we would come to know as the full manifestation of the immortal continuum, expressed through the electromagnetic interference patterns of the tantric union of Earth and Sun, was to become the core of cohesion that allowed us to accept the dark malevolence that had accompanied our experience that day on the mountain.

To our generation, as children of the '60s, the advent of the cosmic Age of Aquarius held the promise of the arrival of a numinous presence, starmen and starwomen who were to deliver messages of Humanity's liberation from suffering, but we were not expecting this. However, on a cellular level, the beings we met on Green Mountain were not strangers to us. We had learned of them when we had been briefed for this mission and, on some level, we knew that every diversion from the living truth of nature, every lie told, every heart broken, every child abused, every drop of blood spilt in war is rooted in our disconnection from the Source of Creation, as a result of the degradation of the Human genetic code which was perpetrated by this race. The evidence of their existence was now forever factored into the whole of our lives. From that time forward, the reverberation of the meeting on the mountain would eat away at all the definitions of normality that came before it. Time and all of life would conspire to draw aside the veil of denial that would expose these beings and what they had done to our race, our planet and our solar system.

The dream that explained it all came to me just before dawn in Kapoho. What dominated this dream was the clear explanation of the intricacies of the higher physics of creation, the cosmic mechanics of the matrix that was to become the schematic for the realization of a new model of existence. It was most definitely an out-of-body experience. The information was not downloaded but imparted by another being during a conversation. As I was merging back into my body and into the morning to which I woke I was still speaking.

"Of course, it's so obvious, so simple, so very simple," I heard myself say as I opened my eyes. Within seconds I forgot everything, but the resonance of the information given in that dream is within me, as it is within us all. It is a question of remembering.

In the months that followed our cosmic conference on Green Mountain, it became clear that our period of grace in Kapoho and the luxury of seclusion afforded by our little shack were to come to an end. It was on the morning of my birthday, shortly before we left Hawaii for England, that I felt the strong presence of my mother's spirit. I explained to Jiva that she had always delighted in giving me particularly meaningful gifts on my birthday.

"She wants to give me something today," I told him.

I answered a knock at our door at around eleven that morning to find a young woman there. As she introduced herself I thought at first that she was nervous, but then realized she was slightly embarrassed. She had brought a message for me and was unsure as to how it would be received. Nina was the partner of

Makua, a well-known shaman referred to in Hawaiian as a Kahuna, who lived not far away. She had a gift for me from my mother. My mother's spirit had come to her very early that morning and directed her to our house. She said this with the slight trepidation of not knowing whether her message would be received with the respect it deserved. I shared with her my intuition that my mother wanted to communicate with me as it was my birthday. Nina handed me a heavy solid silver ring with the face of a woman moulded into it, a face which was an unmistakable likeness of my mother. Nina had had this ring for many years and had been requested that morning to give it to me. This exchange had taken place on the doorstep of our shack and I finally recovered enough from my surprise to invite Nina in. She declined, saying she was needed at home.

We made enquiries among our friends and discovered that Makua was a seventh generation Kahuna of considerable renown who officiated at the major sacred Hawaiian ceremonies on all the islands. He was known to live on the south side of the island, but was a recluse, only leaving his home for official ceremonies. His phone number and address were kept secret.

About a week after Nina's visit, she returned one morning to invite us, on Makua's behalf, to visit with him the next afternoon. Jiva was adamant that he must create a specific gift for Makua and spent the rest of the day making a ceremonial fan out of the wing of an owl he had found on the Green Lake property. That night, I painted the dried putty that held the wing onto the handle; one side night, the other side day.

At the appointed hour in the afternoon we arrived at the home of Nina and Makua, the location of which we were sworn never to reveal. Nina welcomed us into the house which was only barely more substantial than our own. The austerity of the small wooden home spoke of its inhabitants' selfless devotion to the care of others. It did, however, borrow its beauty from the ocean in which it stood - half the house teetered on high stilts embedded in the lava pools.

Framed with the blue sky and the bluer ocean behind him, Makua stood. His presence was larger than life and yet not overpowering. His face was dominated by eyes that had seen much love and suffering and the warmth of a tired but sincere smile. At first, I thought he was wearing a feathered cloak, but then I realized it was a tattoo of a ceremonial feathered garment almost covering his entire body, a mark of honour conferred upon Kahunas of his standing. One of his legs had a massive dent with extensive scarring around it, the result of a shark bite. The shark was Makua's Amakua, both his ally and his nemesis - a powerful and exacting Medicine to carry - one that had given him immeasurable gifts at great cost.

Makua's majestic demeanour derived not from any personal contrivance of his own sense of importance, but from his heart and soul, and from the grace he had gained from surrendering to the extraordinary and difficult life the stars had conspired to bestow upon him. As he welcomed us to his home the air around was thick with a sense of the pre-ordained. We introduced ourselves and Jiva offered Makua the brightly painted owl-wing fan. Makua held it delicately in his large gentle hands as tears filmed his eyes. He nodded slowly as the gift spoke words to him from beyond the event of its giving. Jiva had so perfectly anticipated the medicine of this owl-wing's resonance with Makua's spirit. He looked deeply into Jiva's eyes and asked,

"How did you know?"

For the next five hours Makua 'spoke story'. We learned of many secrets of the shamanic Hawaiian tradition. Some of his stories revealed the concerns he had for the future of his islands and his people. Their spiritual lifestyles and Ohana traditions were eroding with alarming speed. Most of Hawaii's real-estate was owned by the Japanese and its infrastructure was run by America. Racially motivated violence was endemic. As he told his stories, Makua was backlit by the ever-changing colours that washed the sea and the sky behind him. As evening graciously gave way to night, clouds gathered darkly, under-lit by the last of the light as the never-setting Sun slipped beneath the ocean rim to begin its journey under the world to bestow upon other lives the blessing that is morning's first light, to illuminate other sacred gatherings of Earth's children, telling stories, keeping the faith.

It seemed there was a specific body of information that Makua was compelled to transmit and, when his lilting voice slowed and came to the end of another story, we felt it was to be the last and we should leave him to his much-needed rest.

As we were leaving, Jiva asked him if he was familiar with a particular ceremony that was held here in Kapoho in which three groups of people participated, each wearing a different colour with matching banners. Makua was taken aback and asked in surprise how we knew of this. He explained that it was an ancient ceremony practiced by the ancestors of the three tribes of this area, a sacred and magical ceremony of unification and renewal that was said to reach across the divide to the ancestors. We told him of what we had seen on Green Mountain. We had 'lifted the veils of time', he said, and had witnessed the old way of opening portals into the past. Jiva and I sent an unspoken message to each other and Jiva then told Makua of our encounter with the beings we met on Green Mountain. It was at this point that the deeper reasons for our meeting were revealed to one and all and its palpable portent gathered around us in the candlelit darkness of the night. Makua picked up the owl fan as though he was inspecting our credentials and weighing up how much he could trust us. He told us that the 'Kapu' warning sign at the entrance of the Green Lake property was because of the stories that had been handed down by the Hawaiians about 'monsters' that lived in the lake and in the mountain. Some people who had gone there had disappeared. These beings had also been seen on the north side of the mountain. Several people had come to him, as a Kahuna, to relate their experiences with these beings. He himself had seen one as his headlights picked out its strange form late one night. No one knew where they were from, only that they came out of the ground and the water. Makua's final advice to us that night was to honour, acknowledge and act upon our initiations.

"Ride the wave," he said, "or the next one will be bigger and may drown you!"

The sharing of our experience on Green Mountain with Makua and having his supportive feedback meant a lot to us. We did not see Makua and Nina again for several months. We were busy getting ready for our journey to England. The end of our time in our sanctuary was rushing towards us. Although we were not party people, we had family and many friends on the Big Island, mostly met through the reconnection work I had been doing, and we decided to throw a going-away party.

A couple of days before the gathering I called Nina to invite her. I invited Makua also but let her know I was doing so only as a gesture of respect, knowing that he rarely left his home other than to officiate at ceremonies. She told me that was pretty much the case, particularly as he was to officiate in Maui, Oahu and Molokai that same week and would only just arrive home on the day of the party. His leg was giving him a lot of pain and she anticipated the exhausted state he was usually in after such an expenditure of energy.

Before anyone arrived, we held a small ceremony using incense and an eagle feather to appeal to the mosquitoes to take a break that night.

We were surprised when at least forty people turned up to the party. Our tiny home seemed to stretch with each arrival. We had stipulated that the catering was 'pot luck' and on every possible surface was a sumptuous vegetarian dish. One friend who supplied the health food stores with cakes brought a mouth-watering array. At around ten o'clock everyone deserted the house to watch Stan, a fire juggler, perform on the lawn. Near the end of his performance I slipped quietly through the glass doors into the house.

Standing in the centre of the room was Makua. He had come straight from a ceremony on Molokai and was dressed in full ceremonial garb. A cloak of feathers that mimicked his own tattoo was draped over his shoulders and in his hand he held a burnished and intricately carved staff, its handle worn smooth with years; hanging from his waist was the owl fan. He was magnificent. The noble stance of his being transcended the obvious pain he was in and the exhaustion that hung around his eyes.

"They told me I had to come," he spoke softly, resigned yet happy to be there. I built a tower of cushions in front of the only chair for his leg to rest upon. The room was highly charged, and I could sense a gathered presence giving him energy. The colour came back to him and he seemed comfortable and relaxed.

Soon the revellers began to return. They responded immediately with silent reverence to Makua's presence and wordlessly gathered around him, some on the floor, some sitting on the kitchen counter, others standing, as Makua told the stories of Hawaii, its true history and the magic of its Kahunas. No one spoke, no one even asked a question of him - they did not need to, as Makua's stories were as one long song, seamlessly strung together with a melody of meaning that told the tales of his ancestors.

When he was spent and had once again honoured the sacred responsibility to which he was so dedicated, we walked out to the front of the house with him to say our goodbyes. The three of us stood in starlight and silence; between us, a well of understanding. A palm tree whispered as a fragrant breath of night air caressed us, when from Makua came the lilting sounds of his own language. The words he spoke circled round us, weaving us into their meaning. After another silence he spoke again.

"I have adopted you. You are now held in my circle of love and protection as a Kahuna of Hawaii. This is your home. Come back soon, you will always be welcome." We would learn the depth of the power of these words when we returned to Hawaii, seventeen years later. Aloha, Makua…aloha. We would never see him in body again.

It was 5am as we re-entered our little abode to find the rooms still filled with people. The room glowed softly with candlelight, but more than that: it shone with the love of friends and family, it burned with the incandescence of all that had transpired within it over the last two years - the transformations, the realizations, the love born and shared. The reconnection of circuitry that all present had experienced was in no small way a contributing factor to the harmony that wove them together. These people, friends and strangers, had opened the secret recesses of their lives to me and to the mirror; all the pain, the tragedy and beauty of being Human. I recalled our arrival in that empty room, now so filled. My heart broke to leave it. As the last person left, he turned at the door,

"I have lived in Hawaii for twenty-two years. The meeting here with Makua was what I have always wanted and dreamed of. It was the ultimate Hawaiian experience. Thank you."

Amazingly, the mosquitoes had bitten no-one that night.

The rest of our departure from Hawaii I cannot share with you. Too many goodbyes...Monkey...it is too sad. I've never been able to handle goodbyes.

9

DEEP IN THE WATERS OF AVALON

OUR EXPERIENCE ON GREEN MOUNTAIN had stirred memories of our quintessential identities and our reasons for being here on Earth in this time period. This was to be the bedrock that gave us the strength to endure all the trials that were to come our way in the years that followed, as we were given more and more information and trained to contain and embody it. This was a not-so-gradual process of shock treatments that came by way of a pestilence of initiations. Our training ground was to be a deceptively enchanting place; Glastonbury, the Isle of Avalon in Somerset, in the Faerie-drenched West Country of England. Any romantic idea we had of this ancient spiritual centre was to be quickly swept aside.

Some months before we had realized that we were to leave

Hawaii for England we had been given Marion Zimmer Bradley's book 'The Mists of Avalon' to read and had envisioned ourselves living on the side of the Tor, an ancient pagan earthwork that is the centre of the Isle of Avalon, dominating the landscape. I had spent several summers in the West Country when I was a teenager and to me it was the heart and soul of England.

In my vision I saw our home on several acres of land with a long driveway on the side of the Tor. I was told by friends who had been there that it was difficult to find anywhere to live at all in Glastonbury and that to be right on the Tor was virtually impossible. Nevertheless, within an hour of our arrival we had rented 'Chalice Lodge', a large house on four acres of land nestled between the Tor and Chalice Hill. It had a long driveway and the view of the Tor imposed itself through almost all its windows. The house had just become available on the day before our arrival.

About the potency of Glastonbury much has been written by many. It is the pagan interpretation of Glastonbury that comes closest to translating its living truth. Even so, as with all systems of belief in this distorted dualistic paradigm, the simple legitimacy of nature as an expression of the genius of Source Consciousness is burdened with an overlay of hierarchical doctrine that eventually serves to empower some and not others. In the absence of the electromagnetic connection of circuitry that would deliver the energetic nature of Source Consciousness into the individual auric field, drawing the Human heart-body-mind system into the divine immortal continuum, providing an organic non-theistic self-realized state of Samadhi, paths of convolution are created instead and layered with the various archetypes of the angelic-demonic conflict and the do's and don'ts of duality.

There are sites on this planet that offer more energy and clarity than others and yet even they cannot escape the dense mantle of dissonant frequency that cloaks the Earth in a mutant reality. The holonomic symbiosis between all forms of manifest existence within our solar system is the core matrix that orchestrates and organizes our evolution. The original pattern of this interaction has been disrupted and perverted into the dualistic conflict-riddled world that we are presently experiencing. In the years to come we would learn how this disruption was executed and how the mutant realm was stabilized.

In Hawaii we had learned from various sources, including a mainstream science magazine, that of three billion base-pair chemicals in our genetic code only sixty million are active, around only 2%. The science magazine referred to the remaining 98% as 'junk DNA' that was most probably there to kick in at some future point in time when we might need extra defence against disease. If this was the case, then surely, with AIDS wiping out generations of Africans, this material would have kicked in?

As Jiva and I began working more with circuitry, it became obvious that the disconnection of circuitry and the modification of the genetic code were related. Much more than this, the disturbance in our electromagnetic energy field and the mutation of our genetic codes are reflected in all aspects of our existence and perception. The interference patterns created by the confluence of Earth and stars mirror this distortion within our genetic codes, our divine blueprint, our behavioural reference points and in the geomancy of our Earth's natural expression. How could that not be so, given the holographic nature of the universe? The portal that is Glastonbury is no exception. The light that pours into this stargate comes with its dualistic counterpart. Glastonbury calls out to those who recognize the power of the elemental alchemy of natural magic. Some have hearts big enough to translate this powerful energy - many do not.

The attributes that clothe the archetypes of the Isle of Avalon are not simple lore and legend but have been fashioned by the translation of its modified geomagnetism and by the erroneous definitions of god and goddess that have, as elsewhere, been inserted into the pantheon of archetypes via a modified and sometimes entirely false recall of history. There are sagas of kings and courts, struggles and tribulations. Often, the full chronicle of events and conditions linked to these legendary times are romanticized, their grim and grisly aspects sanitized. It was power and control that motivated spiritual, social and political structures and it was war and more war that prevailed because of it.

If all was as it was originally designed in the creation of the Human masterpiece and its relationship to Sun, Earth and stars, the archetypes that permeated the morphogenetic field of Glastonbury would be very different. There would not be, in all of the Isles of Britain, any need for a figurehead that represented the insanity of individual supremacy - a king, no matter how great his lion-heart. For a true Human needs no governing: no kings, no queens, no priestesses, no priests. These iconic personalities are caricatures arising from the mutant Human condition and yet everywhere in Glastonbury they are lauded, revered and cherished, as people attempt to reunite these attributes into a whole self. The resurrection of the original Human masterpiece which is sovereign over its own existence, and which is connected to the Benevolent Source of its Creation without mediation or censorship, is the ultimate journey of reconnection that is offered through any portal that bridges this mutant paradigm to all the time and energy levels in the universe. The true raw energy of Glastonbury is the non-theistic organically present sacredness that needs no translation, a magical proximity that is as potent and tangible amid the blossoms and pastel skies of spring's Beltane as it is in the depths of a bare and cold winter solstice. On any day in between, as you step out of a pub or supermarket, it is there to greet you, a lingering recollection that pervades the most mundane day and compels you to experience all things as sacred.

As with all small town communities, the macrocosmic influence of the world is mirrored in the microcosmic amphitheatre of the mini-morphic field. The turgid Human drama of Glastonbury, however, has a unique flavour. Its particular eccentricities take nonconformity to outlandish proportions. The gossip on the High Street has more to do with who is channelling the dark side, holding black rituals or working with dubious extra-terrestrials rather than who may be cavorting with whom, although that is also of great interest to one and all. Loiter long enough to scratch the surface of the spiritual façade in Glastonbury and you will soon find you are playing with fire. If you don't have the time and courage to go within and make the adjustments and realignments demanded by the energies of this portal in order to gain equipoise in the eye of the storm, best move on quickly.

After our first few weeks there, that was without doubt my desire. It was Jiva who talked me into staying. To this day I cannot say I am totally glad we did. Surely there was an easier way? It would have been a gentler ride if we had slipped quietly into the weave of Glastonbury's rich and pernicious tapestry, keeping a low profile. Instead, we went like lambs to the slaughter. We did not understand the deeply ingrained territorial behaviour patterns of the white Anglo-Saxon mindset that, entrained by a long history of invasion, does not welcome strangers. Jiva's Texan accent was a give-away and, although both my parents were thoroughly Irish, I had been raised in the Far East and attended several American schools and I too was considered an outsider. Our lack of conformity in this area could have, to some degree, been overlooked and forgiven. However, through a myriad of synchronistic events, we found ourselves the guardians of an ancient sacred site - the White Spring. This was the spring at which Morgane, the priestess of 'The Mists of Avalon' was scrying. It was clear to us that this was a position we had come to take up. We were not aware of how difficult it would be.

The White Spring is a sacred spring that has flowed from the base of the Tor since time immemorial. When we were called to be its guardians and to honour it as our teacher, it was encased in an old stone building with turrets. The spring flowed through and out into Glastonbury at the rate of seventeen thousand gallons a day.

We became much immersed in the mystery and the simple power of water. Water…caressing new life in the womb, destroying and levelling mountains and villages…giving and taking life. Gentle rains that implore shoots to unfold, crashing waves that grind great rocks to sand - its range is total and complete, flowing ceaselessly as time itself, its melody the theme-tune of life on Earth. Three quarters of the surface of this blue-green jewel of the galaxy is water, the liquid cohesion that binds all life together; every drop sacred, every drop a living entity, the blood of Mother Earth.

This spring existed long before we were able to form the words we use to name it, or the town it graces. The extraordinary quality of the White Spring has not been fashioned by legends, but by the combination of the unfathomable magical properties of the element of water itself and by its positioning between Earth and stars. It is the magnetism of this land and the power and purity of its waters that have drawn legend to it. The Celtic priestess of the past gazed upon the crystal clear waters of the spring to transcend the time-space continuum and to view the future, her trance state created by an infinite succession of reflections, removing one by one the obstacles of time, that she might delve deeper and deeper into the memories held within the libraries of her genetic codes, accessing the story of this blue-green globe spinning in the galaxy, linking her awareness into the wheel of eternal existence. Through her body, seventy-five percent water, she experienced holonomic resonance...oneness. The distinction between awareness and that of which it is aware dissipated as she unified with the flow.

Water makes life on this planet possible. Our entire ecosystem is a dance of life in which water is the rhythm. Because it has become so available to us and we are able to simply turn on the tap without any thought as to where that water has come from, we have come to see it as ordinary, when in actuality it is one of the strangest substances known to science. One of the properties that make it so extraordinary is that water has memory. Potently impressionable, it is able to store electromagnetic and biological information as it is imprinted with zones of coherence, its microstructure retaining information concerning substances with which it has been in contact. It is able to communicate with the cellular infrastructure of the Human body, giving it bio-informational signals, just as it does to plants.

The waters of the White Spring gestate in the womb of the

Mother beneath the Tor. There it matures by absorbing the characteristics and properties of all it encounters. Enriched with trace elements, minerals and salts, it rises freely to the surface to do that which it does best...nurturing, nourishing and rejuvenating. It emerges alive and infused with properties both tangible and intangible, for it carries not only elemental nourishment but also the memory of its journey through the land of the Faerie, of every stone and every starlit night.

St Michael's church, built hundreds of years ago on Glastonbury Tor, has been eroded by the forces of nature, the wind and the rain. The very stone used in its construction holds more information regarding the true nature of Humanity than does any temple or church it has been used to build. If you break it down to its molecular beginnings you will find the form of the star tetrahedron. There, in geometric language, is the interaction and union of the male and female potencies that are at the Heart of the Cosmos.

However, a living symbology that is as potent today as it has always been is within the properties of the 'red' and the 'white' waters of Chalice Well and the White Spring. Infused by deposits of iron and calcium, they are said to be symbolic of menstrual blood and semen, the male and female potencies. These waters are the physical manifestation of these two energetic functions within the alchemical brew of creation, the opposites a living reflection of the divided aspects of the Supreme Individuality that has polarized in the Human male and the Human female for the purpose of enjoying love. The positioning of Chalice Hill and the Tor and the proximity and union of the Red and the White Springs creates a potential between polarized and attractive energies, the perfect portal through which the solar system can activate the sacred marriage on Earth and within the Human race. It is the propensities of the red and the white that make Glastonbury a cauldron of living vibrant energies. Look closely and you will see that the waters of the White Spring are not only white, for the waters of the red and the white have found each other and emerge unified beyond the laws and politics of Humanity.

Red and white represent the Faerie world. In Glastonbury, the world of the Faerie is still much revered, for the veils between the worlds are at times as fine as the mists. Those that inhabit this world are not the diminutive beings of English fairy tales but entities of great stature and supernatural knowledge and power, able to practice the art of harmony, to identify their consciousness with various resonances and therefore ride those frequencies to different levels of reality. They were and are the worldbridgers.

Over the years the natural environment of the Isle of Avalon has been destroyed by the same disregard for sacred space that allowed a village to be built in the centre of the Avebury stone circle. The site of the White Spring has not escaped ignorant intervention either. In the 1870s the Water Board built a stone reservoir over it to supply the town of Glastonbury. Initially, there was an outcry by those of the community that valued the traditions associated with this spring, but over time those voices were stilled, and it passed out of mind. The pleasant peaceful rocky coombe strewn with flowers and moss that cradled those gurgling waters was buried beneath the stony structures of an over-populated age. The profundity of the White Spring passed into obscurity. The reservoir was not used for long, possibly because the calcium-rich water quickly blocked pipes. It remained unused until the mid-1980s when it was sold to a private purchaser, who then constructed within it a café and a shop.

On November 1st, 1992, Celtic New Year's Day, Jiva and I

became leaseholders and guardians of the White Spring. Drawn as we are to the deep end of things, we threw ourselves into the task with passion, excitement and naiveté. Soon we began to experience physical, mental and emotional disturbances that did not seem to originate from any internal conflict of which we were aware. Jiva experienced a continual sharp pain in the middle of his back, as though someone was stabbing him, and I suffered inexplicable and prolonged headaches. We were soon to learn of one of the favourite pastimes of some of Glastonbury's denizens: psychic attack.

One afternoon we were paid a seemingly friendly visit by a well-known local couple. They said they were patrons of the White Spring and wanted to meet us. We invited them in. The conversation that followed was innocuous enough and I offered them tea. In my absence the woman asked to use the toilet. As I was returning to the front room with a tray of tea I passed the bathroom door which was ajar enough for me to see her crouched over the wastebasket, retrieving what appeared to be hairs from my hairbrush. I was puzzled, but too ignorant to be alarmed. Before leaving, the man asked if he might leave his crystal on our altar to 'absorb the energies of the Tor'. How charming, we thought.

Soon after this strange visit we had another one. This time it was from a likable fellow who had been working with us and had recently quit. He identified himself as a working Druid. It was obvious that the message he had for us was difficult to give and he was torn in this task. He eventually informed us that there was a group of locals who were heavily against our presence at the White Spring as it was felt we were not, in their estimation, eligible for the position of guardians of an English sacred site. Furthermore, a coven had been formed to drive us not only from the Spring but from Glastonbury altogether. Effigies had been constructed to be ritually used to this end. Our Druid friend confessed he had been a member of this coven but had, now that he knew us, decided to leave. When he had learned that a mirror had inexplicably fallen off the wall onto our cat, breaking her back, he felt the need to warn us. He suggested several ways to protect ourselves and our home.

We had been devastated by Minky's accident. Jiva, Zak and I had spent the night sleeping in a circle around her on the floor and at morning's light set off for the vet. After x-raying her he informed us that if she was lucky she might walk again after about four weeks. Miraculously, she was up and about in five days.

Up until then, I had been letting Jiva know that I wanted very much to leave the Spring and Glastonbury and now I had more understanding as to why. However, this was the turning point for me. Forewarned is forearmed and I now had the measure of the hearts and minds of those I was up against. The situation pressed us to look deeper into the reason for our presence on this portal as guardians of such an intense initiation cave. We agreed that we would stay, no matter what. We remained the guardians of the White Spring for ten years.

I won't drag myself or you through the details of the long chain of events and initiations that delineated the gladiatorial arena of Glastonbury, for it was the treasures we came away with that mattered. One of the greatest of these gifts came disguised as loss and sorrow. My father, James William Tobin of Southern Ireland, had come to live with us in Glastonbury as he had broken his leg and could no longer do those small but important tasks that had allowed him his much-valued independence. He rapidly descended into depression and his health suffered. On March 15th Jiva, Zak and I took his ashes up to the top of the Tor to release them. I had mentioned to a couple of people who came into the Spring that I would be doing this at sunrise, and, to our surprise, when we reached the tower on the Tor at around 5am, there to greet us were two fellows we hardly knew. One of them played the conch shell as the Sun rose and under-lit the morning gathering of clouds. The other fellow played his didge as we began to release the ashes. A mist came down upon us all and within its moist shroud we found ourselves isolated, each of us with our own struggle to comprehend the abomination that is death.

I had known that the ashes of my mother, Valerie, were not to be released in Hawaii and had kept them with me these five years. We liberated them on Chalice Hill. This done, in my bed in the valley between the Tor and Chalice Hill, I dreamed of them both.

It was then that a key turned, and the land opened her heart to me that spring and summer. 'You and I are one,' she said. Had we been offered a ticket to anywhere in the world that summer, we would not have budged from the grounds of Chalice Lodge. The garden hedges were swathed in blossoming vines. Bluebells and foxgloves grew profuse and unrestrained around the perimeters of the garden which was carpeted with daisies. The plum orchard, heavy with sweet aromas, gave and gave. Someone had told Jiva that faeries abhorred lawnmowers and he had readily latched on to this convenient tale - the grass grew long and wild. It seemed the Sun shone all summer as the rolling hills around us languished in hazy tranquillity.

I have travelled throughout my whole life, as my parents lived like gypsies: I had circled the world twice by the age of seven. I went to school on large ocean liners and can remember camels on the shores of the Suez Canal before it was closed to the West. But it is here in the British Isles that the land speaks to me, a seed language that resonates with my own codes. Behind the exhaustion of a land that reeks of ownership is the still-beating heart of the Mother that beckons Her children to shelter beneath Her tattered skirt of green. It was not the land that flourished under the 'divide and rule' ethos that enslaved half the world. Within the wind that whispered through the trees there was no talk of Empire. That was a Human agenda, an agenda now bent upon the subjugation of those who live outside the sanctioned perimeter of a morality stabilized by a guilt that smothers our dreams, and behind this agenda is one not-so-Human.

Our presence in Glastonbury was no accidental connivance

of circumstance, nor was it coincidence that within only a few months we were living, working and dreaming in the very lap of the Isle of Avalon. We had come to tread between the worlds, between agony and ecstasy, between the dream and the nightmare, to become strong and courageous, to surrender any shallow dream of happiness, cruelly torn away as the light and the shadow fashioned our joy and sorrow in equal measure, to fall deep in the waters of perpetual renewal and be weighed not against the laws of man but by the sacred law that exists beyond the rule of culture. In Glastonbury you may experience bliss as you catch your breath between initiations, but you will never be happy. Happiness is for children. To reach for its sticky sweetness in the midst of an age of obvious terminal decline, whilst wars and genocide rage a short plane ride away, is to reach for the snooze button. Happiness is a dangerous seductive detour; a way to make your prison more comfortable, the lies more palatable; to make this mutant paradigm, riddled with abominations, work for you personally by ensuring that all your ever-expanding comfort zones are satiated through a hollow consumer-based definition of abundance. All the conditional components of your well-being need high maintenance to perpetuate this erroneous form of stability on the tightrope of survival between the cradle and the grave. Happiness is for mortals. Bliss and ecstasy are not reliant upon the arrangement of circumstances but are realized by the loss of denial rather than adherence to it.

Intellectually, I know that it is against the flow of the wide, deep river of life to harbour regret and yet to this day there are words, deeds, moments that I would unashamedly reclaim from time's steely hold...if I could. In my mind and heart, I have re-written some parts of the play and yet if it were any other way, would I be here today? I treasure the shattering of my heart that rendered it able to hold more and the 'divine ambivalence' I gained, allowing me to find equipoise in the midst of bedlam and injustice, that I might care deeply and yet not give a damn.

And then there was the gift that was at the epicentre of it all. It was on this sacred land where the Celtic doctrine of immortality is still felt and seen in the never beginning, never ending knot-work, cryptic in the limbs of yew and in the runes masked in the boughs of oak, that elemental alchemy imbued our consciousness and stirred in the temple of our remembrance...a memory...the memory of ceremony.

10

ALCHEMICAL CEREMONY

BY THE END OF SUMMER, I began the mirror work I had learned in Hawaii. My first client was newly out of prison where he had spent six years. I didn't ask him what he was in for but waited for him to surrender that information. He had gone through a metamorphosis in the time that he had been in an isolation cell and since his release had been hungrily devouring information to assist him in integrating the newly discovered facets of his identity. He was a middle-aged working-class fellow with worn shoes, whose austere and traumatic introduction to an alternate reality had caught him devoid of the pretentious flannel that often coats the neophyte. He was a very genuine person and I liked him immediately.

He expressed to me a need to forgive his father, who, he

said, had sodomized him when he was two years old. I asked how he knew this; did he remember it? Did his father confess it? Or someone else in the family? No, he said, a psychic he had been to see at a healing centre had 'channelled' it. He was shocked and deeply pained by this revelation, as he had been very close to his father. At this point he let me know that he had been imprisoned for a murder which he had committed. His lack of self-worth and his inability to trust his own knowing in the light of this terrible act had undermined his own authority and he was vulnerable to and impressed by the 'spiritual glamour' of this flamboyant New Age centre, its extravagance designed to bolster the sham and the charlatans. He had put himself, his memory, and his life, into their hands.

Using the mirror, he accessed his own body-truth via his eyes and the testing process of kinesiology. Opening the vault within the temple of his remembrance he was able to retrieve the loving relationship he had shared with his father. There had been no sexual abuse. As he stared into the windows of his soul he reached the full implications of his transgression within the entire sphere of his existence. He accessed the divine worth of the life he had taken from another and swam deep in the ocean of shame and guilt. Finally, spent of tears and heartbreak, he drew himself on to the shores of forgiveness, forgiving himself and all the deviations from love that had set him upon the path of destruction.

My second patient was a quiet, gentle yet powerful woman in her mid-thirties who had recently learned she had a tumour in her breast. She had been sexually molested by her father from a very early age until she was sixteen years old. He had preserved this harrowing evidence of a lost childhood through photographic documentation. It was several hours before she was able to look at herself in the mirror. It took two five-hour sessions for her to come to the point of understanding, integrating and forgiving what had happened to her; a forgiveness that existed before either she or the one who had given her life had taken one breath, a forgiveness that integrated the whole Human predicament. Thus, she ceased to be overwhelmed by the personal import of her ordeal, granting this forgiveness neither to exonerate her father's behaviour, nor to allow him impunity for the deed; not through the intellectual evocation of compassionate understanding, but through an innate comprehension of his need for healing and an appreciation of the hell he must have known. More than this, she retrieved through this shamanic forgiveness a lost aspect of herself that existed beyond the pain of a mutant Human. She was carried above herself, her sorrow-filled home, the streets of her childhood, her past identity, to unify with her divine immortal self that played among the stars, re-establishing her innate self-worth, a divine gift, not only intellectually and emotionally, but also via the electromagnetic energetic nature of Source Consciousness delivered and integrated through her reconnected circuitry.

Her tumour disappeared within forty-eight hours of her last session. She was a friend of the editor of a popular magazine who then contacted me for an article on my work. After its publication I was booked three weeks in advance. This form of one-on-one 'therapy', quantum as it was, was still very draining and I would find I had to lie down for at least an hour between patients. One afternoon as I was doing this, stilling my mind and drawing in the free Earth energies that emanated from my garden, it came to me that there were more circuits and with that remembrance came an immediate impression of where they were. The test points for these circuits were at the third eye, crown and throat and six to eight inches above the crown in the auric field. I eagerly awaited Jiva's return, so that I might use him to test these circuits.

When Jiva returned he was as excited as I was and yet, when I asked to test these points on him, he laughed and said I would need to use someone else as he had twenty-five years of meditational practice and these points on him would be strong and connected. I suggested we test them, just for practice. His circuits were extremely weak.

"Test me again," he said with a look of confusion and disbelief.

As the Sun rose the next morning, I downloaded the sonic code that would trigger a harmonic within the cerebral cortex which was resonant with the function of the Third Eye, Crown, Throat and Auric Circuits, as stipulated in the original Human blueprint; our Soul Covenant, prior to our genetic modification, returning coherence to the relevant circuitry that would 'load' this divine data into the Human bio-computational field.

Closely following the code was a piece of information that took me by surprise. I didn't reject this information, but it made me strangely uncomfortable. The sonic code that was to reconnect the four Air Circuits was to be interfaced with via a ceremonial schematic. The impulse of my western mind was to validate experience through intellectual analysis. I was yet to learn that ceremony is not exclusively of the mind or the emotions or even a combination of both. It is an alchemical coalescence, a wedding, which inspires a brain chemistry that unfetters the intellect from its dogmatic entrenchment within the linear space-time continuum. Ceremony bridges the chasm between a culture bled of its elemental consciousness and its ancient shamanic roots.

Most people are more trusting of a sanitized clinical environment in which to regurgitate the endless dramas of lives whose lack of fulfilment lies deep in the roots of their genetic modification and their separation from Source. They surrender their pain into the hands of a therapist who is willing, for the allotted hour, to climb into the pit of their misery, to look for the misplaced trust, the ruined innocence, the lost childhood, in a search for the beginnings of loneliness and disassociation, not knowing that it began long ago with separation from the embrace of a divine immortal continuum.

As Einstein said, the solution is never found at the level of the problem. Ceremony is a language that transcends time and culture, the solution that exists outside of the problem. Our analytical skills evolve from brain four fifths of which is inactive. Thus, to psychoanalyze our problems is to utilize a solution that exists at the same level. Unlike therapies that thrust us time and again into the trauma vortex, steering further into the turbulent waters of insane conflict, ceremony takes us into a higher vibration of healing that honours us as magnificent masterpieces of impeccable Human design and allows a graceful movement into a state of original innocence. Resonant with the richness of the transformational Age of Aquarius, this higher-frequency healing shifts our focus to the cerebral cortex, denying the reptilian brain its monopoly over our conscious perception. Over-stimulation of the reptilian brain is both initiated and stabilized by worldwide, self-perpetuated 'terrorist' concerns, by erroneous archetypal definitions of God, by the consumption of slain flesh and by the retardation of the Human ability to translate light. This manipulation of frequency is galvanizing, within the collective psyche, a sense of shame and guilt. The dominance of the reptilian brain is triggering adrenal toxicity, a powerful hormonal imbalance that is causing a myriad of physical, mental and emotional diseases.

The cerebral cortex is the temple of remembrance that holds the original Human blueprint prior to genetic modification. This blueprint defines the Human entity as an emissary of Source: it is the potency of god and goddess. As the arena of reference for this identity, the cerebral cortex, is stimulated through ceremony and through the influx of the electromagnetic life-force system that carries the immortal harmonic, the quintessential Human definition is reaffirmed, not only intellectually, but physically, emotionally and hormonally in resonance with the original Human blueprint. The alchemical combination inherent within a coded ceremony reaches deeper than psychoanalysis and galvanises a new behavioural concordance within the archetypal arena of the psyche. Rather than trying to adopt a new behavioural 'sanity' through an intellectual idea of it, ceremonies are alchemical affirmations that celebrate the inherent perfection which resides in the innocent heart of each Human, raising the desired model of Human behaviour beyond the intellectual arena and into the field of experience.

The modification of our DNA was not perpetrated by the use of laboratory technology alone, but also through sound. It is sound that will return us to the magnificence of our original design. Contemporary scientists who are looking into the 98% of disconnected material within DNA have begun to understand that this is not junk DNA as orthodox science would have us believe. It holds the same properties and abilities as the percentage of DNA that is now being used. They have discovered that this dormant material is a code that will respond to a 'resonant language'. They stress, however, that this language must hold the correct frequency. The linguistic code in the Template ceremonies which we were to receive over the next sixteen years is patterned in such a way as to create this required resonant frequency. The content, structure and cadence of the sonic linguistic code accessed in the ceremonies hold a fractal harmonic of the creation code present within the Soul Covenant embedded in the Human matrix.

Although DNA modification has altered the helix and endocrine function, the light-code of the full Human magnificence is out of the reach of manipulation and exists in its entirety, holographically, in our every cell. To resurrect this original blueprint that is the light body we create a mirror waveform of its intelligence, to entice it back into this frequency zone through resonance... through alchemical ceremony.

We were to discover, through collaboration with the Consciousness that represents the Template ceremonies, that it is not only the resonance of sound that is necessary to resurrect the dormant DNA; the sense of sight [1] and the visual embrace of the elemental components of the creation matrix are also required within the alchemy to catalyse the sonic code and stabilize transformation. Thus, the manifest presence of the elemental components of creation, Water, Air, Earth, Fire, Ether and Stellar Radiance, in both their earthly manifestations and their geometric formations, are a physical alchemical presence in the ceremonies, not merely on paper or on a computer screen, but as real objects in space-time. The Template ceremonies are an animated, alchemical mandala that create the mirror waveform of the creation frequency. The interference pattern between the original Human blueprint and the ceremony code conceives a vesica piscis through which the original Human hologram is resurrected.

It was to take me some time to truly appreciate the full spectrum of the value held within the mechanics of ceremony. However, I had already begun to streamline the mirror work I was doing to reconnect the Water Circuits. After listening to the many stories brought to me I had begun to sense that they were, at their

---

[1] Unsighted people use the sense of touch instead.

core, the same story with different names, places and degrees of intensity and abuse. At the heart of each person's story was the lack of connection to themselves, to each other, to their Source and a resultant lack of acceptance, power and love. The abuse they endured was due to the conditions plaguing those who were supposed to love and protect them, as these patterns of behaviour passed from generation to generation. It seemed that to give people the space to throw themselves once again into the trauma vortex of their personal tragedies was to reinforce the cellular memory of these events as valid points of reference for the future. For some, the story would take hours and tears to repeat and their body language would signal the decline of their energies and the lowering of their vibration.

With some, it was obvious that they had become addicted to their stories and had lost their identities within them. I facilitated the mirror work with a friend whose father was a well-known member of the Hollywood elite and under whose care she had suffered a tumultuous and abusive childhood, the story of which was being made into a film. She identified so strongly with this drama and her identity was so woven with it that when she had forgiven all those involved and laid aside the burden of its harm upon her, she no longer knew who she was. For a couple of weeks, she was very angry and called me several times to complain that she could no longer evoke the strong emotions of victimhood and outrage that had, for so long, defined her sense of self. Soon, however, she began to appreciate the liberation she was experiencing and discovered the self that had been buried beneath the mantle of the victim.

It became important to begin to take a transpersonal overview of the Human predicament. My first move was to take all the furniture out of the room in which I held these sessions, leaving nowhere for people to sit, to indulge. Still standing and having barely removed their coats and scarves, they were led straight to the mirror, to the 'now'. Sessions became invigorating, swift, clear, activated. I was on the verge of ceremony.

The day of the Air Circuits download I spent building an altar in the session room - an altar so ornate it took up most of the room, whose bare clinical environment was now filled with candles, crystals, flowers, incense and mirrors. That night Jiva and I experienced our first Template ceremony as we reconnected our Air Circuits.

The dissipation of fear was instantaneous. I was not aware until then of how much fear I had been holding in my body, my mind, my heart. This release was not instigated by cataloguing my fears and rationalizing why I should not be afraid. It was a tangible loss of fear-frequency from my field of existence. Fear was eradicated by the reunion with the immortal continuum as my Third Eye, Crown, Throat and Auric Circuits were reconnected into the universal holography of creation. It was the night of the ceremony that I was finally able to let Zak sleep in his own bed for the first time since the Green Mountain experience.

In the ten days that followed I experienced a deep dull ache in my spine that was filled with an energetic heat and a headache that went on and on. The physical discomfort, however, seemed a small price to pay for the awesome release from fear. It was during this time that I began to retrieve some of the information imparted to me in the dreamtime in Kapoho, a process that would continue for the next sixteen years and continues still to this day.

Our recognition that all four Air Circuits fed electromagnetic data to the pineal was to become the kingpin of my understanding of the connection between circuitry, the endocrine system, the DNA and the entry into a new paradigm. With the influx of electromagnetic life-force into my Air Circuits I was more able to appreciate the holonomic system of creation that births and binds the Human hologram and began to see and feel the interconnected, interactive, co-creative individual system of each and every entity as a fractal of the holography that encompasses the subatomic to the universal, for it is the pineal's bio-informational abilities that are a systems-link to our natural state of omniscience which we now tag as a 'special' skill of telepathy.

I understood that 'enlightenment' was not a conceptual mind-trip. It was not having all the answers to all the questions. It was not assuming, through discipline and the right philosophical attitude, an intellectually contrived semblance of spirituality. Enlightenment was literally about light. It was the resurrection of our original ability to absorb, translate and utilize the code of light intelligence that 'in-forms' us. It is the pineal, constructed of retinal cells, as are the eyes, encasing a series of lenses, that translates light into data for the body's bio-informational system to utilize.

The shimmering impressionable surface of the retinal cells that make up the magical pineal gland have become dry and dull, as its separation from life-force heralds its descent into the mortality that is mirrored in the aging and death of its Human vehicle. Its atrophy renders it capable of translating only a limited spectrum of light. As the pineal becomes rejuvenated via the acceleration of electromagnetic life-force delivered by the four Air Circuits, it will begin to absorb a wider spectrum of light information. This form of 'light in translation' is distributed through the central nervous system and into the DNA.

As each piece of information dropped into place, its significance and structure seemed to radiate out in all directions as the holonomic nature of the Template unfolded. As more and more circuits became known to us, the intrinsic value of the endocrine system was revealed as a stepping stone between Source Intelligence and the Human ability to translate that data into the heart-body-mind system and to know itself as an invincible eternal entity.

The prime purpose of our guardianship of the White Spring was to undertake shamanic journeys in the depth of this intense cave of initiation, to receive the spontaneous reconnection of circuitry and to retrieve the codes. This required a degree of ignorance and naiveté, a desire for romantic adventures and total dedication. We were loaded up with all of the above. Although, once through the initial bardos of identity crisis and layers of fear, these journeys were profoundly and powerfully magical, they were by no measure easy. We found the will and intention to summon up our courage because it was our job. The first of these odysseys was to receive the reconnection of the Earth Circuit.

That night, we endeavoured to keep our equipoise amidst the battle of darkness and light that swirled and stirred outside the spring. Some of it slipped under the door, taunting and teasing the deep dark shadows around and within us. Goblin shadows danced along the cave walls in the flickering candlelight and echoing voices whispered about us behind our backs. The spring sang and sang endlessly, a watery song of all the places she had been and all the starlight she had seen. Merging with this watery medium of sound, a sudden diamond of fiery reflection burst upon the surface of the water and its glamour caught my eye.

I fell into the moment and glimpsed a doorway beyond which the goddess Earth beckoned. In a heartbeat, I slipped through. Tumbling headlong into the spiral, taking a wild ride back to the Source, I felt my body shudder as a cellular renunciation of linear, logical reality rippled like a trillion falling dominoes through my being. A circuit of subtle electromagnetic energy was being reinstated through the centre of my medulla oblongata, piercing my pituitary gland and then descending into the ground below my feet. I felt the world. I chose in that moment to honour and realize myself as a child of the Earth and the stars, allowing and giving my full conscious permission for my being to begin to vibrate at a frequency that would attune me with the crystalline core of the planet, establishing the beginnings of an underground grid-work of consciousness, a mycelium of Human awareness.

So engrossed was I in the bliss of reunion, I was not aware of having spoken. The melding between my heart and throat centres was so total that the words slipped out as effortlessly as the bubbling spring that had inspired them. Jiva caught them before they disappeared, and they became that part of the ceremony that would connect the Earth Circuit.

The Earth Circuit enters the body at the medulla oblongata and then circles around and enters sixteen to eighteen inches into the Earth. It is this circuit that reconnects life-force to the pituitary-hypothalamus-pineal complex. This complex is an alchemical laboratory that manufactures our neuro-chemicals and neurotransmitters, setting the subtle ratios that determine the recipe of our hormonal elixirs and their bio-informational signals. These signals trigger resonant receptors within the Human matrix, which in turn set in motion the cogs and wheels of our deepest unconscious programs, programs that instigate and perpetuate the deterioration of the physical body. It is in this complex that we establish the neuro-chemical patterning that weaves the web of addiction.

Our lives are overrun and rooted in addictions that infiltrate almost every impulse, thought process and action. We cannot extricate ourselves from this predicament without a stable support system. The process of moving out of habitual response patterns and into non-dual conscious perception cannot be directed by the intellect alone. We must reconnect the circuits and create the neuro-pathways that support our move away from our addictions, stabilizing the deprogramming process.

At this time, we share a morphogenetic field with those that instigate and carry out ethnic cleansing and set our watches to the same measurement of time that wakes the generals from their slumber. Our seconds keep time with the marching feet of armies as wars rage across the planet. Amidst all this we can no longer chase the shallow dream of happiness, honing our abilities to maintain our ever-expanding comfort zones. We have been lulled by the hypnosis of our social and cultural conditioning to exist within life-styles that have us flailing in a quagmire of object proliferation, weakening us into submission to addictions we are barely aware of having. As we continue to tie our unconscious behavioural patterns into this grid we cannot redirect our instinctual impulses. To extract ourselves from our addictions we must transcend this existing morphogenetic grid by beginning the process of building and stabilizing a new frequency grid-work in resonance with our original innocence.

The reconnection of the Earth Circuit instigates this deprogramming-reprogramming process by establishing the beginnings of an underground grid of consciousness, a mycelium of Human awareness in the Earth and Earth awareness in the Human. As the Earth Circuit is reinstated, the pituitary-hypothalamus-pineal complex is organically attuned to the crystalline core of the planet. Our pulses and impulses synchronize with our Mother and we begin to function on true free energy. This instigates a cellular renunciation of need, bringing us, through organic unfoldment to our core identity, and into a state of needlessness. We and the Tao become one.

When one ingests a psychedelic substance, its residue is found within the pituitary-hypothalamus-pineal complex. It is here that the ingested substance alters the delicate ratios that determine the balance of chemicals resonant with consensus reality. This alters the frequency waves being emitted from the brain and the visual and audible feedback of the environment mirrors this change. We call this hallucinating. Hallucinations are not false realities - they are alternate realities tuned into as a result of a change within the chemical balance of the brain. When we revitalize the pineal-hypothalamus-pituitary complex to its original function we will be establishing new brain chemistry, organically - a chemistry that is in resonance with the full spectrum of light.

As we regain a balance within the whole unit of bio-circuitry as a result of the reconnection of all the major circuits within the circuit complex, the revitalization of the entire endocrine system creates a new body vibration that resonates with the creation frequency. As this acceleration of electromagnetic life-force establishes a frequency that is vibrated by a critical mass of units of circuitry, visual and audible 'mirror feedback' will generate an environment in which anything, animate or inanimate, that owes its existence to the subjugation of the male or female potencies will not be able to maintain its molecular structure.

As these changes gradually and harmoniously take place we

will begin to redefine the way in which we sustain ourselves. We will no longer be able to sustain our molecular structure by the taking of life in any form, as the Human matrix is altered through heightened awareness of its inter-connectedness with all creation. Energy will then be directly assimilated through sacred breath as we internally manufacture, in the alchemical laboratory of the Human temple, elixirs of life. This will not happen through intellectual direction alone but through the harmonious unfolding of organic alignments radiating out from our inner core. As the pituitary, hypothalamus and the pineal are resurrected and returned to their original design, we will discover our synergetic interaction with the Cosmos, understanding its influence upon us, not through historically gathered data, but by direct assimilation of light.

Each Human holds the memory of the bliss of a spontaneously sustained ecstasy that is intrinsic to our original Human design. The memory of this ecstatic state is now evoked by the use and misuse of external stimuli in a desperate attempt to return to joy. The chamber in which we once manufactured rare and exotic hormonal elixirs that played dolphin-like in our bloodstreams is now the birthplace of addiction, the crucible of fear in which we brew the death hormone that drags its trail of tears across each Human face. Our separation from addictions will ultimately culminate in the production within the Human body's alchemical laboratory, of Amrita, the elixir of life, the juice of immortality, propagating life everlasting through sustained ecstasy.

As form follows frequency, once your vibrational field is

attuned to the crystalline core of this planet, your Human embodiment will be graced with the swan-like beauty of your Mother Earth. She in turn will gaze through your eyes, see her own beauty and be inspired to reveal more of herself, laying bare from her body the constricting garments of the environmental abuse of history. She will awake through you, shifting, changing, erupting, flooding, burning away the superficial debris of what man has come to believe is his culture. She will destroy civilization and replace it with a wild tribal tapestry springing from the loom of our combined instinctual natures...as she slips into something more comfortable.

11

CEREMONY IS A SEED

CHALICE LODGE WAS TO BE SOLD. For several weeks we fooled ourselves into a fragile belief that we would be the ones to buy it. After exhausting various avenues through which we imagined we could raise the funds, we finally came to accept that the ownership of this magical sacred place was not a part of our destiny. Simultaneously the 'instruction' came to sell everything we owned down to the last knife and fork, to take the proceeds to Bali and to live there as long as possible, as I was to write a book about the work we had been doing with circuitry. Looking back, I am amazed at how insistent I was about this, how quickly and fully Jiva agreed to it and his total faith that I was capable of writing a book. We opened our doors for the sale of our belongings and put the White Spring in the hands of our manager.

Leaving Chalice Lodge was more difficult than we had ever imagined. Never before or since have I felt such a connection to a particular piece of land. It was the Celt in me that felt my heart was being wrenched from my body. It seemed to me that my place should have been between those two hills, between the ashes of my mother and my father, between the worlds. The night before we left Jiva had to summon a doctor to the house as I was seriously ill with fever and could not stop retching, as my whole being rose up in mutiny against this terrible leaving. The next morning, we left on a cold and misty dawn, the raised land on which the house stood rendered its own little Isle of Avalon. The world withdrew and allowed us to bid farewell to this beloved home in a private place of sorrow… never to return.

While we were still in Hawaii my elderly father, who lived in England in a small cottage I had bought for him in Lincolnshire, had a serious fall and could no longer live alone. We had made arrangements for his care and sold the cottage. After various bills had been paid there was a modest sum left for our use. Since our previous source of 'employment' was absolutely no longer an option, we decided that we would invest these funds in a business. Several of our friends had been to Bali and they raved about how easy it was to establish manufacture and export businesses there. We had been designing our own line of picture frames for the Hawaiian tourist trade and decided to go to Bali to have them crafted there. Rather than go through the usual manufacturing routes in which profits would go to comparatively wealthy factory owners, we wanted to know the working conditions and rates of pay made to the workers involved, so we wanted to find a family in a village that could make our frames in their compound.

We landed cold, without a single lead. After a couple of nights in the city of Kuta we headed for the hills, to the cultural centre of Ubud, a rich community of painters, dancers, sculptors and carvers. We stayed in a $5 a night room on the famed Monkey Forest Road. The next morning, we made inquiries of the young man who brought us towels and soon we were traveling the back roads further up into the mountains to a small secluded traditional Balinese village. After several days of meetings with the head of one of the village compounds we struck a deal that made him and his extended family very happy and most probably the wealthiest in their village.

The frames we designed were made from 'Femo', a substance that needed to be baked in an oven. This they did not have, so one was purchased in the capital of Denpasar and, with much fanfare, ceremoniously delivered. It was the first manufactured oven ever seen in their village and the entire population turned out to welcome it. Several hours were spent gathered around the oven as the villagers discussed the portent of its sudden and opulent presence in their midst, an obvious omen of future abundance. Many small and beautiful offerings were piled upon its shiny white exterior. Jiva and I sat quite speechless. It was one of the most surreal moments in our lives to see such homage paid to an electrical appliance, a testimony to the Balinese instinctual impulse to see the sacred in all things.

This time, arriving in Bali from Glastonbury, we headed straight for Ubud and quickly found a fairly isolated thatched bamboo cottage in the rice fields two miles outside the town. It took a couple of days to recover from jetlag and a couple more to pull out of that wonderful state of disorientation called culture shock. The 'time is money' creed that drives the western world machine came apart in the slow warm somnolent days and was replaced by jam barate, Balinese for 'rubber-time'. By eight in the morning the risen Sun was already hinting at the savage white heat that would bring the day to a halt by noon, when shade and cold drinks would be sought. Our points of behavioural reference melted in the humidity and readjusted themselves to the exotic and relatively logic-free morphogenetic field of this stunning sanctuary of the Bird Tribe. Rising and retiring with the Sun, we calibrated our energies to the rhythms of nature.

At night, waves of sound emanated from a night orchestra that was louder and busier than day itself, composed of raucous frogs and too many kinds of crickets to number. The starry sky kissed its reflection in the watery rice fields. Dainty, bright moving bodies, the fairy lights of fireflies, wove in and around the lotus pond and night blooming jasmine. The thick trim of palm trees that fringed the edge of the rice fields jigged black and mad in the night breeze; their coconuts became the wild bulging eyes of the demons that fill the strange Balinese Hindu pantheon of archetypes which hold them all to ransom. Offerings were made to these demons daily in the hope of buying a little more time on this Earth free of starvation, disease and infant death; all the ills that are the common tragedies of what is termed the Third World.

One evening I let Jiva know that I was ready to begin to write and that he and Zak must leave our home at six the next morning. This they did, bless them, not only without protest or question but with complete faith, respect and not a little excitement. Alone in the house that next morning I took a Balinese shower, called a mandi, dipping a large ladle into a small tiled reservoir of very cold well water. Electricity had only arrived in this village in the late '70s and hot water was still unheard of. The upstairs room was bowed, thatched and beamed with bamboo and palm and felt like the ribbed inside of a giant whale. Several windows framed the terraced rice fields that stretched down to the jungle and the seven magnificent mountains that defined the far horizon.

Until that journey to Bali we did not consciously know where the information we were working with was coming from, nor did we fully understand the implications of the reconnection of circuitry. At that time, we communed only with the fourth member of our family, the domestic ambassador of some vaster body of Consciousness, the guidance we named Sowelu. That morning I lit a candle and burned some incense in front of the exquisite Balinese altar heaped with orchids and white jasmine blossoms that permeated the room with scent, invoking memories fluttering like butterflies just out of reach. As I did this I implored Sowelu to join me and guide me. I had done as I was asked. I waited. And waited. Nothing.

Then it hit me…the insanity of it, the ludicrous, illogical insanity. I thought of Jiva and Zak wandering around the village to give me space. For what? To sit in silly yet tragic silence? To write a book? I could not write a book, whatever possessed me to think I could? About what? What did these circuits and ceremonies really add up to? Who did I think I was? How could I do this to my family?

In retrospect, it's a good thing there were no mobile phones in those days, or I would have called the boys home. Instead I knew I had another four hours before I could share my misery and my shame.

The minutes piled up; time mocked me. Still, I sat and waited in the near empty silence filled only with the hollow beating of my heart: it seemed that even the rice stopped growing in expectation. I cried noisily as, one by one, the reasons I thought I had to live this magical life evaporated. Ever-building waves of insecurity washed over me as I bowed my head beneath their weight and laid my forehead on the floor in submission to my own stupidity. I wept through this little death, my mortal objection to the impossible and, finally, raised my swollen eyes to see upon the altar, in front of which I was prostrate, our large and noble eagle feather. I grasped it as if it were a raft floating on a deep deserted ocean. I drew its potency around my body, touched it to my third eye, washed it over my crown and held it to my heart.

The dam of mistrust broke in a new torrent of tears, very different tears: my breath caught, my pulse quickened and became deep and rhythmic as an energy so clear, so pure, so uncompromising, entered my field of awareness. Just as it had on the morning of our grand initiation in Hawaii, when I looked across the room into Jiva's soft knowing eyes and the room had kaleidoscoped around us, my whale's belly sanctuary began to pixel into fractals of light. Quickly, before another doubt could distract me, I put pen to paper and in that moment my odyssey into language began. I became, as had been agreed in some other time, a writer, a quantum poet. It would be some time, however, before I came to understand my own writing.

In ecstatic states of trance, I wrote. As a child, I had been issued a certificate for dyslexia which I was still using in college so that my exam papers were marked regardless of the implausible mistakes made in spelling and grammar. One teacher commented in her written report that my essays were quite good once you 'broke the code'. I was not burdened by the restrictions of grammar and spelling and still, as my infinitely patient editors will attest, cannot quite get the hang of it. I wonder how much of this 'dyslexia' actually originates from an authentic impediment and how much from a rebellious nature that is not concerned with dogmatic academic parameters.

I will admit, however, that I still don't know left from right unless I stop to consider, which annoys Jiva when I am giving him directions and he often comments that I don't have dyslexia, I have 'lexdyxia'.

In addition, I attended eleven different schools in four different countries and my first language was Japanese. I learnt English in an American army school from an Australian. I am often asked what country I am from, as my accent is unrecognizable. While working as a nurse in London I was asked several times a day where I was from and the convoluted answer was tiresome to both myself and, I suspect, my listener, so I invented a country of origin. Most people, not wanting to appear so ignorant of their own globe, would let it end there, some throwing out a comment such as, 'You must miss the heat', or, 'I hope you're managing to send money home.'

But now, in my bamboo womb in the rice fields, I was not fettered by the expectations of others and dived headlong into expressing the improbable concepts that welled up from a primordial point of reference buried deep, beyond the reach of criticism and judgment. It was because of this that I accessed a language that was tailored to substantiate the spectrum of meanings and feelings being transmitted to me as I reached for sounds to clothe them in the nearest fraction of meaning in this mutant dimension. Even so, I was still restricted to a language passed down by those who would judge me insane. This is most probably the challenge for any poet. Musicians, on the other hand, have the ability to express the wordless in a range of pure sound.

Later, when my work enjoyed a degree of exposure, I found it difficult to deal with the ridicule I sometimes received for the outlandish and arrogantly bold stance I took on certain matters, the most preposterous being physical immortality. I was greatly consoled by a piece written about the responsibility of a visionary which pointed out that it was not their job to censor their visions according to the rationale of others or even themselves, but simply to translate awareness and inspiration into language without weighing it against any possible criticism or expectation. Bolstered by this, I knew then I did not have to be 'reasonable'.

In those first few months I trained myself to trust in the alliance I had made with the Consciousness that merged with my awareness and filled the space around me, to go beyond what I thought and to translate instead the quintessence of what I felt. Thus, I created a conduit of communion with a Consciousness that I believe exists inter-dimensionally. In that isolated and ratty bamboo dwelling I created a bridge between the quantum and the page. Some piece of radiant information would swim into view - reveal itself like a dolphin breaking to the surface, gleaming tantalizingly in the Sun of my comprehension - before diving back into the depths of quantum possibilities. At times a notion would cross my mind like the shadow of a crow; insubstantial, yet heavy with portent and I would strain and struggle to capture it and bring it down to earth, not always with success.

On that first morning Jiva returned home to find me sitting overwhelmed and exhausted with a small pile of handwritten papers before me. I had written of 'holonomically compatible systems' and 'morphogenetic fields of shared perceptions'. Not understanding much of it, I handed the papers over to him saying,

"Well, here it is - maybe you can explain it to me." As he read through the papers Jiva began to smile and then to laugh. At first, I thought it was at me, but then I heard the delight in his voice. He was impressed and moved by what I had written, and I found this so exhilarating that, like an actress on the stage brought to life by her applauding audience, I began to write each day for his pleasure and, to a degree, still do.

With Jiva's easy and respectful approval my confidence grew each day. This part of me would never have come to life if it had not been for his trust and belief in me, his faith, love and the deep spiritual respect he has for all things feminine. This is why he is rightly listed as the co-author of this book, for the merging of his contribution and mine is seamless and indivisible.

It was during this time that we spent in Bali that the origin and fullness of the Consciousness we were working with revealed itself to us. One moonless night, we experienced first-hand the black magic for which Bali is well-known, of which we had heard many tales. It was a form of dark sorcery practiced by elderly men who had matured in a very different Bali; a Bali in which this form of mastery was used to gain position and prestige within their village, a Bali in which for fear of disembodied spirits no one left their home after dark. The spirits of these Balinese that would sometimes inhabit dogs and chickens would wander after midnight into the compounds of extended families to spy and cause mischief of all kinds. In extreme circumstances these forays would end in the death of an adversary. There are also white magic Balinese whose mastery of the elemental laws is used for healing.

It was late enough to be the early hours of morning. We had been celebrating my birthday in the small gazebo that sat in the middle of the lotus pond in the garden. We gathered up our things and made our way across the water to the main house to discover that the electricity was out. Jiva went upstairs to find a candle and suddenly I heard him fall heavily to the floor. He continued to struggle loudly as he tried to get to his feet. I called out to him, asking what was happening.

"I'm caught in the net," he said.

"What net?" I asked. "We don't have a net." We slept upstairs beneath only a ceiling fan. The sounds of his struggle continued. I rushed up the spiral staircase to help him. Every time I thought I had reached the top of the stairs I found myself at the bottom again! After several attempts, I realized I was not going to be able to reach Jiva until I could bring light into the darkness. I remembered the candle on my cake in the kitchen. I rushed in and lit it from the stove; immediately, the entity left and Jiva broke free of its spell.

Speechless, we huddled on the downstairs bed around the form of Zak who, in spite of the commotion, was still soundly asleep. The solid magnetic pull of peace and joy that, from the day of his birth, has been a source of reference for the real, drew us into his silent, innocent nurture.

Once peace and calm settled upon us and the house, we went upstairs and lit more candles and incense. We were shaken, but beneath it all quite grateful for the experience. We decided to read the manuscript I had been writing. The elegance of the frequency that shone through the information spun a vibrant cocoon around us and, when I came to the end of a chapter, the echo of the last words spoken dissolved into the silence. Out of the deep night came a voice, the words uttered from Jiva's lips and yet it did not sound like him.

"You have entered this reality as a virus of holistic consciousness. Ceremony is your seed...plant it!"

At that moment there was a great rush of sound bursting over the house, above the roof. It was the sound of a thousand wings...bird wings...a great gathering of the Bird Tribe. Within this was the call of the eagle and the hawk. We leapt to the window and looked out to see nothing...nothing but the darkest hour before dawn, still studded with the winking of far-away stars.

As we withdrew to the altar, the words that now close every ceremony we hold came into my mind and fell from my lips,

"I honour and acknowledge my physical being as the pinnacle of the manifestation of my spiritual identity." As these words resonated, we felt within us a reconciliation of matter and spirit wedding us to the moment, rendering us stargates within the true continuum of time and space.

I felt impelled to open a book that I had brought with me to Bali. It was 'The Mayan Factor' by José Argüelles. It fell open to a page upon which José spoke of the Ahau Kines, the Consciousness with which the great Mayan shaman kings had conferred to bring through their calendars. I knew in an instant that the Ahau Kines were the Bird Tribe and it was they with whom I had been in communion when downloading the body of information which was to become 'The Template - A Holonomic Model of Transcendence'.

In this moment, many years later, in the same rice fields, as I write these words, two eagles soar above me, calling.

12

CONSPIRACY OF MORTALITY

AFTER FOUR MONTHS IN BALI, our money and visas ran out and we returned to England, cold, penniless and disorientated. Unable to afford a place of our own, we were pressed to take a room in an old farmhouse in a small village on the outskirts of Glastonbury. Although it was in a beautiful area, its charm did not make up for the loss of autonomy. It was a difficult place to live for many reasons, but it was at least possible to escape the over-inhabited farmhouse and its mini-morphic field of endless and petty dissonance by taking walks in the much diminished yet still beautiful forest that was close by.

As the promise of autumn drifted in on the tail of a late summer breeze the strength of the Sun waned, and the trees displayed their mortal shades. The answer to the riddle of death beckoned through the veil of synchronicity and danced out of reach. These variations in environmental stimuli that trigger cyclic programs of bio-informational signals initiating the decline of vital energies stimulated our awareness of the Fire Circuit. We were to learn the hard way that this circuit was blocked by the fear of death.

It was not until later, after our Fire Circuits were reconnected, that it became clear that the reconnection of circuitry was intrinsic to the transcendence of the mortal paradigm. It is not that the Template model is an immortalist movement, focusing on that outcome as its prime objective; it is simply that with the reconnection of circuitry and the resultant rejuvenation of the endocrine system, immortality is inevitable. The physical deterioration that leads to the death of the manifest expression of life, the body, is the result of an unnatural deficit of life-force that occurs as a result of our disconnection from the creation continuum.

The test point for the Fire Circuit is situated in the perineum. This circuit feeds the gonads, which, in unison with the pituitary-hypothalamus-pineal complex, manufacture the hormones that carry the bio-informational signals which regulate the cyclic functions of the reproductive system and initiate the onset of the degenerative phase that leads to death. The present ratio of catalytic alchemical components within this hormonal recipe gives rise to the conspiracy of mortality. As procreation drags behind it inevitable death, love is made in fear.

The reconnection of the Fire Circuit confronts death electro-magnetically. The knowledge that never was there a time when I did not exist…never will there come a time when I cease to be… is no longer only a philosophical or intellectually adopted concept but is vibrating its frequency cellularly within the arena of the perineum. Here the acceleration of electromagnetic input is delivering the full spectrum of the immortal harmonic that will rejuvenate these magical organs which define Humanity as a universal progenitor of life. When the entire endocrine system is resurrected to the fullness of its original capabilities it will manufacture the hormonal elixirs that will imbue the physical matrix with the bio-signalling intelligence that affirms the mandate of physical immortality. Yes, physical immortality: not the lengthening of the life span sought after in the laboratory temples in which man aspires to defeat death with his intelligence to preserve the flesh that bit longer, nor am I referring to the immortal nature of the 'soul', or the conscious return to the 'One'.

Some years later, when we had received the information on all the twelve circuits of the Foundation Ceremony, we were holding a workshop in Bali when someone interrupted our presentation on the immortal nature of the pre-modified Human to say:

"Of course, you are speaking of the eternal nature of the soul."

"No", I replied, "I am speaking of physical immortality."

"Flesh?!!" She spat the word out as though its linguistic

resonance was a putrid substance that was defiling her mouth. In the teaching of most religions and philosophies the soul is always immortal and superior to the flesh and bones of the body. It is the same dualistic perception of separation that defines heaven as 'up there' and hell in the centre of our Earth. It is this focus upon the spirit, the soul, the unseen, as more worthy of our respect and faith than the incarnate disposable fabric of material existence that allows the abuse of our bodies and the desecration of our environment. This iconic separation of spirit and matter robs us of our ability to synthesize the sacred into our everyday lives and to know our bodies as chalices of life eternal.

It is the subject of immortality that confounds many of those who come to the Template ceremonies, for the death program is deep and all pervading. However, physical immortality is not so new and outrageous a concept as you might think. Taoists have long believed that physical immortality can be attained through continuous physical rejuvenation. The reconnection of circuitry instigates rejuvenation via the endocrine system, resurrecting the original Human blueprint and realigning the incarnate body presence with the natural dataflow of the life directive that emanates from the omnipotent Heart of Creation. The natural order of this life-continuum is endless and eternal, without beginning or end. Physical immortality is not a miraculous state of being: it is the natural embodiment of the Benevolence of our Creation, a reunification with our quintessential identity that is defined by our connection to Source.

There are some who attempt to move beyond the fear of death by adopting a philosophy to reconcile them with death by portraying it as 'a final initiation', or 'a great test.' To some, death is a release from the confines of a paradigm riddled with every imaginable suffering; however, the cycle of birth and death is endlessly repeated in this temporal zone. Souls reincarnate within this mutant dualistic dimension due to its disconnection from the immortal continuum.

As a nurse I witnessed close-up the painful and humiliating degeneration that leads, finally, to death. Whatever intellectual or philosophical belief system you may have adopted to evade your true feelings about death, there is a deep unconscious dread that looms behind each thought, that dwells within each breath, as closer comes that day to separate every mother and child, every lover from the last kiss. At a frequency level, Humanity is broadcasting a message of fear, a message that reads: 'I am afraid. I am afraid of annihilation. I am afraid of eternal separation from all that I love. I am afraid of death.' As this wave of fear is broadcast from a few billion units of circuitry, a mirror image of reality supports its validity all over the world, collectively forming and stabilizing a morphogenetic field that forms a cocoon of belief in which the dormant immortality of Humanity never finds its wings but dies over and over again.

The metamorphosis from mortal to immortal will be stabilized when our collective consciousness creates a resonant global structure providing points of behavioural reference that allow the individual unit of circuitry to contain and transmit the higher frequencies which will break the tyranny of the present fear-based mortal consensus – a new consensus reached by a critical mass of reconnected units of bio-circuitry, able to translate and transmit the full spectrum of the creative directive emanating from Source, providing new archetypal reference points in the collective that is the morphogenetic field, breaking the spell of our mortal trance and reconnecting the planetary biosphere to the immortal continuum.

Unaware that our Fire Circuits were to be reconnected, on the autumn equinox Jiva and I spent the night in the White Spring.

There had been a lot of rain that week and the spring, strong and loud, brought with it the energies of the moon, full in Scorpio. A sting of intensity permeated the air and it was with great reluctance that we entered the White Spring long after dark.

The reconnection was one of the most uncomfortable and frightening experiences we have ever had. We went through the mental and emotional torment of facing a seemingly imminent death over and over again, devastated by the fear of an impending eternal separation from all that we knew and loved. All our fears boiled up from the marrow of our bones and bounced and reverberated around the echoing walls of the initiation cave. Exaggerated, they grinned like caricatures out of every shadow and crevice. The momentum of ferocity built in ever expanding waves. We had learnt to ride these waves until they subsided. On this occasion we bailed out.

At around 3am, we burst out of the doors into the cool fresh night in a state of extreme disorientation. Jiva somehow managed to steer the car out of town and we soon found ourselves on the thickly misted moors, the road ahead a ribbon of moonlight that seemed far too narrow and longer than necessary. At last we reached the farm house that we shared with a motley group of individuals. Creeping silently up to our attic room we slipped into our bed wedged under the heavily beamed slanting roof. Zak slept soundlessly on the far side of this huge room. Our eyes became accustomed to the darkness which began to pour into varying degrees of black and charcoal. We lit a tea-light on the altar and the room softly came to life bathed in warm hues of wood and sparkling crystals. The elfin mask on the wall smiled wickedly. We felt safe: it was over.

Our Fire Circuits had been reconnected without our conscious participation and we had travelled the chasm between our conscious and unconscious in a state of fear and confusion. A facet of our trust in ceremony was fashioned as we clearly saw that it bridges that gap, facilitating the integration of the self into the grand wheel of eternal existence, cog by cog, as what you know becomes who you are.

It was not until a month later in the early hours of the morning that I brought forth the alchemical ceremonial code that would reconnect the Fire Circuit. That night we celebrated our wedding anniversary as we had always done, by staying up through the night in quiet celebration of having found each other on this crazy planet. My heart was full and open as dawn dispersed the mists that lay upon the fields of Avalon; the words welled up inside me and flew from my lips as I grabbed a pen to scribble them down, anxious in case they would be carried away on the same magical wave that had swept them in. As Jiva and I spoke together in the gathering morning light we were aware of the linguistic resonance of this immortal sonic code. A tide of endlessness rippled through our cellular consciousness. Remembrance stirred… beckoned from beyond this realm… gathering us up within its eternal embrace.

The treasured codes, recovered in the eye of the storm that is the portal of Glastonbury, did not come easily. They were pried from the jaws of initiation and paid for in a currency that exacted an unsparing demand for growth. At times our endurance thresholds were exceeded and on occasion we considered leaving it all behind for a safer, quieter life, but this was just a flexing of our sense of free will and, beyond all that we endured, was the crystallization of the total commitment in the core of our beings that was initiated when we wound our way down from Green Mountain and spoke the sacred oath. After several years in this emotional training camp I lost my Piscean desire to please, to be approved of, to bond with everyone and began to figure out friend from foe. I made some deep and lasting connections with friends good and true, those whose strength of presence in Glastonbury anchors the light in the midst of all its storms.

The White Spring was inextricably merged into our process of transformation. Unlike the Chalice Well across the road, the White Spring was not walled and did not charge an entry fee. We kept it open 365 days a year and in the long English winter we struggled physically and financially. The staff in both shop and kitchen would freeze on the many days that we would spend money to keep the Spring open without a return of revenue. It was to be five years after we left the Spring that we cleared the bank loan taken out to keep it going.

On holidays, we would stay open giving out food to the homeless and downtrodden, for the White Spring drew and gave shelter to everyone without censorship. Although the use of cigarettes, alcohol and drugs was banned from the Spring, there was nothing we could do about the considerable consumption of all the above that took place in its tiny open garden and in the street that ran a foot away from it. Life in all its artfulness and astounding range went on within the patient embrace of the White Spring, as all the dramas of love and hate and all shades between, played themselves out upon its tolerant stage. Through it all, the spring gave and gave its waters without restraint to wash it all away to begin again each new day. For a time, we lived in a dark damp windowless room above the spring and, when the doors were closed on the last of the day and the final echo of Human voices faded into the gathering gloom, only the water could be heard. In it the cadence of Earth's unfathomable, unceasing, abiding patience echoed in the candlelit stillness.

Whatever might have taken place that day, we never ceased to be in awe of the fact of our presence there. To many it may have seemed that the apparent unbridled chaos that tumbled through each day was a result of our inability to 'organize' it, to render it another conservative 'spiritual' stronghold to mirror the silence of our neighbouring spring, Chalice Well, with its clear boundaries and manicured order; its keep-off-the-grass-ness of an English garden. To us the White Spring's lack of constrained government was obliquely sanctioned by our own lack of respect for authority. It was a free space and we 'ran' it in a glorious state of divine confusion.

You can imagine the amount of criticism and abuse we received both from those whose translation of 'sacredness' was akin to the sanctimonious contrivance of peace that neither served nor offended anyone and, at the other end of the spectrum, from the 'rainbow fascists' who were never satisfied with the extent of our nonconformity and thought that no money should be earned to cover the rent or other utilities, not to mention salaries paid to staff. As the saying goes, you can't please all the people all the time. In Glastonbury it is an achievement to please anyone, ever. However, time has passed and these days we are often stopped in the High Street when we return on a visit to Glastonbury by someone who recognizes what we accomplished there and how difficult it was.

One day a friend told me that we had acquired a reputation

for holding 'black' ceremonies and that this had begun when I had purchased eight black candles from a candle shop on the High Street. At that time, we were holding Air Ceremonies that required a third-eye meditation in the mirror. The ceremonies were held at night by candlelight: I had heard that a black candle created a beautiful light and was inspired to try it out, not knowing the red flag this was going to raise. Someone who had observed me buying the candles had passed on the information and soon the gossip was that we were holding satanic rituals. Those who experienced the ceremonies knew differently, but they were mostly from out-of-town as we rarely worked with Glastonians. We were already considered to be international drug dealers, secret government agents, holders of wild tantric sex orgies, Freemasons and shape-shifting aliens.

That afternoon I sauntered down the High Street, past the notice boards crammed with flyers offering a myriad of services: workshops on sex without guilt, past life obsession, soul dry-cleaning, finding the inner adult, guilt without sex, and time-shares in the fifth dimension. One couple announced in their advertising to having inserted invisible behaviour-modifying devices in people's auric fields during a past Atlantean incarnation. They were now offering to remove these devices - for a fee. I noticed the candle shop was quite busy. After paying for more black candles I inquired of the sales person behind the counter if she knew where I might purchase a goat. She didn't. Telephone networks buzzed, the tale mutated and rebounded off aerials and satellites and by teatime it had reached advanced civilizations in galaxies far, far away.

13

ORIGINAL INNOCENCE

AS WE CONTINUED TO INTEGRATE the energetic nature of Source Consciousness reintroduced by the four Air Circuits that fed the pineal, our appreciation of this master gland expanded. Its ability to decode the data stream of light intelligence defines it as the primary bio-signalling system that determines the dimensional spectrum within which we become conscious. When it is functioning at its full potential, it is a biological time machine.

It is no wonder that the Tibetans were so focused upon this superlative gland. Having realized that the quantity and quality of light to which the pineal is exposed dictates the level of consciousness or 'en-light-enment' one is able to access, they devised long and arduous exercises to do so, sometimes going so far as to physically create an aperture at the crown of the head. In the Template model it is the reconnection of the four Air Circuits that rejuvenate this gland in order to return it to full function. In our appreciation of the Human bio-capacitor as a fractal of universal consciousness, it follows that all its visible and invisible systems are holonomic and so, with each circuitry reconnection, all other circuits are upgraded and so too are the systems they feed. Thus, the pineal is continually recharged with all subsequent reconnections. The advent of the Ether Ceremony, specifically the reconnection of the Solar Circuit, was to augment our understanding of this as we began to appreciate, on another level, the pre-eminence of light.

Light is consciousness transubstantiated into a super-operable holonomic feed for the Human bio-computer to download and utilize. However, each unit can only decode and avail itself of this light intelligence in proportion to the amount of genetic potential that has been activated. These genetic capabilities are reliant upon the amplitude of the individual's electromagnetic 'bank' of Source Consciousness and the extent of this bank is reliant, in turn, upon the integrity of the circuitry that delivers this divine electromagnetic intelligence. This bio-energetic information is raw data supplied to the endocrine system to be translated into the various alchemical recipes of bio-informational signals that transmit frequencies in accordance with the genetic propensities of the collective resonant field. Light is our life-line!

In a nutshell, the Human entity is only able to utilize the power of light in accordance with the amount of genetic material that has not been 'turned off'. The amount of usable light dictates the frequency dimension that entity is able to consciously inhabit.

One very prominent and significant focus that is at the heart of the New Age movement is a passion for 'the light' - and rightly so. It is indeed all about the light. Light is the new faith. Light, as the quintessential form of consciousness made coherent, is the ambassador of the supreme organizing principle, numinously expressed by our Sun; an ambassador that not only delivers the message but is the message and the means through which it becomes manifest.

For Jiva and me it has always been that, before gaining the information that will reconnect a circuit, there is a term of passage during which the consequences of the disconnection of that circuit are fully revealed within our own life experience. Were these circuits to reconnect all at once it would be like smelling many perfumes and trying to distinguish one fragrance from another. While facilitating the reconnection of the circuitry in alchemical ceremonies we are required to present a body of information that outlines the specific Human condition being experienced as a result of the disconnection, the transformation that would be activated by reconnection and the overall impact of this on the collective. Thus, we needed to have extensive and comprehensive knowledge of each individual circuit and that required conscious personal experience.

That spring, spent in the countryside of Somerset, in preparation for the reconnection of the Solar Circuit, I reflected upon my lifelong obsession with the miracle that brings each day...the Sun. We had recently left the farmhouse we were sharing and on the 23rd of March I was introduced to the Solar Circuit as I lay on my back in the neglected garden of our new home, a little old cottage in the village of Butleigh Wooten, whose 'centre' was no more than a red phone cubicle and a post box.

I was mulling over eternity, a concept that gazing into the sky has always inspired in me. The overgrown garden expressed the spring joy of Somerset as she shed her sheath of reserve and tumbled headlong into the tender and vulnerable expression of rebirth, carelessly tossing about her achingly fragile flowers that trembled in the barest breeze, the wistful melancholy of new life stirring a desire for innocence lost, moments of perfection when all things elemental conspire to grant a glimpse of impossible beauty that cannot be caught except in the heart.

Into this reverie flew three large hawks, flying in a tight hypnotic circle directly above my head. On and on they circled, as all around the warm buzzing of tiny beings in busy flight crooned the droning somnolent tones of oneness. I fell soft and deep into trance. The hawks broke their circle of flight and began to swerve and weave across the sphere of space between them, tying knots of movement to undo the memories held within the temple of my remembrance, deep in the future of the long ago past.

A rush of breath filled my lungs; tears flowed in a river of release as my Solar Circuit was reconnected. As this grand Solar Circuit reinstated my electromagnetic resonance with Galactic

Centre via the Sun, a new dataflow of consciousness seeped into my awareness; my sense of self could no longer be contained within the perimeters of my past identity, an identity defined by a culture that has lost its comprehension and acknowledgment of the primary position of the Sun as an emissary of the divine life-force without which all life on this planet would cease.

The seams of my mortal senses tore to accommodate something new and ancient that insisted upon its rebirth. On a cellular level, codes within my DNA, reactivated by the transmissions of light from a newly understood Sun, awakened genetic information. My cellular denial of a greater identity graciously gave way. My mortal disguise faltered, its mask melting in the heat of the Sun.

Our reinstated morphic resonance with the Sun, through the reconnection of the Solar Circuit, inspires a point of expanded reference that dwarfs the petty issues of our Earth dramas and the social and cultural concepts which arise from the illusions of individual supremacy. Prejudice between races, cultures and religions cannot maintain its fabrication in the unifying enlightenment coded into one ray of the Sun's illumination. All endeavours to preserve the dynasties of decadent nuclear empires appear useless, empty and insane, as our impulses synergize once more with the cosmic intelligence projected from the Galactic Centre and translated radiantly through our most illustrious celestial consort...the glorious Sun.

Through the ascendancy of the Sun's full brilliance, we will discover a higher purpose than the struggle for status in the sandbox of society as the Solar Circuit beckons us away from our dramas and invites us to rediscover our function as mediators of cosmic intelligence, projected as light from the Galactic Core, to the planetary mind of Earth. We are, as biological units of circuitry, the transducers of this information matrix. It is in discovering the co-creative nature of our relationship with the Sun and the Earth that our quintessential function is revealed to us. It is through us that the heart of Earth is illuminated by the love of Her Sun.

The Solar Circuit is one of three represented in the Ether Ceremony. It is situated approximately two inches above the umbilical cord in the solar plexus. Testing it through kinesiology reveals that it is strengthened by looking into the Sun or at any piece of geometry that holds a solar resonance. This circuit is our galactic umbilical cord linking the Human complex of circuitry with the Centre of the Galaxy via the Sun.

The Heart Circuit is the second to be reconnected in the Ether Ceremony. When you consciously examine the spoken and silent agreements you make as you barter for your needs and desires to be met in the heartland, you will most probably recognize agendas that are far from unconditional. With the disassociation of the heart from the centres of survival and procreation and the overall inability of the present Human to access the full spectrum of its divine identity, this is hardly surprising. It is noteworthy that many spiritual and religious doctrines require their followers to abstain from sexual relationships. This abstinence is seen as essential in order to realize spiritual progress. It is both ironic and telling that the sacred act that defines us as universal progenitors of life, the very quintessence of our divinity, is judged as an impediment in the process of self-realization.

We became more aware of the deviations and distortions that led to this enigma when, several years later, in the fourth ceremony, we received the reconnection of the Source Circuits and began to investigate the definition of God in the Human psyche. However, at this juncture, we were able simply to acknowledge the disconnection of the Heart Circuit and the inescapable reality of Human difficulty in matters of the heart.

Although Jiva and I have always felt a deep connection to the British Isles, especially the South West counties, we were aware that when the time came to settle down and cease our endless traveling, it would not be anywhere in Europe but somewhere more raw, less populated and developed, as our work required that we disassociate from the manufactured grid. Not long after the Solar Circuit reconnection, I awoke one morning having received in the dreamtime a message that, in a matter of days, we were to see the place in which we would eventually settle. This was puzzling, as we had no plans to travel out of the country.

Two days later, we received a call from a friend in Hawaii

asking us to pick up a valuable and fragile piece of art from her friends in London. We arrived the next afternoon at Danny and Maggie's home, an old converted stable in north London. They had fallen in love with the Australian rainforest and had done very well in transporting it into the heart of London. Several ten-foot tall trees with special indoor lights were placed around the open-plan, split-level room. In one corner a small pool with a little waterfall was home to a couple of psychedelic toads and the stable was filled with chirping crickets for them to feed on. We made an immediate connection with Danny and Maggie. I noticed on the wall a large laminated picture of a land mass. As I approached it my heart missed a beat. It was an aerial photograph of an area of rainforest on the north east coast of New South Wales in Australia. Never having been in the least drawn even to visit Australia I was surprised when the knowledge that this was one day to be my home settled upon me.

We visited Danny and Maggie several times that year. On one occasion we met with them at the Avebury stone Circle and they showed us pictures of the new home they had built in two hundred acres of rainforest. Not only did they invite us to visit them, they gave us the tickets to get there.

We spent some time in Bali on our way to Australia and it was there that we discovered the Heart Circuit. We had obviously been suffering its disconnection all our lives but tuning in physiologically to its weakness made us acutely aware of it. By the time we arrived in Australia, we could think of nothing else.

ORIGINAL INNOCENCE

Danny and Maggie's property was awesome and we spent a week or so with them before realizing that, in order to focus on our work, we needed our own space. Through various synchronistic and fortuitous events, we found ourselves on thirty acres of rainforest, forty-five minutes from the coast. The house was a huge empty barn of a room with polished wood floors and sliding glass doors all the way around. There was a small split-level platform which held a bed, nestled in the high roof: other than that it was unfurnished. Each time we visited the beach we brought back several buckets of sand and soon we had a huge pyramid of it piled up in the centre of the empty barn. Suspended directly above it, hanging only inches from the apex of the sand structure, was a star-tetrahedron that I had made out of cardboard and covered with holographic glitter, mixing some of this glitter with the sand. We decorated this unusual altar with flowers, crystals and candles. As the centre of our space we were drawn continually and irresistibly to meditate on it and it seemed each day was ordered around its presence, drawing us within and without into a place of peace and introspection. Each day we shrugged off another convoluted aspect of the addictive static of life as we eased into a more simple existence. The world fell away, leaving only the bright hot sunshine and the somnolent sounds of the humming rainforest.

One early morning we awoke to the usual dawn laughter of the kookaburra and the sense that, that night, our Heart Circuits would be reconnected.

A short trip was made to the local shop for supplies. On the way home, we came across a four-foot lizard swaying in the middle of the road. As Jiva, Zak and I gathered around him, we noticed a small trickle of blood coming from the corner of his mouth. We sensed his impending death and were touched by the great honour of the occasion. The lizard looked around this strange Human circle. I became aware that the physical manifestations of our bodies as Humans and lizard were costumes we wore for the occasion; beneath our guises we were one shared consciousness. He seemed to recognize and accept that ours would be the last eyes he would gaze into before he retreated back into the dreamtime. All our identities unified in those sacred moments. I like to think that he could feel us loving him in the sad silence. The lizard's eyes locked into Jiva's as he respectfully asked him to bestow upon him with his dying breath the blessing of all the Medicine wisdom that he had carried forward from the first dreaming. The lizard took his last breath and slipped quietly from this world. We carried his Medicine home that morning.

On our arrival at Danny and Maggie's rainforest sanctuary we had been stunned by the beauty of our surroundings. Not only was the rainforest visually magnificent but the frequency was high and clear, a testament to the aboriginal custodians of this land and the impeccable reverence with which they lived each sacred day upon it. The land was unreachable, untouchable, a feast of which we could not partake. The trauma of its separation from those people, the mediators of its symbiotic relationship with the Sun and the stars, was as raw as the first days when the genocide of its race had been committed, for these wounds cannot be healed by time.

The forest was, to us, a great sentient being in the throes of grief and it was with sadness that we dwelt within it...until the morning of the lizard. That day the land opened her heart to us.

We spent the rest of the day in preparation for the visitation we knew was coming. By nightfall we were ready. Once Zak was asleep, we arranged ourselves around the shimmering altar and slipped into meditative communion. Not yet realizing the full import of the star-tetrahedron or the pre-eminent position it was soon to take in our existence, we allowed it to fill our vision. It became everything; spinning gently in the warm currents that drifted in from the rainforest, its presence speaking volumes as it gathered and projected fractal beams of light into and around us, its form telling a wordless story of life that was in perfect resonance with the seething sounds of the jungle night shift.

Mesmerized, we waited and waited. The events that had culminated in our being there crowded into the space, the vision and the reality coming into alignment. The night was charged with the primordial magic of the Aboriginal dreamtime that seemed to swell with each breath and finally brimmed and spilled through the glass doors. Our total isolation came home to me as two large fruit bats flew into the room, circling and circling around us. My whole body began to shake in the warm tropical air as another frequency joined us. Its vibration drew near to blend with my own and I began to make, on many levels, the adjustments necessary to resonate with this Consciousness. Welcoming this blending into myself, I felt an expansion in my heart and relaxed into its awareness.

What followed was in its way as momentous as the event that took place on Green Mountain. It was not as dramatic or as dangerous, but it provided a pivotal point of reference for my understanding of the capacity of a regenerated Human, functioning on its full blueprint, an awesome insight into the potentiality of the transcendental Human and the holographic nature of creation, the resonant-field model to which I was an apprentice. When the convincing illusions of this world have beaten me into near submission to belief in my mortality, to question my sanity, it is the memory of this experience, so simple and yet so profound, that inspires me to continue to work with a paradigmatic visionary model that seems at times fantastical.

I was breathing with my heart. I know no other way to describe it. Every breath brought immense energy and light into my being, effortlessly. I was weightless. I was ecstasy. Each breath was all there was and held everything within it. Sometime after this experience I realized that, in that state, I would not have been able to communicate in language as we know it, I would not have been able to eat, to drive a car, to do any number of things that define our present mode of existence. And yet it was a very physical sensation. I was not 'out of body', but for the first time, fully present in it. Unusually, Jiva did not share this experience with me, but he did observe it. He told me later that as my breathing altered so did my physical appearance. My face became sharply defined and ageless: 'elfin', was the word he used.

The experience was all too brief and, as I came out of my altered state, my body once again filled with the magnetic density of this dimension; the tension that is always present in this dualistic reality returned. The ceremony to reconnect the Heart Circuit was upon us and, spontaneously, Jiva and I began a litany of renunciation that invoked love to take precedence over all other allegiances and agendas, each of us realizing that detachment was a prelude to full acceptance, that there was no separation, that all was simultaneously one and different ... to love was to be love.

There was no sleep that night and soon the kookaburra changed places with the bats as the night shift crawled under rock and leaf. Every tree and blade of grass welcomed and absorbed the coming light that touched them tenderly with exquisite hues of peach and pink. Blues of promise kissed the sky: then it rose; the golden orb of life, pulsating rays of cosmic intelligence, the miracle once more, the Sun!

Jiva and I sat on the deck that circled the house to greet this rising Star, still in awe of the night's visit and feeling very open, understanding more and more of the message. Through the blending of our energy with the Consciousness that had come to us that night, we were given a taste of ourselves in the future, a taste of what will be when our fully reconnected circuitry is activated - a state of total synthesis and integration of all our centres and circuits.

A few days later we discovered the third and final circuit of the Ether Ceremony, the test point for which was at the tip of the pubic bone. However, it was time to return to Bali and we accepted that our reconnection would take place there. Four days later we were turned away from Brisbane airport: there was a small problem with Zak's passport which, because it was Easter, would take ten days to sort out. Danny and Maggie had returned to England to visit family and, fortunately, they offered us their home.

Fourteen river crossings deep into the box canyon of Wilson's Creek, Danny and Maggie's home was far more isolated than our previous house, the rainforest wetter, older and denser. As the Sun penetrated the forest canopy its inner world gleamed with rich jewel-like colours. Pristine and crystalline, this world teetered on the brink of a transcendent realm. They had done nothing to tame the land around their home but had built it in, with and of the jungle. A wide wooden deck encircled the house. We had slept our first nights on this deck a few feet away from a coiled ten-foot python. I would wake to the rush of air around my face, as huge bats feasted on the mosquitoes that wanted to feast on me and felt the spirit of the snake stir in the warm night. Now, as we wound our way up the creek, the frequency of the Pubic Circuit reached out to us and the next day we prepared for our reconnection.

The energy that night was different from the night of the Heart Circuit: it was raw and primal. In truth we did not feel quite ready, but we were aware of the many synchronicities precisely calculated to create the combination that would open this window in time. All that was needed were Human units of bio-circuitry to receive the download and anchor it into this dimension. That was our job. We knew very little about this circuit and entered the encounter quite blind to the implications of either disconnection or reconnection.

The myriad species of giant ferns reached out to hold the house in a dense cradle of wild foliage. The absence of electricity rendered the night sky glass-black, strewn with points of diamond light. Our lack of knowledge with regard to what we were entering into distorted our sense of time which seemed to be rushing on with great speed and, before we had a chance to reflect upon the occasion, we were in the thick of it. We were both physically jolted at the moment of reconnection. It was as though history was heaving up out of our memory banks in waves of ancient programs projected inside our third eyes and enveloping us into the centre of an ever-evolving hologram. I reached out to somehow slow down the images, but they eluded me. Not realizing that my eyes were closed, I was disorientated as I opened them to a sudden quiet stillness.

A few weeks later, back in Bali, the mystery of the Pubic Circuit began to unfold. We were staying in the mountain village of Penestanan when, one night, three thousand Balinese converged in truckloads on the village. They had come to participate in an intensely powerful ceremony. Usually the Balinese are very open and sharing with their rituals, but that night was different. There was an unusual air of solemnity about them. The event was a Kris Knife ceremony of a magnitude that happened only every seven years. It was shrouded in secrecy and foreigners banned. None of those who took part could leave the temple until four in the morning, as this would break the spell that was to take all participants into trance.

The force and power of the event was compounded by the grief and pain of a people whose country had just been bought by the World Bank and whose sacred rice seed had been taken from them and replaced by a genetically modified imposter. The absence of integrity in this, their main source of sustenance, was breaking down their immune systems and their spirit, just as surely as the ecosystem was deteriorating with the toxicity of government-issued fertilizer and insecticides. These were doing their job only too well. Where there were once a hundred fireflies, there were now only two or three; where once the frogs and crickets drowned out the Human voice, a whisper could now be heard.

The life style of the Balinese is one of balance. All to them is ebb and flow. Even the western world's most advanced computers could not come up with a program that could improve upon a water system which ribbons through each and every village, running only on its own power to bring water to all its inhabitants; water that they drink and in which they wash their babies, in total trust. That water may have been unfit for tourists, but its 'pollution' was of an organic nature that did not threaten the Balinese. That same water is now poisoned by chemicals which are tearing down the walls of their resistance to disease.

All this grief was expressed consciously in their ceremony that night. The sounds they made as they went into trance and bellowed their frustration, confusion and rage shook the whole village.

Something in the force and potency of that night brought our attention to the significance of the Pubic Circuit. Suddenly the sounds from the village stopped and in the heavy silence, Jiva began to recite part of the biblical Genesis. My body began to shake as it recognized, buried in this creed, the abuse of Human innocence. I was shocked at the flagrant and transparent language that spoke unmistakably of the disempowerment of Humanity. The next day we acquired a copy of the Bible from a second-hand bookshop in Ubud and read in chapter three of the book of Genesis,

'...Now the serpent was more subtle than the beast of the field which the LORD God had made. And he said unto the woman, Yea, hath God said, Ye shall not eat of every tree of the garden? And the woman said unto the serpent, we may eat of the fruit of the trees of the garden. But of the fruit of the tree which is in the midst of the garden, God hath said, Ye shall not eat of it, neither shall ye touch it, lest ye die.

And the serpent said unto the woman, Ye shall not surely die. For God doth know that in the day ye eat thereof, then your eyes shall be opened, and ye shall be as gods, knowing good and evil. And when the woman saw that the tree was good for food, and that it was pleasant to the eyes and a tree to be desired to make one wise, she took of the fruit thereof, and did eat, and gave also unto her husband with her and he did eat.

And the eyes of them both were opened, and they knew that they were naked and they sewed fig leaves together and made themselves aprons. And they heard the footsteps of the LORD God walking in the garden in the cool of the day and Adam and his wife hid themselves from the presence of the LORD God amongst the trees of the garden.

And the LORD God called unto Adam, and said unto him, Where art thou? And he said, I heard thy voice in the garden and I was afraid, because I was naked and I hid myself. And he said, Who told thee that thou wast naked? Hast thou eaten of the tree, whereof I commanded thee that thou shouldst not eat?

And the man said, The woman whom thou gavest to be with me, she gave me of the tree, and I did eat. And the LORD God said unto the woman, What is this that thou hast done? And the woman said, the serpent beguiled me, and I did eat.

And the LORD God said unto the serpent, Because thou hast done this thou art cursed above all cattle and above every beast of the field upon thy belly shalt thou go and dust shalt thou eat all the days of thy life.

And I will put enmity between thee and the woman and between thy seed and her seed: it shall bruise thy head, and thou shalt bruise his head. Unto the woman he said, I will greatly multiply thy sorrow and thy conception: in sorrow thou shalt bring forth children: and thy desire shall be to thy husband and he shall rule over thee.

And unto Adam he said, Because thou hast hearkened unto the voice of thy wife, and hast eaten of the tree of which I commanded thee saying, Thou shalt not eat of it: cursed is the ground for thy sake: in sorrow shalt thou eat of it all the days of thy life.

Thorn also and thistles shall it bring forth to thee: and thou shalt eat the herb of the field. In the sweat of thy face shalt thou eat bread, till thou return unto the ground, for out of it wast thou taken: for dust thou art and unto dust shalt thou return. And Adam called his wife's name Eve: because she was the mother of all living. Unto Adam also and to his wife did the LORD God make coats of skins and clothed them.

And the LORD God said, Behold, the man is become as one of us, to know good and evil: and now, lest he put forth his hand, and take also of the tree of life, and eat and live forever: Therefore the LORD God sent him forth from the garden of Eden, to till the ground from whence he was taken. So he drove out the man; and he placed at the east of the Garden of Eden Cherubims and a flaming sword which turned every way to keep the way of the tree of life.'

This text is a veiled account of the degradation of the divine Human potential and was the catalyst that began our exploration into the manipulation of Human consciousness through religion and the origins of the modification of our DNA which has resulted in a mortal slave-race. In coded language, the 'tree of knowledge' and the 'tree of life' refer to those fractals of the holonomic

Human symbiotic covenant that resonate with the geometric codes in light which define the Human as an immortal progenitor of life. 'The tree of knowledge' is the genetic information within the DNA blueprint that enables us to procreate. It was this fractal of Human potential that was reactivated in order to expedite the agenda of those responsible for the modification of the Human prototype, to further engender a slave-race. In this chapter of Genesis, the reactivation of this natural divine ability is shrouded in shame and guilt and portrayed as a self-instigated act of defiance and disobedience by woman against 'God'. For this she is cursed to be ruled by her mate and to give birth in great suffering.

'The tree of life' is the genetic information within the DNA blueprint that activates the bio-informational communication which prompts the perpetual rejuvenation that would include the Human electromagnetic field in the self-sustaining continuum of the universal holography. The re-instigation of the Human/slave prototype's ability to achieve its divine gift of procreation is described as a wilful liberty taken unlawfully and, because of this, steps are to be taken to ensure that the modification of the 'tree of life' is left unaltered: our progeny are cursed to die, and Humanity's mortal program is maintained.

It was not long after our focus was drawn to this passage in the Bible that we were introduced to a lengthier version of the story of Eden. This alternative account was presented as a more accurate portrayal of the incident, one which disclosed that the reactivation of the modified Human's capacity to self-propagate was a reverse procedure of genetic engineering carried out by a member of the same race of beings who perpetrated the original modification. This rendition of the account of Human genesis was allegedly translated from a series of pre-biblical chronicles inscribed upon 'lost' tablets and other artefacts unearthed in the Mesopotamian desert, a region now known as Iraq. Over the following years, these annals of information would become better known and were scrutinized by anthropologists and independent researchers into the truth of our origins. We were to explore this data as it emerged in correlation to the reconnection of major circuitry.

At this juncture, within our discovery of information pertinent to the circuitry of the Foundation phase of reconnection, we focused upon the relevance of this passage of Genesis in regard to the disconnection of the Pubic Circuit. Even at this point we knew enough to realize that the reactivation of the 'tree of knowledge' was a genetic reversal and we speculated upon the motivation behind the biblical account that portrayed this episode as a heretical act carried out in defiance of the wishes of the 'Lord God'. The answer lay in the multileveled and far reaching impact this interpretation has had on Humanity's capacity to accept its own 'fall from grace', its 'original sin'. It is one of the primary programs in the manipulation of Human consciousness through religion.

This programming exists not only in the Bible but also in many other ancient texts. Most religions insinuate that union with woman will impede man's spiritual evolvement and so it is that the celibate priest never looks deeply into the eyes of the one whose love can truly transform him. The divine act that he is convinced conceived his original sin, holds his original innocence.

This programmed emotional pattern of shame and guilt is intrinsic to the disconnection of the Pubic Circuit. This circuit, in unison with the Fire Circuit in the perineum, is the delivery system for the electromagnetic feed which animates the fractal of the holonomic Human blueprint that characterizes the true transcendent tantric Human.

We are a slave race functioning on just enough circuitry to propagate our species. The pure nature of our sexuality is diverted into the neurosis of survival by the suppression of bio-informational signals that have the capacity to trigger a spontaneous tantric mode. Our lack of self-knowledge is complicit in a planned obsolescence created by the 'gods' who gave death to Humanity and kept eternal life for themselves.

The church regards all experiences of sensual pleasure as sinful, attacking, to the point of extinction, the pagan faiths that anoint sex as a central holy sacrament. It has claimed that Adam lost both his innocence and his immortality when Eve introduced him to sex. Thus, woman brought death into the world and sex perpetuates it. The patriarchal religions that dominate most of this planet are bent upon the subjugation of the sensual feminine principle which is said to deter man from his spiritual path.

It is no longer necessary to read these texts to be

manipulated by them, for they exist within a morphogenetic field whose grid-work provides the scaffolding for this patriarchal age. Powerful forces with interests vested in Humanity's ignorance of its original and true potential have made it so. Even in those rare moments when we have felt our bliss, we have heard footsteps in the garden, footsteps not of our maker, but of our manipulator. We did not 'fall'...we were pushed.

14

TOTAL ECLIPSE OF THE SUN

BACK IN ENGLAND AGAIN, we left Heathrow airport to cut through the wet worn suburbs of the city and head out through the diminishing signs of over-civilization into the village-dotted countryside, all awash in the weary grey of England in the last dragging months of winter. We arrived late that night at the faerie fields of Avalon, bathed in the insistent and timeless peace of its soft hills and coombes steeped in age and legend.

Since our mission began, whatever funds we had managed to raise we ploughed back into the work and, with all the traveling that was required, we could not afford to keep a regular home waiting for us in Glastonbury. For several years we had lived in curious and eccentric dwellings that included a cave and an ambulance. This may sound like a charming gypsy life, but I can tell you it was not. The constant upheaval was, and still is, a high price to pay.

A couple of miles from Glastonbury we turned down a rutted dirt driveway, past an apple orchard and a field that was home to a couple of donkeys. We pulled up to the tiny wooden bowered bridge that spanned the stream running beside our cabin nestled under the limbs of an oak. We had arrived home at 'The Dove'.

The Dove Centre, so called because it is located in the sign of the Dove in the Glastonbury Zodiac, is a farm which had been bought by an artist couple and turned into a commune for other artists and musicians. Bronwyn and Roger were now its only occupants. Bronwyn was a painter of some renown and Roger made exquisite dulcimers. We had arrived at their farm one sunny summer's day after a trip to Bali, having seen their sign from the road into Glastonbury. Something told us to ask the taxi driver to pull down the long dirt driveway, at the end of which stood Bronwyn with a puzzled yet welcoming look on her face. The three of us spilled out in a disarrayed jumble and introduced ourselves. We had just arrived from Bali, we explained, and had nowhere to go; did she have a space for us? This was quite out of character for us and perhaps for Bronwyn too, but she found herself offering us the use of a tepee until something else could be arranged.

I was relieved when we were eventually able to leave the tepee. The flap at the apex of the structure that let out the smoke from the fire in the centre of the room was just as effective at letting in the rain. With all our suitcases we felt like square pegs in a round hole. Jiva received permission from Roger and Bronwyn to build a temporary structure in their field to get us through the spring months. This he did in three days. We retrieved, for £5 each, twenty-three old front doors from the reclamation centre and Jiva erected them around a wooden platform. Each door had a window and the front of the cabin was all glass. The roof was a huge canvas thrown over a lattice work of wood slatting. There was no bathroom or even running water. We were very much off the grid. Our cabin sat at one end of a lush green field with a Celtic tree circle of thirteen different trees that Bronwyn and Roger had planted twenty-two years ago. In this modest yet powerfully peaceful sanctuary we fell asleep to the haunted calling of owls and awoke to cooing doves, the cawing of crows and pheasants pecking at the door to be fed.

This humble little shack that was meant only as a stop-gap for a few months was our refuge, off and on, for several years. On one occasion we traded homes with friends in Los Angeles. Luxuriating in their spacious mansion with a swimming pool, we were astounded to learn that their week in our shack had been the best and most magical part of their tour of England.

That year we returned from California in the wet and grim but, mercifully, not-too-cold late winter. Winters in the cabin were brutal when frost formed on the inside of the windows and we had to burn a wood fire to defrost the fuel in the gas heater. The outer layer of the many quilts on the bed would be covered with a frozen sheen of moisture. We wore woolly hats to bed, otherwise we would wake with terrible headaches from the numbing cold. It would take some time to get to the point when we could bear to make our way to the outside toilet and shower a couple of hundred yards away in Bronwyn and Roger's studio courtyard.

We spent the next few months holding workshops and training new ambassadors and then we turned our attention to the White Spring. Our growing dedication to the ever-evolving Template was steadily taking over our lives and the White Spring was left in the hands of the manager and staff. We did, however, continue to create unique and intricate wands and jewellery to sell and this provided the financial backbone that kept the Spring open. Our work with the Template waned in the summer months and we were content to stop traveling a while and enjoy our cabin, which became a perfect studio for our craft.

The total solar eclipse of 1999 was a week away and, unbeknownst to us, was to herald the coming of the 13th Circuit of Activation and Integration. The first twelve Foundation Circuits had been hard won and we were basking in their nurture. Their reconnection had provided a stable platform of key elementary reconciliation of the fundamental Human condition on which to stage the emotional resolution that would allow for the retrieval of a more expanded identity base.

With the reconnection of the Water Circuits we had forgiven those we loved and those we did not. We had accepted that life was not happening to us, but because of us; that mother and father are sacred and, despite what we may or may not have enjoyed or suffered under their guardianship, they were the stargate through which we entered existence and that, beyond the wounds and scars our parents carried from their own inability to flourish in this mutant, dualistic paradigm, they loved us more than life itself.

With the reconnection of the Air Circuits we forgave those dark power-holders who had, down through the ages, caused fear to enter our vibrational fields. We empowered ourselves with the conscious knowledge that we were the Source generating all the experiences that we had.

With the Earth Circuit reconnected, we fell back into the lap of the Mother and reaffirmed our allegiance to our emerald-blue planet spinning through the galaxy. We reinstated an electromagnetic conduit into the very body of her wisdom, allowing a sublime influx of Earth awareness to deliver its simple natural truth into the pituitary-hypothalamus-pineal complex, rendering ourselves sentient instruments through which Source Consciousness could interface with this planetary bio-computer.

The Fire Circuit broke our covenant with death. In one aesthetically compelling moment of ceremonial awareness we introduced the frequency of immortality into our field of perception and into the entire planetary biospheric membrane. Never was there a time when we did not exist...never would there come a time when we would cease to be! This immortal creed challenged in one poetic sweep the greatest deceit ever perpetrated upon Humanity.

With the reconnection of the Ether Circuits we revealed and denounced guilt and shame, inviting light to enter our hearts, placing love as the central cohesive sacrament which defines our core existence.

We did not know it, but we were now ready for the 13th Circuit.

Jiva and I had decided to view the eclipse from Glastonbury Tor, where we would witness a 98% eclipse. That would have to do, as the report from Cornwall, where the total eclipse was to be seen, was of water and food shortages and day-long traffic jams. All hotel and bed-and-breakfast accommodation had been booked up for several years. To be honest, we were not particularly drawn to the event and were disinclined to undertake the arduous pilgrimage to Cornwall.

Three days before the eclipse both Jiva and I awoke just before dawn to an intense and insistent Presence in our one-room cabin. Reluctant to leave sleep and the womb of our warm bed, we arose and lit a candle on the altar that was framed by the melting night sky as another Avalon dawn slowly illuminated our secret field. The visitation was unexpected. Usually we would be aware a day or two in advance that a communication of some intensity was approaching and would prepare for it on various levels. However, that dawn found us disorientated by the residue of sleep that still clung to our thoughts, clutching hot mugs of tea, the steam spiralling up to merge with the incense lit on the altar. Welcoming and resisting the event, we slowly became present.

A momentum of vibration built and set the cabin thrumming around us. As the sky became soft with the promise of day and the leaves of the oak whispered in the first morning breeze, the living truth of creation beckoned us to trust. We rode our breath through the stargate of time and space into the embrace of the moment, each breath releasing tension and resistance and adherence to the norm, leaving room for the impossible. The Awareness in the cabin merging with our own, we shared a vision that slipped seamlessly into our consciousness.

The scope of the vision radiated out in a holographic panorama from the third eye in a spherical projection that held us in its centre. I was the centre of the universe (as I had always suspected), as was every other point of light. Wheels within wheels... all around were the churning interactive fractals of co-creative consciousness establishing the mechanics of resonance that govern the synchronomic forces of manifestation, light informing transmissions of divine cognizance pulsating through the hyper-mandalic holography of the one matrix, the geometry of it making all things simultaneously and inconceivably one and different.

We were backstage at the continuum. The centrifugal crystalline generator that received, translated and transmitted the divine hyper-coded life covenant into usable data for our solar system was the grand Maha-spheric gateway to the Heart of the Cosmos...our Sun; the womb from which all is birthed into time and space. This was our first visionary introduction to the symbiosis of the holography that forms the matrix of manifestation. It would be some time before we came to understand that the symbiosis of our solar system had been adulterated to create the dualistic fear-based paradigm which Humanity now inhabits.

Opening my eyes, I saw that the Sun had risen and splayed its honey fingers across the altar, causing the treasures upon it to glint and glimmer.

"We'll use the rent money," Jiva said, bringing me back to earth.

"What for?" I asked.

"The petrol to get to Cornwall," he said.

We headed down to the south Cornish coast with tent and sleeping bags in a state of high excitement. Warriors, we would battle the traffic and walk there if necessary.

As always Cornwall was stunning; a Tolkien tome come to life, its powerful cliff tops strewn with crumbling castles, soft undulating hills rolling down to the havens and coves where ancient fishing villages sat timeless and still. Miniature rose-wreathed thatched cottages, from which you might expect a hobbit to emerge, lined narrow cobbled lanes.

We had brought Zak with us, now a teenager, and several of his friends, and met with our friend and webmaster, Laurence. By sunset we had set up camp in a farmer's field by the ocean. At ten the next morning we were gathered and waiting on a castle-crowned mount with a view of 360° that included the ocean, surrounded by several hundred people.

Some years earlier, in 1990, we had witnessed the total solar eclipse on the Big Island of Hawaii. This was our first experience of an eclipse and Jiva and I had many expectations of the event. Looking back, I remember hoping for some high spiritual experience that would galvanize my sense of being a galactic Human. At the darkening of the light the jungle around us was plunged into sudden, total and heavy silence, each living entity shocked and confused by the unexpected gloom. The phenomenon of a mass so gargantuan as to blot out the rays of their Sun was not a part of their souls' original evolutionary covenant with light. All was suffused with a deep-sepia wash that took the day. An inexplicable sense of shame and guilt churned in the pit of my stomach and I felt the need to weep for something lost long ago. Even as the Sun returned its light there was an oily clinging residue of misery over everything. 'Eclipse' is defined as: 'blot out, cloud, darken, dim, extinguish, obscure, overshadow, exceed, outdo, outshine'; terms of disempowerment, very different from conjunctions and alignments which imply interactive equal cooperation.

That morning on the mount in Cornwall before the eclipse began, the air was filled with expectation and a respectful deference. In the split second when the eclipse began a hush fell upon every living thing and a great ominous shadow slipped across the land like an ancient spell. I was intent on tuning in to the event in the expectation that I would experience a more activated sense of being a co-creative part of the universal holography and, in so doing, feel closer to the Source, closer to an expanded sense of identity beyond that portion which had awoken within this mutant paradigm. Instead, I found it difficult to focus on the eclipse itself as, essentially, I was not impelled to do so. My attention was drawn time and again to the people around me: I was being heavily buffeted by great waves of emotional turbulence which rose from the crowd. With so little time to make arrangements, we had not been able to find a more secluded spot in which to experience the event. In retrospect, I can now see that the response of the crowd was an important aspect of what I had come to learn.

Overwhelmed, I found my computational awareness shifting into hyper-drive and I began to tremble, not because I was attempting to integrate some higher frequency generated by an acceleration of life-force from the eclipse, but from the sheer force of un-integrated iconic recognition boiling out of the collective unconscious. As I surveyed the sea of faces around me raised to the heavens as one great expectant entity, I felt disempowerment settle like a film of grime upon us all - a miasmic communal paranoia. The field was a great confessional filled with the penitent. Upon many a face I saw a battle between the desire to remember and the desire to stay in denial of something which, if it were acknowledged, would change everything. The entire gathering was keeping at bay, in the deep recesses of things forgotten long ago, a collective secret; something unspeakable; something perpetrated upon the entire Human race and its Mother planet – as the moon snuffed the light of the Sun.

The Sun shone on beyond the moon as the Earth became a silent darkened stage. A break in the continuum of light reaching Earth's crystalline heart as a coded reinforcement of her terminal decline was mirrored in the mortality of her inhabitants. The moon was rendered a dark and vast archetypal configuration, penetrating all bardos of consciousness to reach the depths of the spirit and imprint upon it its dark geometry, visually exposing the phenomenon of its power to shadow the light. As the Sun was once again revealed in its totality, the light returned, and a roar of approval rose from the gathering as though they had witnessed a gladiatorial triumph. And yet no elation could wipe away the travesty that had occurred. A sense of futility and disappointment lay over the dispersing crowd as some smiled thinly: the occasional laugh could be heard, nervous and hollow.

The day-to-day domestic existence of Humanity is so filled with the endless tasks and distractions of survival that little thought is given to our symbiotic existence as fractals of the whole holographic cosmology. An eclipse returns us briefly to the awareness of and appreciation for the stupendous cosmic interference patterns which weave the infrastructures that dictate the paradigm matrix. It is the celestial proportions of the solar eclipse phenomenon that draws people away from their homes to travel great distances to witness the event and yet it is the daily rising of this numinous cosmic entity, gifting us the day, which is the true miracle.

Just days before writing the account of this eclipse I wrote a morning ceremony to be performed at the rising of the Sun. It is included in 'The Template - A Holonomic Model of Transcendence', as part of the Sacred Day Ceremony.

This sacred day
My communion with Earth's Sun
brings my full conscious awareness into the moment,
honouring my physical being as a portal
through which divine Consciousness flows,
a stargate in time and space.
My every breath crystallizes my presence
as a co-ordinate in the divine immortal continuum,
cleansing my emotional body.
My mental body breaks free of its mortal confines
as I remember my quantum identity,
awakening my fearless self.
Love is my protection.

Imagine if this recognition, focus and gratitude were collectively offered to the sunrise each morning.

In India, the solar eclipse is accompanied by much chanting and ritual. This is usually interpreted as homage, when in fact the eclipse is recognized as a highly inauspicious event and the 'holy names' are chanted to reverse the negative influence as the Sun is darkened.

When we returned to our tent, we felt a particular

exhaustion that heralded the need to integrate something we were not yet consciously able to assimilate. We lay down on the ground, falling instantly into deep sleep, and woke three hours later, both having had the experience of downloading coded information which, in the light of further data and experience, we would be able to retrieve and comprehend. As we left Cornwall for Glastonbury we felt rejuvenated but did not yet realize that we were 'pregnant' with the coding for the next phase of the Template model of transcendence.

The solar eclipse had stimulated our inherent knowledge that the original Human, prior to its genetic modification, was coded to evolve through its symbiotic relationship with every point of light within the embrace of the solar system. It had not accomplished this by revealing a convergence within this unified symbiotic field in which every animated point of creation is a sensory organ of Source Consciousness, expanding and evolving through the absorption, translation and transmission of light, received as information from the Sun. Instead, the total eclipse of the Sun had visually divulged the breach within the divine immortal continuum, a breach that is illustrated by the eclipse, but is by no means restricted to the ecliptic event, for the moon is continually eclipsing the function of the Sun...electromagnetically. The breach within the immortal continuum is itself continuous and is creating a mortal paradigm. It would be several years before we would learn the full implications of this and its impact on Humanity, Earth and the solar system, and discover the circuitry within the Human electromagnetic field that would ultimately heal the breach.

In the meantime, the solar eclipse had set in motion the retrieval of information and codes relating to the original genetic blueprint embedded in the Human matrix. As the saying goes, 'You don't know what you've got 'til it's gone.' It was the withholding of light that catapulted us into a receptive mode for the 13th Circuit, now registered within our cellular consciousness.

15

THE HOLOGRAPHIC SOUL COVENANT

FOUR YEARS BEFORE the 1999 Solar Eclipse, we had come to the realization that there were further circuits involved in the resurrection of the Human electromagnetic field. A component within the alchemy of the reconnection of these circuits was to be ceremonial communion with sacred symbology. We were in total resonance with this information and made it our priority to discover the nature of this 'symbology'. The autumn equinox was approaching, and we decided to access this portal to gain further insight.

Once again, we spent the night at the White Spring. On this night we were not sitting at the mouth of the cave with the water, but had built an altar at the very back, deep under the Tor. It was a heavy night with a hollow chill in the air that crept into our bones.

Our clothes were almost wet with the damp as a fine sheen of spring water covered the walls. The altar reflected the heavy autumnal night that marked the descent into the demise that is winter. Set in the centre was the skull of a she-wolf.

That night she had fervently tried to impart something to us as Jiva and I took turns holding her skull. Convinced that she held the key to the reconnection of further circuitry, we wondered if perhaps the perfect symmetry of her exquisitely balanced skull was forming some sacred symbol which, if we could only discern it, would trigger some deep coded genetic response. I laugh to think of it now, but at the time it was immensely frustrating, and the night was spent going around in confusing circles, time and again returning to the wolf skull, turning it over and over in our hands, willing her to speak to us, inviting the perfect balance of her skull's structure to activate some long-lost knowledge. She patiently offered the answer plainly displayed in her construct as she stared sightlessly, winking knowingly, the candlelight rendering her eyeless sockets dark hollows full of meaning. It was four years later, two months after the eclipse, when the answer dawned on us.

We had just watched the autumn Sun set behind the Celtic tree circle when it all fell into place. For the past two weeks the words 'occipital lobes' kept popping into my mind. I reached for the wolf skull on the altar, turned it over…and there it was! The skull was not showing us the symbology that would reconnect the circuit, but the point at which it entered the body, the occiput at the base of the skull where the spinal cord joins the brain; the axis point between the left and the right, the male and female, the above and below. This point marks the present moment, the culmination of past and future; the portal to the immortal, our point of orientation as we navigate the inner and outer landscapes. The occipital end of the 13th Circuit is the point of entry through which the stars imbue our psyche as stellar radiance triggers our DNA.

Three months later, on the winter solstice, the activating occipital end of our 13th Circuit was reconnected. We had decided not to brave the heavy cold damp White Spring and chose instead to experience the solstice in our cabin in the warmth. It marked the thirteenth anniversary of our meeting and the thirteen-year point until the culmination date of winter solstice, 2012. I think we both knew the gift that night would bring, although we did not dare speak of it.

Long tendrils of ivy had squeezed through the many gaps around the picture window and tenderly enveloped the altar, wrapping around the coiling stem of the candle holder and creeping out of the eye socket of a Peruvian peyote mask. Crystals nestled in the antlers of a carved wooden stag. A South American beaded jaguar head glowered at the badger skull as our massive eagle feather swayed in the heat of the wood-warmed room. Thick forest-green and wine-coloured velvet covered the twenty-three doors and draped beneath the canvas roof to keep in the warmth from the wood stove. Night fell, soft and silent, and the energies of culmination built in ever-tightening spirals as the cross-quarter drew near.

The solstice, marking a transitional point in Earth's communion with her Sun, brought focus to our own need to resolve residual inner conflicts; to face fears, which, when embraced and released, allowed us to harmonize with the celestial rhythms of a new cycle. Breathing deeply, I moved through each emotional barrier that denied me the ability to embrace, without censorship, the moment. Opening my eyes, I could see Jiva in a similar process. This almost unbearable discomfort eventually passed as the hour slipped beyond midnight and we broke through the various bardos of ego into a place of peace and a state of deep samadhi...to commune with the Consciousness with which we had collaborated throughout this wild adventure, a presence that made sense of a world deep in the insane grip of terminal decline. My shoulders finally relaxed as I looked at Jiva. He was smiling with relief and bliss.

We were seated across from each other as a large star-tetrahedron slowly turned between us, first one way and then the other, creating a variety of changing forms, expressing the symmetry of unity perfectly. As it took us deeper and deeper, we felt a sudden sense of disorientation as though past points of reference had been swept away. Our focus never left the star. We could see it now as an archetypal resonant field, resolving, through its definitive configuration of Unity and Trinity, all inner sense of conflict and duality. I reached for a way my mind could interpret this, only to find it had transcended my polarized thought processes: there was no available language.

As form is the shape of consciousness, the consciousness expressed by the total and seamless unity of the star-tetrahedron is the tantric pulse that births all forms of life. That night, as its geometry transmitted its intelligence data, it created a vortex of coherence that engaged our own fields of awareness. By virtue of its supreme and overriding integrity, it commanded resonance. Thus, the resonant field for this divine frequency, dormant in the geometric Soul Covenant embedded in the Human matrix, was reactivated. As a conduit of coherence between our conscious selves and our original blueprint was re-established, the occipital terminal of the 13th Circuit of Activation was reconnected.

The immediate sensations from this reconnection were more extreme than any others we had experienced. We were truly disorientated, not understanding until much later that, through the download of electromagnetic energy into the base of our skulls, we were experiencing a higher dimensional vibration that was already overriding dualistic points of reference and were embodying the frequency of a new paradigm. Shimmering in front of us, the star-tetrahedron, the geometric conjugal mediator, had synthesized within us the tantric friction of opposites to conceive, through the sacred marriage, the divine androgynous Trinity.

It was, of course, not symbology we were reaching for that autumn equinox in the White Spring, but geometry. A symbol is emblematic, expressing its meaning through reference and suggestion: it represents something rather than being it. Beyond symbolism, sacred geometry is both the Source and its creation in different stages of manifestation.

Once, someone asked me how to program a piece of geometry I had given her.

"You don't", I explained; "it is the program." Sacred geometry is the universal language of light, the manifest expression of the underlying organizing forces of life that energetically defines all of creation. The mathematical laws of sacred geometry govern every system of growth, every motion in the universe, from atomic bonds to spiraling galaxies. All life-forms function upon the vibratory infrastructure of geometrically organized hyper-cooperative pathways of electromagnetic energy.

Until that solstice night we had had very little exposure to sacred geometry other than to the star-tetrahedron which had been gracing our altars for the past few years. Rather than immerse ourselves in books, we were compelled to discover the meaning of sacred geometry from the forms themselves. To become co-creative with any system it is essential to first discover and understand its construct. As you expose yourself in states of openness to sacred geometry, it will expose to you the deepest composition of life itself, showing it to be an ingenious web of relationship. Because sacred geometry is a configurative representative of the elemental components of the creative force, it offers, through its simple presence, a direct conduit to Prime Consciousness. Bypassing the dogmatic perimeters of the intellect, it transmits knowledge that exists beyond the reach of religion, philosophy, belief or disbelief. It is a pure language.

Two days after we had experienced our activation, I was working alone in the White Spring. There were quite a few people milling about and several shoppers perused the crystals and carvings for sale. I found the frequency of their presence growing more and more intolerable and, finally, I broke. Even though it was only 11am, I announced that due to circumstances beyond my control everyone had to leave…'right away!' In a greatly agitated state I found myself prizing crystals from the hands of willing customers and shuffling them, protesting, out of the front door. At last alone, I sat for a long while, head in hands, allowing the sound of the spring to wash over me. I was having a very difficult time integrating this new circuit and the energetic information it was introducing into my electromagnetic field. Even so, it was an exciting sensation. At the time, we simply thought that the lack of grounding we were experiencing was due to the fact that we had not yet integrated the reconnection ceremonially. There are innumerable nerve endings culminating at the base of the skull as the spinal column enters the brain and it is a highly charged terminal. Reconnecting this point to an influx of ultra-energized life-force was exceptionally stimulating. We slept and ate very little.

The spring and summer that followed the activation of the 13th Circuit were exciting, energetic and dynamic. The most compelling aspect was the introduction of a spectrum of the creation frequency that was the first taste of the Trinity as, through the activation point of the 13th Circuit, we embodied the frequency of a new paradigm. It was a summer filled with grand visions, a sense that it would never end, of invincibility. We were withdrawing more than ever into our own world, feeling ever more alienated from everything other than nature and each other. On occasions when we found ourselves in social situations, interactions seemed pointless and they grated. We felt impatient and intolerant. After that morning in the White Spring when I had thrown everyone out, I never worked there again.

We continued to believe that the electrifying and un-synthesized aspect of the 13th Circuit would eventually mellow out, not yet realizing that there was a magnetic integrating terminal that was the counterpart to this circuit. As autumn finally approached, oak and hawthorn shed their summer dresses and the land itself beckoned us into a place of introspection. We realized it was time to tune into the ceremonial code to activate the 13th Circuit.

It was not difficult to locate the five Platonic solids that provided the geometric resonant component within the alchemy of the Ceremony of Activation, as the Platonic forms are the focus of most who are involved in geometry and there was a shop in Glastonbury that sold them. However, to bring through the sonic component that would complete the alchemical code for the activation of the 13th Circuit, we returned to the peace and quiet of the Balinese mountains. In our bamboo sanctuary we withdrew from the many distractions of everyday life and immersed ourselves in the natural world.

We rose with the Sun and fell into sleep soon after its

setting. The rhythm of natural light assisted us to slowly release our addiction to the over-stimulation of external influences. It took a while to surrender to the long Sun-drenched days, passed in virtual silence. Everything reduced to an elemental simplicity - a cloud sailing by the bamboo window frame, a dog barking in a distant village, a child crying, the gamelan choir drifting in on the eventide as another soft jasmine breeze drew in the night.

In the cradle of this vibration our relationship with geometry was nurtured. Our knowledge and understanding of this phase within the whole system expanded and integrated, not only through the accumulation of information, but through the direct experience of that information as it was translated through the Human condition, particularly through the emotional body and its effect upon our relationships with ourselves, each other and with reality as a whole. It was a visionary process that required us to release established logical notions and to embrace without restraint the pure transmissions offered in each moment. The distillation of this phase of the Template was accelerated by our exposure to sacred geometry as solid forms in time and space rather than on paper or computer screen.

Seeds of our future comprehension of this massive body of information were sown in the solitude of the Balinese mountains and the most fundamental understanding that was to form the foundation of the Template of our resurrection was revealed to us. We came to understand that the 'soul', rather than being an ambiguous censoring device that registers all your good and bad deeds, is an organizing schematic of encoded information that is embedded in the Human matrix. This is the most fundamental infrastructure of the Human identity - a creation mandate that spells out the full spectrum of potential encoded into the original Human blueprint. This holographic covenant is written in the geometric language of light. Due to the disconnection of circuitry and the modification of the DNA, there are fractals of this covenant that are inactive. The geometric codes we were downloading would resurrect these dormant fractals.

When they arrived, one morning, the words of the Activation Ceremony were strange to me. The language was very different to that employed in the Foundation Ceremony. It spoke of an aspect of Human identity that was as yet unfamiliar. We are so used to hearing Human beings explained in terms of inadequacy; fallen, guilty, shameful, weak and mortal. The words of the Ceremony of Activation employ a language that defines the Human as an exemplary paragon of galactic propensities, affirming the Human identity beyond its function in this mutant dualistic paradigm and honoring its celestial seeding and its soul's lineage.

The ceremony begins with the geometric configuration of the tetrahedron, the most autonomous and fundamental building block of manifest creation. In the ceremony the sonic code, the spoken words, invoke the frequency of sentient sovereignty as the participant consciously recalibrates their resonance with the universal reservoir of pleasure and causal desire. Within the geometric Soul Covenant, embedded in the Human matrix, this activates the library of resonant harmonics stored within the tetrahedral fractal of this holonomic blueprint. As the ceremony proceeds, the coded language defines the transcendental Human identity in terms of pure empowerment. The frequency wave of this ceremony opens the portals to the very infrastructure of the DNA to trigger a profound and immutable genetic response.

Our journey of discovery had occupied the two-month duration of our visas and we returned to Glastonbury to share this incredible ceremony in a state of electric excitement. The first Ceremony of Activation was to be held on the Isle of Avalon, in a geodesic dome in a picturesque field next to the Chalice Well Gardens. It was the spring equinox. Miraculously, the Sun shone that morning and did its best to dry up the muddy field through which we all slipped and slid to reach the tent, whose sides had to be propped up to accommodate the sixty people that filled and spilled out of it. This group had all experienced the reconnection of the twelve Foundation Circuits and some had waited more than a year for this 13th Circuit.

Finally, I was free of all the many preparations involved in creating this gathering. All the panic, chaos and hurry ended abruptly in a sudden silence, as I found myself the focus of a sea of expectant faces and trusting eyes. Suspended from the centre of the tent was a nesting of the five Platonic solids with a star-tetrahedron in the centre holding within it an octahedron. This three-foot gold-plated nesting turned evocatively in the still silence. The silence deepened as I realized I could think of nothing to say to this lucid group of journeymen and women. I was overcome with the sheer honour of their presence. The length of the silence grew somewhat uncomfortable before it was finally accepted and we all fell softly into it. The magnetism of meditation rendered the air potent and heavy, the silence now filled with birdsong and buzzing insects enjoying the warmth of the spring morning. As the Celtic past of this ancient and sacred place crowded into the space, we became aware of the exquisite synchronicity of our presence and the sacred coded ceremony in which we were about to take part.

Our introduction to the ceremony was brief, as that morning words paled in comparison to the event. The group surrendered into conscious communion with the geometry; the vibration of the exquisite spoken sonic code took their bodies into perfect resonance with that which their eyes beheld. The silence that followed the closing of the ceremony was filled with an unfathomable remembrance. The reconnection of the occipital point of the 13th Circuit had reinstated the coherence of a conduit of consciousness that began the reconciliation of the quintessential Human identity with the holographic universal mechanism of creation on a fractal level not experienced since the separation that began with the modification of the Human blueprint and the creation of a slave race.

The scale of the reunion encompassed the historic scope of the Human tragedy down through the ages and reached across time into a future that was endless...eternal. The peripheral frequency of the immortal Human identity touched each one present there that day with the promise of the liberation we hardly dared dream of: the liberation for which the resonant template already existed within the original Human blueprint, and which had, through this alchemically coded ceremony, begun its activation

16

THE TANTRA OF CREATION

SOON AFTER HOLDING THE FIRST Activation
Ceremony we began to receive feedback from the participants.
There was unanimous appreciation of the exhilarating injection of
energy, a heightened feeling of interconnectedness and a sense of
the holographic nature of reality. Many people experienced
enhanced psychic abilities: one woman went on to assist the police
in searching for missing persons. There were, however, those who
also commented that they were having trouble maintaining aspects
of their lives that required a certain degree of linear thinking and
were having to make lists of their lists to stay on track. One couple,
who ran a retreat centre, experienced difficulties in interacting with
their guests and keeping up with their paperwork; so much so that
they closed down for a time. We discovered that one of the

characteristics of activation without integration is a sense of invincibility that can border on arrogance and we found that the problems were more often with males born under certain astrological signs - their egos were going haywire. It finally sank in that the problem was not transitional.

By this time the sweet sorrow that is autumn had shifted sharply into winter. We found ourselves, one late November morning, forced to face the true nature of the situation. Having prepared the space and ourselves for receiving information, we quickly became aware that there was another point involved in the reconnection of the 13th Circuit.

It was Jiva who tuned into the integration point at the base of the spine in the coccyx, and on testing it, found that this point held very little energy. We had been investigating the Archimedean solids in a pictorial geometry book and found that we were able to temporarily bring life-force back into this point by focusing on these forms.

It was distressing to us that we were not given both the occipital and coccyx points with all the relevant geometry and reconnection codes at the same time. It would have been easy to blame ourselves for this and, indeed, we did feel the responsibility of it very heavily. However, when we investigated, it was not surprising. It became apparent that we did not have a point of reference for comprehending, in any conscious way, the integrating aspect of Archimedean geometry which we would come to know is feminine and magnetic. For in this patriarchal age it is the Platonic, electric, activation geometry that is at the forefront of our consciousness. Very little is disseminated about Archimedean, magnetic geometry. This limitation is mirrored in the macrocosm of the present global condition. It is the over-emphasis on the male, electric, activating property, devoid of the feminine, magnetic, integrating aspect, which allows the desecration of the environment. The reference to the supreme Godhead as male is a further galvanization of the iconic imbalance that lies at the very core of the terminal decline that grips this planet.

The lack of information about Archimedean geometry was underlined sometime later when we met a mathematician and geometrist called Jain, who lived in Byron Bay. Having attended our ceremonies, he invited us to peruse his extensive library, a good-sized room housing books on geometry and mathematics from floor to ceiling. He had said that he had some books on Archimedean geometry: as it turned out, these comprised only two very slim volumes by a physicist.

It would not be until the integration point of the 13th Circuit in the coccyx was reconnected that we would be able to understand and synthesize the collaborative dynamics of the occipital and coccyx points with the co-creative tantric function of the Platonic and Archimedean forms. A portal of opportunity to receive the reconnection of the integrating terminus of the 13th Circuit was opened to us at sunset on the 11th of November.

As always, when the time of reconnection draws near, we are filled with a strange mixture of excitement and apprehension. I imagine the prisoner feels this as the day of release approaches – the freedom so longed for brings responsibility and inevitable change.

We had been assured of a clear, bright cloudless sky that day and so it was. As the afternoon drew on we came up with several reasons why we were too busy for this appointment, feeling a greater resistance than usual. Running out of anything resembling an intelligent excuse, I mentioned to Jiva that we were out of several provisions and a run to the store was needed. Looking up at him I caught his eye and saw in it the mirror of my own ridiculous defiance. We both laughed and got on with the business of setting the stage for transformation.

We bundled up in warm clothes and tumbled out of the cabin into the sharp bright blue-gold late afternoon and set off to the Celtic tree circle at the bottom of the field, where we built a small wooden pallet to serve as a platform. On this little stage we waited, in meditation. Sundown was an hour away; the high heavens melted into deep turquoise as the Sun approached the Celtic tree circle on the near horizon. There had been little direction given as to how we were to receive this connection. Our eyes were drawn to stare into the Sun. Almost immediately, we were able to differentiate the beams of light that pulsated so miraculously from this grand star as liquid gold fractal transmissions; an unremitting, endless code of light Intelligence. We recognized this light code to be a cascade of radiant matrices holding the evolutionary harmonic. This electric activating transmission merged with the magnetic life rhythms pulsating out from the Earth's biospheric aura. Our 13th Circuit integration points in the coccyx reconnected. We were not only witnessing the sacred marriage of the Mother of Form and the Father of Consciousness, we became it.

I felt a new solidity become a part of my body presence. A magnetic facet of ultra-Earth awareness seeped through every level of my being as I was drawn into the great Maha Gaia Tantra of universal creation – electromagnetically. I understood my connection to the Earth and the Sun, not as some bystander, but as a conjugal mediator. It was through my very being that the courtship of creation was taking place. My consciousness was a symbiotic component of creation. I felt the great love between these two sentient sovereign celestial and earthly entities imbue my physical matrix with the Amrita of an immortal continuum.

Light, as the geometric primal life impulse, endlessly transmitted from the galactic directive and transduced by our Sun, holds within it codes which reach out to our Earth for resonant fields with which to create. The world of nature that surrounds us revealed itself as an endless labyrinth of energetic interactive co-creative consciousness, exposing the holographic nature of the matrix. The tantric interference between the Solar and Gaia potencies of creation forms the womb from which all cosmological transmissions are birthed into time and space, the crucible in which the recipe of life is determined. Manifest existence is the result of the interference patterns created by the interplay of codes and frequency resonances that develop, between them, a matrix of archetypal patterning which translates this relationship into the principles of matter; expressing this tantric union as life-forms that walk, fly and swim, clothed in fur, feather and skin … trees, flowers and shimmering wings, all sprung from a palette of light.

I saw so clearly the folly of thinking there could be activation without integration. The cosmic directive that is the light code was one of two interactive, co-creative waveforms within the quantum tantra of manifestation. The convergent pattern between the two creates a vesica piscis; a yoni through which the fertile impulses of creation are expressed in form.

The electric seed transmission of the information that is light remains non-manifest until it unifies with a magnetic resonant field. Through the embrace of this field, the hologram of manifest existence is conceived as the egg-like feminine receptors provide the integrity of form through the integration and synthesis that takes the electric light directive of the seed-impulse through its iconic and embryonic stages into crystallization. This explained why the activation of the 13th Circuit without integration resulted in an ungrounded state: exciting as it was, it was a trip going nowhere; a cause with no effect.

The integration point of the 13th Circuit drew our electromagnetic fields into the deep recesses of the Earth's consciousness as a sovereign, sentient, celestial entity. For Jiva and me it was a deep and welcome homecoming. After the experience on Green Mountain, we understood paradise to be a simple quantum flux away. Earth was, and is, the garden of eternal bliss dreamed of throughout Humanity's long imprisonment in this mutant mortal realm. Earth is the stargate to every time and energy level in the universe. It is on the starship Earth that we will gain re-entry into the divine immortal continuum.

However, for some who had previously experienced the activation of the 13th Circuit, the reconnection of the integration terminus marked the end of a phase that had allowed them to explore their disassociation from Earth and they experienced a 'coming down', a wet blanket. Due to the fear-based paradigm we now inhabit, with war, disease, genocide and the countless manifestations of the modification of our genetic propensities, it is understandable that many people cleave to the myriad of philosophies and processes that they believe will free them from this body, this Earth. Some await a fleet of spaceships to 'ascend' in. Religions teach that this life is a punishment for our sins; a way to work off 'bad karma'; that our bodies are made of weak and sinful flesh that will lead us, through its natural instinctual impulses, into corruption and degradation.

Through our reconnection of the 13th Circuit and our work with geometry, it was with deep resonance that we discovered that we on Earth, in this space-time frequency, are not experiencing the third dimension. We inhabit a lower octave of the third dimension - duality. The challenge for Humanity is not to 'get out of' or transcend the third dimension, but to create it, for this dimension is the stargate to every other level of manifest experience. The third dimension is where the party is!

We did not find ourselves in this immeasurably privileged position - embodying an instrument of sentient capability, each one of us an autonomous instrument of sensuality, of divine Consciousness, seeing beauty, feeling love - so that we could, upon finding ourselves challenged by the shadow, run 'home', back to the 'One', to the Void, to the undifferentiated ocean of potential. We belong here; this is our home. We must challenge the darkness and win back the true time-space frequency zone of conscious evolution for our people and for our planet.

In the full manifestation of third dimensionality, coexisting with all other prime dimensions, there are trees so deeply green they are almost as blue as midnight. Each leaf is as a facetted jewel that, when slightly turned, emanates a fractal beam of deep violet with a golden hue shining out from its core...and suddenly there for a moment is the most brilliant opal-hued silver flash! Water...liquid crystal...lavender beams swimming in its depths...becoming pink and palest blue and creamy opal white: geometry dancing beneath it all as every living thing celebrates together the conscious ceremony of life eternal, for here there is no shadow...no separation. So much light, as the grand Maha-spheric Sun embraces you, each beam of light a thousand loving arms...a cosmic embrace. And when it sinks away into the turquoise indigo night of a billion stars, you will not sleep, but awaken into a realm of celestial dreaming, listening within the cathedral night to the starry orchestra, starchild that you are, riding on the alpha-wave of deep inner star-studded space to the shores of morning light; and there again, the Sun that never left, but only withdrew, that you might know it through its starry consorts, returns now as dawn's caress upon this beloved Earth, as sunrise brings the promise of another day filled only with the joy of living and loving.

The potency of this multidimensional realm is geometrically coded into the quality of light. Our challenge is to reconnect the delivery system in order to 'reboot' Source Intelligence; resurrecting within our endocrine systems the ability to translate that light into the bio-signals that will reanimate our dormant genetic material. A fully resurrected Human blueprint transmits the harmonic of the universal design principle: a critical mass of resurrected Human units of circuitry will broadcast a collective frequency which will find resonance with a multidimensional unified field, thus drawing into manifestation a transcendent Earth.

17

FORM: THE SHAPE OF CONSCIOUSNESS

IN THE DAYS THAT FOLLOWED our integration of the 13th Circuit, the pale Sun was a brief visitor in fragile winter skies as the days almost ended before they began. The cold of the canvas-roofed cabin was debilitating and inhibiting. Our focus was to bring through the Integration Ceremony as soon as possible. As well as a clear and secluded space in which to download the codes, we also needed a full set of thirteen Archimedean geometries. As lovely as the cabin was, it was too cold: neither could we find any Archimedean geometry, nor anyone who could make it. Back we went to Bali.

The usual adjustments were made as we settled into the bamboo cottage in the mountain. It was monsoon season and our simple thatched home leaked in the torrential rain as thunder shook the flimsy structure. We stuffed plastic bags into the holes in the grass roof and did all we could to avoid the fevers that the monsoon invariably brought. There was much to achieve in the two months that our finances would allow us to stay.

Immediately, we set ourselves to finding someone to create the geometry we needed. It is believed that if you need something, someone in Bali will make it for you. We held tight to this legend and our adventure began. The mission took on an 'Indiana Jones' quality as our suspension-free jeep rattled around the deeply pitted mountain roads as we chased the flimsiest of leads. We tried silver-workers and iron welders: most shook their heads, others laughed. A few actually put their hands to creating a piece and the resulting 'geometry' may well have had the ability to disconnect circuitry.

One evening, while sitting in a café in the main town of Ubud, we noticed that the candle holder was a stained glass semi-geometric form in a metal frame. The waiter gave us the name of the craftsman and directed us to his workshop. Despite our combing the island for several weeks, our future sacred geometry workshop was to be three rice fields away in our own village. We brought our designs to the owner of the small workshop and as soon as he saw them, he smiled and assured us he could make them all and anything else we desired. And so he did. That was the beginning of a great partnership that smacked of destiny. The people of his village had named him

'Ting-Ting', as that was the sound endlessly emanating from his workshop as he made his various stained-glass creations. As the geometric combinations came through, Jiva would sprint across the rice fields to Ting-Ting's workshop to deliver the geometric formulas we needed and in a couple of days the finished pieces would be ready for us.

There have been many junctures in the long adventure of the unfolding of the Template model when we would marvel at the pristine intelligence of the information, as it revealed itself, fractal by fractal. The all too brief months we spent surrounded by stunning pieces of sacred geometry in the seclusion of the Balinese mountains was one of the highlights of our journey. As the days passed, we immersed ourselves in the challenge before us. Shutting out all other stimuli, we lived and breathed ceremony, codes and geometry.

Specific combination codes of Archimedean geometry in elemental progressions woven with their Platonic counterparts revealed themselves in nesting formulae. In the soft, starry and melodious evenings Jiva began his endless love affair with sacred geometry. He would sit in long silence with a particular piece turning it over in his hands to see it from every possible angle and I would hear from him intermittent sounds of progressive revelation, appreciation and resonance as each form drew out timeless memories from his cerebral cortex, his shoulders heavy with knowledge that he could not yet express in language. It was then that Jiva began his dreamtime visionary journeys in which he travelled through labyrinths of sacred geometric realities, dreams that continue today and have bled into his waking hours.

We refrained from referencing written material on geometry as our impulse was to build the forms and listen to their unmediated communication. The integrity of our blueprint was continually reinforced by the resonant feedback between our field of awareness and the transmissions emanating from the complex nesting of Platonic and Archimedean geometries that spelled out the magnificence of our original design. Coupled with this, the occipital terminus continued to deliver the raw electromagnetic input from the universal grid: the coccyx integrated this geometric information into comprehensive data for our computational matrix to decipher and utilize and thus we more fully understood the mechanisms that govern the implicate order of manifest existence and the full Human potential within this whole system of holonomic evolution. With this heightened appreciation of the relationship between geometry, creation and the Human entity, we were able to download the sonic code that would activate the resonant receptors in the coccyx terminal of the 13th Circuit. We were also able to appreciate the stages through which the geometry morphed as it moved through the iconic to the embryonic and, finally, into the crystallization of matter.

These realizations affected the way in which we perceived the capacity and function of the geometry and it soon became obvious that we needed to rename them accordingly. The established names did not express the essential qualities of these forms as they related to their purpose within the Soul Covenant, nor did they linguistically recognize the male and female differentiation of Platonic and Archimedean geometry, or that they formed the two potencies of the tantric components within the alchemy of creation. The orthodox names express these geometric forms by explaining their visual and constructive nature but not their esoteric function. They do not touch upon the fact that sacred geometry is the language of light. I say we needed to rename them, but actually I did not need to think about the names we were to use for these geometries; they were simply there.[2]

We had decided to take this ceremony to Australia before returning to Glastonbury, as a group of people who had previously experienced the Foundation phase, the Ceremony of Original Innocence, had organized themselves and requested us to come to Byron Bay on the east coast of New South Wales.

The ceremony was to be held once again in the rainforest retreat of our friends Danny and Maggie. The thirty-two participants passed over the fourteen river crossings in a determined cavalcade of four-wheel force and descended upon the beautiful round house in a collective state of celebration. As we all sat in a large circle, every one of them shared their gratitude and amazement at the transformations they had experienced since the Foundation Ceremony.

Jiva and I were nervous, as we had left Bali in such a flurry of activity that we had barely had a chance to tune into this ceremony and, frankly, we were experiencing a lack of trust that we had got it right. As I endeavoured to present the information which

---

[2] See 'The Template – A Holonomic Model of Transcendence'

accompanied the 13th Circuit, my tongue felt thick and dry in my mouth, my wits slow and reluctant. Like a fish out of water I flapped about, doing my best to explain my as yet unformed understanding of the information associated with the Ceremony of Activation and Integration. I contained within me the full vision and comprehension of what I wanted to explain to the group but had somehow not yet caught up with myself sufficiently to translate this understanding into language. My lack of faith in my own abilities compounded the situation, so when I found myself in the middle of the ceremony, having spoken the sonic code resonant with the fifth piece of geometry that Jiva was holding up, I was not surprised when the room was filled with a strange garbled sound as though the group was being collectively strangled. Looking up from the page, I saw a room full of contorted faces; everyone seemed to have a mouth full of peanut butter. They were communing with the geometry but could not speak the code that was its consort. Searching for Jiva's reaction, I saw a worried man. The room burst into nervous laughter. As I looked down at the page I felt not only huge relief, but also the playful yet practical spirit of the Consciousness we were working with. Aware of my doubts about the precision of the ceremony we had downloaded, they had arranged a mischievous way to show me that not only did it 'work', it was precisely constructed to the exact degree. I had jumped ahead one piece and read the sonic code for the sixth piece of geometry. As the room calmed and everyone, including Jiva, was staring expectantly at me, with conviction and joy I read out the fifth sonic code. Immediately, not only did everyone understand what had happened, they also appreciated the jewel contained in my 'mistake'. With gusto they spoke the fifth code as they communed with the resonant fifth geometric form of consciousness that was a fractal of their Soul Covenant.

The spoken code of the 13th Circuit Ceremony of Activation and Integration redefines the quintessential Human identity not as an 'Earth orphan', lost in linear space-time, but as the transcendental Galactic Human, affirming its symbiotic evolutionary relationship to Earth, the solar system and the entire universal holography.

As the electric solar energies within the Platonic geometric code transmit the iconic form of individualized sovereignty, the magnetic Gaia energies within the Archimedean code integrate this autonomous awareness into the primal field of conceptual existence.

As the electric solar energies within the Platonic code transmit the heartbeat of the Cosmos, the magnetic Gaia energies within the Archimedean code synthesize this pulsation with the microcosmic field of awareness into the matrix of form.

As the electric solar energies within the Platonic code activate awareness of the interconnected, interactive relationship with Source, the magnetic Gaia energies within the Archimedean code seal this emanation into the crystalline matrix of the Human-Earth hologram.

Back and forth the ceremony wove, between the electric and

magnetic, the male and female, activation and integration. Deep in the heart of the primeval rainforest, as one Human voice, filled with the exultant cadence of unity that has forever lifted the Human spirit from the suffering of this fear-based paradigm, we swayed euphorically between Platonic and Archimedean, between Sol and Gaia, between form and spirit, matter and consciousness, rocked in the cradle of creation as the energies built in spiraling circles of revelation, activating and integrating the geometric blueprint that lies at the heart of the Human masterpiece.

18

BREATH, THE UNSPOKEN VOW

AFTER RETURNING TO GLASTONBURY with the ceremony that reconnected the Integration terminal of the 13th Circuit, we held a series of workshops and quickly made a U-turn back to Bali. This was to become the pattern of our lives, traveling between Bali, England, Australia and America, never spending more than a couple of months in each country. The endless traveling was far from the glamorous lifestyle that many thought we lived. There were constant upheavals and farewells, our few belongings stored in other people's attics and basements.

With the reconnection of more and more circuits, the influx of life-force enhancing electromagnetic energy boosted our endocrine systems and enabled us to withstand the viruses one can become vulnerable to when traveling, continually changing time zones and weather conditions and being exposed to considerable amounts of radiation on airplanes. When we did complain, we did so half-heartedly, knowing that it was an incalculable privilege to have the job. Although we stayed in many grim and cheap motels and spent endless hours on monotonous freeways, we also found ourselves in beautiful homes in rain forests and rice fields, by secluded beaches and lagoons inhabited by giant turtles. Our travels were seldom prearranged, and we would often land without any idea where we would be staying, acting on trust and relying on good fortune.

Once we were back in Bali, it quickly became apparent that there was another ceremony that was also a fractal of the Activation and Integration phase, a ceremony which was to reconnect the circuitry intrinsic to our ability to engage in a holistic mode of breathing that was inherent in our original design.

Since our experience in the Australian rainforest on the night our Heart Circuits were reconnected, we realized that breathing was a function which involved far more than the diminished process we are capable of in our present modified state. That night in Australia I could feel the full activation of my endocrine system, as my body was flooded with endorphins and my heart centre expanded to envelop my entire being. Each breath I took accelerated the spin-frequency of all my energy centres, activating their ability to receive and transduce electromagnetic Source Consciousness… bliss.

We knew then that breathing was the system of synthesis which activated the Human holonomic system, rendering it able to calibrate the frequency of its electromagnetic field to resonate with other dimensions of consciousness. It was the key to our ability to transcend this mutant paradigm and resurrect our light bodies. Once having experienced a holistic mode of breathing, it became obvious to me that, due to the disconnection of circuitry, various components within the bio-mechanism that metabolizes our breath are no longer employed. As a result, we engage in shallow, unconscious breathing, absorbing just enough of the catalytic agent of oxygen to decode the minimum of pranic nourishment necessary to maintain the degree of consciousness resonant with a genetically modified, disconnected Human, hallucinating a mutant reality.

The full spectrum of the holonomic system of breathing revealed itself as all the components of the Sacred Breath Ceremony became clear to us in Bali. After holding the first Ceremony of Activation and Integration of the 13th Circuit in Australia, we were aware that the reconnection of life-force into the occipital and coccyx circuits activates the two ends of an energetic column or causeway that encases the spine and that this column is a component of the pranic mechanism. Within days of our return to Bali, we discovered seven new circuits, all of which feed various organs of the endocrine system and are systemically connected to the pranic causeway.

Mapped throughout this causeway are ultra-sensitive nodal receptors that correspond to the entire endocrine system. Each receptor is programmed to identify a resonant fractal of the bio-signalling transcendent intelligence that is the geometric infrastructure of the pranic code. Each node is a resonant receptor that responds to a like resonance within this code, a code that communicates the immortal frequency. As the node receives the pranic signal, it is transmitted to the relevant endocrine organ. The more capable the receptors are of receiving the full spectrum of the pranic code, the more bio-informational life resonance is available to the endocrine system to translate and utilize.

For the first time since beginning our work with the Template, the chakra system became a specific consideration as it became clear that this system is a component of the pranic mechanism. Prana is drawn into the body from the heart chakra centre, from the central fractal of the Human hologram, the portal through which the pranic creation code emanating from Source interfaces with the chakra system. The combination of the pranic circuitry, the chakra system, the endocrine system and the pranic causeway together comprise the holonomic system that is the pranic mechanism. The more that circuitry is connected into this mechanism, the more the chakra system is able to decipher the pranic code and more of this code can be utilized within the pranic causeway.

As we delved deeper into the pranic mechanism and its interface with the forces of creation, we found its holography to be so complex and intricate that it defied explanation in isolation, or in terms of linear thinking and dualistic language. The chakra system is particularly enigmatic, verging on unfathomable. Its construct and function as a holonomic system of energy transformation is a field of multidimensional interface. The chakras are interdimensional portals that link the body from one dimension of expression to another.

Each chakra is hyper-elemental, with whirling opalescent rainbow hues of never-still, light-refracting labyrinths of multilevel energy-transforming components. These dataflow translators are portals between the divine mandate of the life-directive and the manifestation of that directive as an incarnate living entity. As the electromagnetic dataflow is accelerated, through reconnected circuitry, so the chakra and endocrine systems are activated, resulting in the embodiment of a wider spectrum of the divine immortal blueprint.

Once we had received the pranic circuitry we turned our focus to geometry. It was immediately apparent to us that all the pieces, except one, would be Archimedean and all would be stellated. There were fourteen stars in all.

We were soon able to match the geometry to the circuitry. With this information, I spent the next couple of days in isolation and emerged from it with the sonic code to reconnect the pranic circuits. That night we prepared ourselves for the Ceremony of Sacred Breath.

Each ceremony has its own distinct flavour. The Ceremony of Original Innocence holds the essence of emotional resolution and forgiveness. The 13th Circuit Ceremony is an exciting and disorientating ride as it recalibrates the electromagnetic field to the full spectrum of the third dimension, breaking out of the dualistic paradigm. The Ceremony of Sacred Breath is a euphoric and joyous celebration that instils the sense of having reached a point of no return on the journey of liberation.

As you weave your way through this blissful ceremony, unifying with the cosmic directive, embracing the Earth pulsations, immersing yourself in the rhythmic tides of prana, merging with the never-ending, one eternal breath that is shared by every living thing, drifting beyond the reach of time, you feel yourself a part of the spherical mandala of the universal hologram as it unfolds and displays to you its fractal composition in a starry array that stirs remembrance…awakening your quintessential identity, the sense of separation falling away, star by brilliant star. Weaving in, through and around each utterance, each form beheld is the divine cohesive influence that ignites the passion of life. Breath, the bridge to consciousness, the cohesion that crystallizes spirit into form, the medium through which we witness the daily miracle, the unspoken vow of spirit and matter, the sacred wedding that weaves the matrix into form, the catalytic component that activates the alchemy of light and consciousness.

In the Ceremony of Sacred Breath, the seven circuits reconnected into the pranic mechanism are the Lung, Roof of the Mouth, Fontanel, Penis/Clitoris, Testicles/Ovaries, Sacrum and Umbilical Circuits. Through the stimulation of accelerated electromagnetic input, these circuits activate and integrate a wider spectrum of the pranic code that holds the immortal harmonic.

The holonomic template embedded in the Human matrix begins to reveal itself dynamically. The reconnection of these circuits makes available a wider spectrum of the dataflow that is prana and a holographic comprehension translates into our daily experience of life. When the Human bio-computational unit of circuitry is fully connected into the creation mechanism of universal holography, it will then be able to decode the full spectrum of intelligence-data present in prana. The immortal harmonic synthesizes and crystallizes with the incarnate body presence, unifying the physical matrix with the design pattern of the original blueprint present in the geometric Soul Covenant, resurrecting the light body.

As we integrated more and more of the data delivered by the reconnection of the pranic circuits, we were to determine that it was the stellation of the forms that brought in and synthesized a sixth element in the alchemical brew of creation - Stellar Radiance.

Stellar Radiance is that form of light which carries the creation code of prana. Prana is the primal form of light before it is transduced into the differentiated spectrum of colour that we know as visible light. The light we see and decode, emanating from our Sun, is the Sun's translation of the pranic code emanating from the Heart of the Cosmos. As this radiance enters the heart of the solar hologram, it is translated through the Sun's pineal-like lens system and is retransmitted as the solar matrix of the immortal continuum. Thus, our Sun is the mediator of Galactic Intelligence, projected as radiant light from the Benevolent Source of Creation. This radiance then becomes accessible for the Human unit of circuitry to decode and utilize; a code to activate the symbiosis between the Human entity and the solar system. Each one of us is a star projecting the intelligence specific to planet Earth. It is the presence of these geometric formulae of radiant light that activates and integrates the resonant stellar code within our Soul Covenant.

Stellar Radiance, translated by and emanating from our Sun star, is absorbed by every infinitesimal point of awareness within the unified field of manifestation. Each point of light is a component in the holonomic function of conscious evolution. The formulae of light, translated through the symbiotic relationships of the original planets of this system, propagates the birth of animate life and creates a fecund environment in which Source Consciousness can differentiate and thrive in the countless forms of conscious awareness that are the sentient emissaries of its divine potency.

During the following months of integrating the dataflow of Source Consciousness particular to the pranic circuits, we enjoyed a steady increase in the benefits offered by an acceleration of pranic nourishment. We had more energy, our muscular frames became stronger as we were more inspired to be physically active and we had far more resistance to viruses. We had less tolerance for situations that did not support our ability to experience deep rhythmic breathing.

On our travels, we had met many who claimed that having experienced DNA activation processes they now operated on twelve strands of DNA. From what we had understood of frequency resonance between the Human electromagnetic field and the dimension of consciousness experienced, it made sense that if you were functioning on that much genetic material you would be vibrating at a frequency that was resonant with a far more holistic paradigm than this one. It was some time after the reconnection of the pranic circuits that, through the testing procedure of kinesiology, we found that codons in our dormant third DNA strand had been reactivated. Although the reactivation of a dynamic ratio of helixes in the dormant DNA code would require critical mass and a resonant morphogenetic field to stabilize this transformation, the upgrade of pranic nourishment instigated by the reconnection of pranic circuitry rejuvenates the endocrine system, rendering the pineal able to translate a wider spectrum of light. This light is then distributed through the central nervous system and into the DNA to reactivate dormant codons. This may not be enough to resurrect whole helixes or to affect overt changes in environmental feed-back, but it is a beginning and a very real sign of what our future holds.

We held Sacred Breath Ceremonies in Australia, England and the USA and many people reported back that they were experiencing improved health and vitality. Margo, our good friend, ambassador to The Template and our administrator in the USA, decided she could no longer live in Los Angeles, as she felt she could not breathe there. She soon left her home and job for the hills of northern California.

For many it was after this ceremony that they began to

understand that their bodies were the pinnacle of the physical expression of their spiritual identities. Death was not the natural culmination of life but the breakdown and defeat of it, the slow steady deterioration experienced as a result of a disconnection from the true continuum. For them it was the reconnection to the constancy of life through circuitry that led them to the conviction of the inevitability of their immortality. Some understood this through the intellectual analysis of the process they were undergoing and others through the download of Source Consciousness encoded into the electromagnetic information delivered by the potent circuits they were reconnecting. Their ability to access a wider spectrum of prana was quickening the integration of this divine Intelligence, awakening their innate knowledge.

Two of the stars used in the Ceremony of Sacred Breath are Stars of Immortality. [3] These intricate and dazzling forms of sacred geometric information transmit an immortal harmonic that activates, within the divine blueprint, the Human geometric Soul Covenant, the frequency that defines the Human as a conscious conduit of life eternal. As a result of this, circuits into the fontanel and roof-of-the-mouth are permanently reconnected, delivering a continual data-feed of Source Intelligence that constantly informs the Human electromagnetic field of its inclusion in the immortal continuum. Among other transformations, this frequency download alters the alchemical ratio of bio-signalling emissions

---

[3] See 'The Template – A Holonomic Model of Transcendence'

created by the endocrine system, rearranging the hormonal recipe which instigates the deterioration that culminates in physical death, to one that supports eternal life.

Many participants who experienced this ceremony became vegetarian. This was not surprising, for as the immortal resonance integrated by the reconnection of circuitry infiltrates consciousness, it stimulates the desire to transcend the way in which one is physically sustained. The heightened awareness of interconnectedness, brought on by our inclusion within the divine immortal continuum and the reunion with all creation, elicits the desire to refrain from the taking of life. The integration of an expanded spectrum of prana activates the cerebral cortex, reducing the aggression aroused by the over-stimulation of the reptilian brain, leading to an enhanced sense of compassion as all the senses become refined and the inescapable cruelty inherent in the eating of murdered flesh can no longer be denied.

The more ceremonies we held, the more we came to understand and appreciate what it means to engage in holonomic breathing. Although it is undeniably beneficial to practice holistic breathing techniques that will serve to energize the entire body system, bringing more mental clarity and even physical rejuvenation, the activation of the pranic mechanism to its full capacity was not to be achieved through a discipline directed by the mind. In the early days of the Sacred Breath Ceremony we attempted to teach the 'Breath of Immortality', but eventually we realized that our perception of breath was still dualistic. Holistic breathing is a state of holographic infusion, a flow that has no beginning or end; not a discipline, but a way of being. It will require the resurrection of all the sub-systems and hyper-systems of the Human complex to be energetically re-integrated, actuating a mode of seamless breathing that gives and receives 'life-love-breath,'[4] a spontaneous method of activating prana that creates, and is, a torus[5] with the heart at the centre, functioning as a holographic hyper-infinity figure-of-eight that embraces the Human energy field.

Jiva once told me that in the Hindu tradition it is believed that you are born with a predetermined number of breaths and that yogis who practice slowing and extending each breath are attempting to extend their lives. That night in the Australian rainforest when I had spontaneously entered a mode of holistic breathing, my breath did not begin or end. I did not take my breath, I was my breath.

Each breath affects the whole because we are the whole. We are the Source. As the holographic emissaries of Prime Consciousness, we are fractals of the One, of the Monad. The degree to which we are able to translate the pranic code is the degree to which we integrate, synthesize and crystallize the monadic Prime Consciousness transmitted by the Benevolent Heart of Creation, thus reactivating the Human template,

---

[4] See 'The Template – A Holonomic Model of Transcendence'

[5] See 'The Template – A Holonomic Model of Transcendence'

becoming conscious conduits of light and love, becoming our light bodies, embraced within the immortal continuum. With each holistic breath we partake of the one eternal breath that is shared by every living thing on every planet in every solar system, in every galaxy of every universe. Our breath weaves our individual energy fields into the holographic template of all manifest existence.

We are not only ourselves … we are the Universe.

19

MUTINY: THE NEW WORLD DISORDER

EARTH'S POSITION WITHIN THE SOLAR SYSTEM at this point in history has rendered her a stage upon which the celestial influences, through an ever-building friction of grand planetary alignments, create a kaleidoscopic fulcrum and focus as she aligns with the Galactic Core, opening a grand starry avenue of coherent communion to the very Heart of Creation.

This activation portal began to dilate as, in the mid-twentieth century, the periphery of the 13th baktun awakening-code approached the outer reaches of the Earth's biosphere. A flood of photonic light information funnelled into our solar system and a massive archetypal cleanse began as, with the acceleration of Source Consciousness, social, political and sexual dynamics began to recalibrate.

MUTINY: THE NEW WORLD DISORDER

In the western world a grass-roots revolution was set in motion - an uprising of the socially disenfranchised, whose beliefs and convictions were written in the neon-lit tunnels of subways, on the crumbling walls of the architecture of poverty, in the disintegrating tenements of misery. Graffiti was the medium that expressed the civil unrest which simmered in the ghettos, a bare and angry syntax that spelled out in primary colours the bold audacity of a demographic that had nothing and nothing to lose. The mean streets belonged to this legion of youth who had neither time nor space to be young, to be innocent.

Their graphic call for justice and equality did not go unheard. The cause was carried forward into the public domain by men and women, black and white, whose names are still evoked as icons of freedom; those whose violet-indigo light shone too bright, who ushered in a new age and lost their lives because of it. We hear them still. They are among us today, reborn, the seeds of their lives planted in our children, our grandchildren; their dreams and visions live forever.

The acceleration of conscious evolution, riding in on waves of light of a new spectrum of violet radiance, liberated creators of art, music, film and literature to express a vulnerable honesty. Fed on this, the new youth generation reached for mind-expanding substances and eastern philosophy, disassembling past patterns and reinventing themselves according to the primal resonant integrity of their celestial seeding, as their Bird Tribe identities were awakened within the starry nights of sensual freedom and the stirring melodies that awakened the heart.

This generation broke out of the fear, shame and guilt-based parameters of the orthodox religions, as they invoked the purity of the natural world to define their understanding of Source. The impulse that drew so many to vegetarianism in those years was resonant with a deeper respect for life and the innate knowledge that to consume slain flesh was to defile the temple of the body and to further disassociate the electromagnetic field of awareness from the divine immortal continuum.

As they peeled away layer upon layer of the falsities that had been imposed upon their sense of self through the indoctrination of their 'education', some hit upon the very bedrock of the deception that has, down the corridors of time and history, torn the world apart... the erroneous definition of God.

Repulsed by religions that were operated and managed by celibate priests who condemned the natural functions of the body and named woman as the obstacle between man and spiritual attainment, they turned away from church and scripture. As the ratio of alchemical components within their brain chemistry was altered, they freed themselves - if only momentarily - from the dominant patriarchal consensus, to dip their toes into the quantum, into the reservoir of pleasure and causal desire from which they had emerged into physical reality. Their heightened sentient awareness of the fear-free vibrations emanating from the natural world informed them that God was not the administrator of punishment and damnation, an angry, manipulative, judgmental, jealous and vengeful control freak. They saw 'God' in a flower, in the shimmering wings of a dragonfly, in the never-still patterns of consciousness sharing spatial cognizance in the living ocean of the geometric matrix of eternity. They sensed the endlessness of their true immortal nature - then awakened to the prison of their mortal realm in states of disorientation, desperation and depression. The seeds were sown in their cellular memory and passed on to the next generation. The infrastructure of Humanity's fraudulent history and the erroneous definitions of the Benevolence of Creation were dissolving.

Many friends I had in those heady days of mutiny have lost the thread of their intention to erode the status quo that gave respectability to racism and war. Defeated and betrayed by the futility of taking up arms against a faceless machine that now has the world in a cyber straight-jacket, they have succumbed to the social hypnosis that has convinced them that their 'idealism' is not viable. Exhausted by the basic tasks of survival and sensing the end of their mortal sentence, they focus now on how much they can squeeze in before the vice tightens, before the dam breaks against the tides of war, genocide, famine and disease that threaten to engulf the world beyond the daily illusions of their domestic charades of 'normality'. They see now that in the arena of direct action their hands are tied. There can be no more bank-burning, no more peaceful sit-ins. We cannot take up arms against this sea of madness. The prison we inhabit has no bars, only barcodes. The paradigm itself is our prison. We cannot fight our enemy through direct action. We must transcend the space-time frequency zone and its mutant mortal parameters.

For many young people dodging conscription for the war in Vietnam was not a mental decision, but arose from a newly nurtured appreciation of creation, rendering them incapable of taking life. War; what was it good for? It was good for the economy, for the subjugation of the Human spirit, for the culling of the population and the continuance of conflict. War is the sanctioned arena in which the mutant genes that drive man to murder are exercised.

The ban-the-bomb contingent of the youth of the '60s attempted to delay the nuclear future by dancing barefoot circles around the icons of destruction. They thought they could cancel the coming of Kali and find freedom within this mutant time-space frequency zone, not yet realizing that there could be no peace in this dimension. However, many corrupt regimes are overthrown, however many warlords are put on trial, many more replace them, for their existence is not simply the result of a confluence of degenerate circumstances and environments that can be eradicated by peace talks and the gathering of the United Nations. Many of these contaminated governing systems are being supported by those who subsequently make the pretence of policing them.

There is no political answer to this demonic behaviour. It surfaces just as diabolically in the rich white world of western politics as it does in the corrupt administrations of the third world. The dark power holders are expressing a genetic mutation, a parasitic consciousness arising from the splicing of their genetic blueprint.

The world governing systems are the way they are because they are programmed to be so. Politics provides Humanity with a power placebo, a means to divert and placate our sense of outrage and helplessness; to give us the fallacious impression that we have a say in our own governing, an influence over our future. Anarchy, a lawless rebellion, is futile and dangerous and may well accelerate the process of terminal decline. The constriction of free movement is already widespread through the chimera of terrorism.

As a spokesperson for the Template, am I saying that we are helpless victims? Not at all. I am shining some light into the shadow to illuminate the Machiavellian victim-predator, good cop - bad cop infrastructure of duality that traps some into believing that peace can be found by entering the conflict. My intention here is to better explain the path of transmutation of this fear-based paradigm. There can be no revolution. To 'revolve' means to go around in circles, to spin, to gyrate. Revolution is the program sanctioned by the warmongers that takes and wastes our energy, our time, our focus and, worst of all, our children.

There must be evolution - an evolution that comes from breaking the codes of creation, freeing us from the mortal paradigm, redefining self and Source, awakening us to the magnificence of our true identities, the electromagnetic fields of our radiant incarnate presence superseding the phantasm of the present mutant mortal paradigm.

The new model of existence will not come from better

government, stricter policing, or a properly organized global community. It will arise from a community that needs no governing at all. The new paradigm will be spun from the amalgamation of awakened consciousness transmitted by a unified people whose collective connection to Source will be fed into the biospheric membrane of Earth's morphogenetic field.

In order to enslave a race, you take away its past, its memories, its ancestry, its identity. Humanity's release from slavery must include an awakening to and a retrieval of our true history and, thus, in the collective Human psyche, a redefinition of God. Peace cannot be measured by the absence of war. Liberation and freedom are not political issues: they are intrinsic to the definition of the divine Human blueprint prior to its modification. The reconnection of Source circuitry instigates the delivery of the energetic nature of Source Consciousness into the Human electromagnetic field of awareness. Source circuitry reaches the deepest strata of the Human infrastructure where the meaning of God will not be named but will unfold to you, within you. When a critical mass of units of Human circuitry integrates and synthesizes this Source Consciousness, the actualization of Human transcendence will crystallize the 'new world disorder'.

20

'GENESIS REVISITED' - REVISITED

PRIOR TO OUR EXPERIENCE ON GREEN MOUNTAIN, information from various sources regarding alien abduction, cattle mutilation, UFO sightings and the extra-terrestrial infiltration of political and military organizations had been brought to our attention. We did not reject this information, but we did not focus on it either. Aware that we did not have enough knowledge to holistically integrate these matters into our perception of ourselves, our Earth, our past, present and future, we compartmentalized it.

After the crash-course of the Green Mountain event, the compartment labelled 'extra-terrestrial' split its seams and burst its content into our everyday estimation of reality. You can read about these things and see the footage, but nothing compares to meeting an extra-terrestrial face to face in broad daylight. The event became a measure through which we discerned the real, not only in regard to the beings we met, but particularly through the dimensional shift that gifted us with a touchstone which would forever give us a point of reference to our true identities and the proximity of a paradise that is a collective perception awaiting only our cognizance of its existence. Our footsteps upon the Earth took on a new lightness as a 'divine ambivalence' tempered our awareness of and reactions to the sometimes frightening reality of the global deception. The knowledge of Humanity's ultimate transcendence of the fear and suffering our race has so tenaciously fought against for eons was almost tangible. It would happen. We had been there, seen and felt it.

In one intense afternoon on a mountain, memories of past and future were activated. However, many more questions arose from the event than were answered by it and, to this day, we are unpacking its implications. Although we were aware, on some level, of the spectrum of oppression, brutality and control inflicted upon Humanity by the race to which the aliens we met belonged, we could not completely integrate the full ramifications of what we had experienced without being consumed by the intensity of its import. So we set ourselves a safety net of 'creative denial' in order to focus on and achieve the work that lay ahead.

In the months that followed, it seemed that a floodgate was opened, and information poured in from a variety of sources. Some smacked of disinformation - some, particularly the notion of 'ascending' out of the mess on Earth on spaceships, seemed reckless, irresponsible and desperate. The more grounded and well-presented information came from courageous 'whistle-blowers' dedicated to assisting Humanity in deprogramming their social, political and religious hypnosis. We felt our bodies come into easy resonance with this material and filed it away for a later time.

It was after the reconnection of the Air Circuits in Glastonbury that our acceptance of the existence of the alien agenda transformed into an objective, far-reaching and pre-eminent concern, a field of enquiry whose investigation was fundamental to our obligation within the context of the Template mandate and so we dived into the matter. We have since discovered much information, but the entire picture has not yet been revealed: there are many false memory inserts to deprogram and knots in time to undo. Total recall will require total reconnection to the 'living' truth through our own bio-computational awareness. The reconnection and integration of the 33rd Worldbridger Circuit is assisting us to identify the 'spin' that is being placed upon the account of our history, especially the various re-interpretations of Genesis. What we are clear about now is the connection between the modification of Human DNA, the disconnection of circuitry, the stabilization of a false time-space frequency experience and the extra-terrestrial presence behind the agenda.

It was when we came across the works of Zechariah Sitchin and Laurence Gardner that we were able to put a name and an origin to the beings we met on the Mountain; the Annunaki. This name, according to Sitchin, is translated as 'those who to Earth from heaven came', the mother planetoid Nibiru being 'heaven'. Time and again we were led by our collaborating Consciousness to the books of these authors: however, with each appeal to examine these versions of our drastically revised history and ancestry, came a resolute disclaimer, a strong warning that at the very core of the revelations was a dangerous, malevolent distortion that was designed to perpetuate the disempowerment of the Human race. We tuned in for more specific details and found that although we were not quite ready for the full picture, we did glean a major piece of misinformation that pertained to our original blueprint prior to our genetic modification and the splicing in of so-called 'superior genes'.

Inevitably, the subject of Human DNA modification came up at every workshop. We were clear that the disconnection of circuitry was intrinsic to the modification of our genetic code and questions were always asked about the who, the when and the why. We did our best to give general answers, but also made a point of curtailing any long-detailed discussions as there were blanks in our understanding.

One Easter weekend we held a Ceremony of Sacred Breath very near the Avebury stone circle in Wiltshire, not far from Stonehenge. It was a powerful and focused group who were familiar with Sitchin's 'Earth Chronicles'. After the ceremony most of the group stayed behind to discuss his interpretation of the genesis story which is based on the Sumerian texts that were incorporated into the Old Testament version of Genesis, and which reveal the extra-terrestrial identities of the 'creator gods' that much of Humanity has adopted as their true benefactors of life; gods that are widely recognised and worshiped by the predominant orthodox religions. Known by different names, they are identified in the Sumerian material as one entity, the Annunaki chieftain, Enlil.

It was late when we set off for the long drive home and we did not arrive until 1:00am. Zak was still awake, watching a film on his tiny portable television. We sat up with him until it was over, when a program that followed grabbed our attention. It was a series called 'Phenomenon - The Lost Archives'. The first program in the sequence was called 'Genesis Revisited' and included pieces by archaeologists, anthropologists, astronomers and linguists, with the emphasis on the work of Zechariah Sitchin. We were astounded to find ourselves watching this controversial program on mainstream television and I was glad to have Zak there with us to witness it. After the credits rolled Jiva and I sat in stunned silence before expressing our tired amazement and falling into bed. We lay in the darkness exhausted by the long, arduous and significant day, our bodies buzzing madly. As we breathed ourselves into relaxation, we were gently, but with clear insistence, informed that it had become our responsibility, as Template ambassadors, to procure this program and show it at our workshops. This transmission was followed with the now familiar warning that there were treacherous deceptions within the presentation and that we must do our utmost to discern them and to expose them to our groups. We fell asleep with a sense that we were moving closer to a more comprehensive and integrated phase of our ability to accumulate and share the whole Template model of transcendence.

The next day we began to chase down the Phenomenon program. I enlisted the help of our administrator and other people who were connected to the television industry. We all came up against a brick wall and the segments that were to follow in the series were cancelled. We speculated that whoever was in charge of late night TV had carelessly put on what they thought was another package of intriguing but innocuous documentaries, but when someone heard the words 'genetically modified race' the series was axed and buried. A couple of weeks later we were holding a small ceremony in Glastonbury and shared the story with our group. One of the women taking part told us that her son had intended to tape the movie that had been shown before the documentary, but her recorder had malfunctioned and taped the 'Phenomenon' program instead. A couple of days later a copy of it arrived in the mail. Later, our American administrator Margo was able to buy a DVD to send us.

For some time, we had been studying the six volumes of Sitchin's Earth Chronicles and his book entitled 'Genesis Revisited'. Although we appreciated the life-time commitment that Sitchin has undoubtedly made to produce such a prodigious and comprehensive body of work, the minutely detailed and ceaselessly cross-referenced books repeated the same points again and again and were a chore to trawl through, their deeply alarming core revelations buried in mountains of data. However, the 'Genesis

Revisited' program was a distilled and briskly edited compilation, covering a considerable amount of varied material in 40 minutes. Its credibility was supported by the various qualified professionals who presented their information with intelligibility and authority. It had a powerful effect on the groups of people who saw it, moving them at a profoundly archaic level. The reactions in the early days were dramatic; some people wept with remembrance and relief, feeling that their unconscious knowing was verified, others were surprised and shocked, but there was always somehow a sense of relief that the alien under the carpet had finally been identified.

We continued to deliver our disclaimer, a disclaimer that over time became more defined and more disquieting. To begin with, we had felt that the evidence presented by Sitchin and the growing number of others proposing various 'Interventionist' theories, were, in good faith, attempting to illuminate the true origins of the Human race. Later, after the fourth ceremony of reconnection to Source, it was to become evident that these revelations were being presented knowingly or unknowingly with a specific 'spin'. Once again, Humanity was being dangerously misled about its origins.

The body of evidence that has been unveiled by the eminent scholars of many disciplines who are prominent in the Interventionism arena is intended to show that the 'gods' of the Old Testament are, in fact, extra-terrestrial colonizers and, furthermore, that we owe them a vote of thanks for our present state of 'elevated' existence. The deception to which we had been alerted is not about the existence of these extra-terrestrials, but in the claim that they were our benefactors, the creator-gods of the Human race, who genetically engineered a slave workforce for their mining operation by splicing their superior genes with the DNA of the primitive hairy ape-like beings, which, they maintain, inhabited Earth at that time. Also deceptive is the story of their 'accidental' arrival in our solar system.

Insights into their true agenda on Earth came to us as we received the Temple of Time Ceremony code, geometry and circuit points. The information was actually hidden in the 'Genesis Revisited' program, but we were not able to discern it until we had the Temple of Time co-ordinates. With every viewing of this documentary, more and more levels were revealed to us and to our core group of Template Ambassadors. It seemed that the reconnected circuitry was awakening authentic organic points of reference that enabled us to break the spell and uncover the fraud. With each viewing of the documentary more was unveiled as our programming was undermined by the energetic truth of creation.

The enslavement and genocide that continues to be perpetrated upon many of Earth's people has been systematically contrived by the removal of the knowledge of our ancestry, history, language and thus, identity. On an all-encompassing scale, this program of subjugation and manipulation has been carried out upon the entire Human race in our current paradigm, and the versions of Interventionism that are being revealed at this time are perpetuating the program as we continue to be fed a false history.

'GENESIS REVISITED' - REVISITED

At the core of these revelations are the Old Testament accounts of our genesis. For time out of mind these texts have been recognized and accepted by Judaism and its branch, Christianity, as a common denominator of true ancestral history; a history whose implicit fundamentalism has been translated globally as a dominant principle of ubiquitous patriarchal religious indoctrination. The Genesis story has been left long enough now to steep in the Human psyche in order to breed its program of shame, guilt and belief in the doctrine of original sin. It is now known to be an abbreviated and misleading version of a fuller rendition of Earth and Humanity's beginnings, deriving from Sumerian cuneiform texts, a story that has been translated through the mythos of major religions.

However, amongst the recent proliferation of scholarly and popular works purporting to throw new light on Humanity's history, a so called 'lost chronicle', said to have been unearthed out of the Mesopotamian and Syrian deserts, is now being presented as the true story of Human genesis.

In order to further the plans of the Annunaki, the existing, relatively homogenized program of 'god' and 'heaven' must now be expanded upon. It is now inevitably time for the tactical revelation that the 'god' worshiped as an omnipotent benefactor, the giver and taker of life on Earth, is a member of a technologically superior extra-terrestrial race. The timing of the 'discovery' of the 'hidden secrets' of our past has been exactly arranged to suit this specific phase within the Annunaki breeding program which is soon to accelerate. Nibiru, the planetoid headquarters of the Annunaki, the Planet X reported to have been identified in 2000, is coming into close proximity to Earth and Humanity is now being prepared for its arrival.

In the documentation of our history as upgraded apes who have their Annunaki 'benefactors' to thank for our advanced state of 'civilization', not once is it mentioned that this so called civilized world cannot feed its own children and is on a path of terminal decline. These writings cite our age of technological development, our capacity for space flight and genetic engineering as the legacy of our Annunaki genes and the measure of our progress, never once mentioning that our planet is in the grip of widespread war and genocide, that the insanity of paedophilia is rampant, that the African people continue to be mercilessly annihilated by a plague manufactured for the purpose, leaving orphans who have nowhere to lay their heads. Our seas and rivers are contaminated daily, our forests casually levelled for the raising of cattle sacrificed to sustain the addiction to flesh and for growing tobacco to inhibit our sacred breath. Is this the 'civilization' for which we should be so thankful?

It is non-symbiotic Annunaki genes, spliced time and again into the original masterpiece of the divine Human blueprint, that has caused us to veer off the path of conscious evolution into this heartless nightmare of so-called advancement. It is the Annunaki gene code that drives us to solve conflict with murder, to rape children to satiate the festering sexual insanity born of the disconnection between the heart and the divine procreative centres.

It is the Annunaki consciousness that riddles and plagues our literature and film with endless scenarios of cop shows and serial killers. The around-the-clock transmission of negative dramas and loveless, abusive pornography is beamed through our homes and our bodies by satellite broadcasts that saturate our airspace, incessantly stimulating the reptilian brain and triggering adrenal toxicity. Our obsession with death is their legacy, for it is they who brought to Earth not the seed of life, but the obscenity of death.

The unveiling of the Annunaki story at this time is intended to compensate for and override the acceleration of light information and the opening of the 2012 portal of evolutionary opportunity; to expedite our cooperation in their desire to gain not only total control over our planet and our race but to gain entry into the very recesses of our Soul Covenant, our symbiotic relationship with light within the solar system. They want Earth for their home.

To this end they have been carrying out an extensive breeding program over a long period of time, a program that has required splicing and re-splicing the Human gene code over and over again to create a biological compatibility that would allow for the Annunaki consciousness to interface with not only the environment, but also to become part of the symbiosis of the whole solar system. This has also required an agenda of time-travel to create varied influences that would bend and sculpt the false memory inserts and deep subliminal programming of Humanity through the insertion of erroneous archetypes parading as deified entities. These programs instil, through mass religious hypnosis, the pseudo-spiritual hype that annuls individual sovereignty, triggering and stabilizing pathological obedience.

And so, the sons of 'god' 'mated' with the daughters of Eve, spliced themselves into our hearts, bodies and minds, to see through our eyes and feel through our emotions. Will this agenda work? Take a look at Mars for your answer. There, exhibited on the devastated landscape, is the manifestation of the inability of the Annunaki to interface with an ecosystem that is incompatible with their genes and mirrors their inability to absorb and utilize the coded Intelligence present in the quality of light that informs and compels our solar system. Ultimately, this agenda will result in the subsequent loss of eco-symbiosis that could eventually wipe out the Human race and its Mother planet. The Annunaki do not have the Soul Covenant, the blueprint that would grace them with the capacity to absorb, translate, utilize and transmit the intelligence which defines the masterpiece of the Human design and its function as an alchemical component of conscious evolution within the entire solar system.

The major religions that are used as the chief and crucial behaviour-modifying tools of consciousness control have, at their centre, the punishment-reward system, a system that triggers compliance and conformity. 'In the beginning God created Heaven and Earth'. Heaven; liberation, freedom, paradise, a promise of a future prize for good behaviour, as you might promise a child a treat for obedience, a reward of deliverance bestowed only after the slow deterioration of our weak and sinful flesh, only after death. We search for self-realization and bliss beyond the very sacred enclosures in which they exist, the meaning of God stolen from the realization of it in every simple astounding breath and commandeered by the individual supremacy of a saviour, a redeemer, who listens with a censoring ear to our pleas, our prayers, for a morsel of joy, a momentary cessation of suffering in this mutant realm of 'His' creation. Heaven, of course, could not be here - could it? Here, on this emerald-blue planet of stunning grace and eloquent expression, in her fragrant blooms, her cooling pools of water, rushing rivers, seas and oceans, fecund forests and jungles, in her supportive solid earth and soft sweet air. Could heaven be hidden in the tantric potencies of our bodies, made to love, to create? Is heaven to be found out of our bodies in some ambiguous cryptic state?

The intention of the Annunaki is that we will integrate into, or be overwhelmed by, their genes. Perhaps there will be a massive culling to this end. Then they would take Earth for the heaven that it is but cannot so remain in their possession.

There are those whose life work has been to reveal the Interventionist information in order to assist Humanity and there are those who are working to sustain the wardenship of the Annunaki over the mortal prison they have crafted through frequency control. There may well be threats to those who have taken up the task of revealing the most malignant deception ever perpetrated upon Humanity.

To harness support for the atrocity committed by the Annunaki against Humanity, a 'good cop, bad cop' scenario is being aggressively perpetuated along with the tale. The story is told that there are two 'royal' Annunaki brothers responsible for the creation and breeding of Humanity as a hybrid slave race; one bad and one... not exactly good... but apparently not quite so bad! Enlil is the more ruthless brother and Enki is the master 'creator' geneticist who is now sorry for the part he played in the manipulation of Humanity. His move to save the hybrids from total annihilation by commanding Utnapishtim of Ur, the biblical 'Noah' to build the 'Ark' and preserve the gene pool is being cited as proof of his big-heartedness. The Ark story only stands up if it can be believed that the myriad assortment of life forms from all the continents could have been gathered, fed and preserved on one wooden boat and kept from attacking each other. It is more likely that, in the event of Earth's inundation, DNA samples were retained for reseeding, as is suggested in Sumerian texts. It is hard to see the trees of truth in such a forest of lies, especially as total recall of sequential continuity has been diverted through time travel, endless memory inserts and the undermining of our sovereignty via the inserts of false archetypes that usurped Humanity's inherent knowledge of its origins.

In this era of transformation inspired by the stars, with the intensification of the Aquarian Ahau awakening codes pulsing through our neighbourhood, the mask of 'god' is slipping. In the light of the acceleration of conscious evolution that has been activated by the new intensity of creative data present in the bands of photonic intelligence radiating through our solar system, there are many who are not going to swallow the spin. The revelations designed to introduce us to our 'benefactors of life', the patrons to whom we owe our 'upgrade', have instead revealed the pseudo-divine prototypes that have been transliterated into religion as manipulative imposters: God impersonators.

This usurpation of the position of Creative Benevolence within the minds and hearts of Humanity is possible only because we are a stolen race on a stolen planet. Most of our electromagnetic circuitry is switched off, the greater part of our genetic propensities modified. Thus, we have been disengaged from the divine immortal continuum, from Source. Without its connection to the Heart of the Cosmos, Humanity is orphaned and disoriented, searching blindly for a point of spiritual reference in order to know itself and evolve.

This jewel, our Earth, is the manifestation of the ultimate confluence of Source Consciousness, realizing a perfect interference pattern of spirit and matter; a stargate through which the undifferentiated potencies of creation finds tender birth into time and space in order to experience relationship. It is prime real-estate and the Annunaki want to call it home. It cannot be fought for, but it can be retrieved; not through any battlefield but through the unified field - through the resurrection of the divine Human blueprint.

With the reconnection of circuitry, you instigate an acceleration of electromagnetic Source Consciousness into this time-space frequency zone, undermining the present predominant fear-based, conflict-riddled world structure simply by being; each one of you adding a fractal of consciousness to the required critical mass of the new paradigm hologram. This will create, ultimately, a stable resonant field of evolutionary opportunity to transcend the mortal paradigm.

21

THE SOURCE

THE TEST POINTS FOR THE SOURCE CIRCUITRY, their resonant geometries and the information associated with their disconnection crowded into our consciousness and once again we returned to Bali to clarify the information and receive the Source Ceremony.

Bali was in mourning, not only for those who had lost their lives in the Kuta bombing, but also for the loss of an innocence that had sheltered them from the storms of war-riddled reality beyond their sequestered shores. The cultural centre of Ubud, usually bursting with creativity and bustling with tourism, was a virtual ghost town. Many shops had already gone bankrupt. The always desperate tone of the street hawkers had reached a new fervency as starvation became a real threat to them and their families. Collectively, they feared for the overall future of their country: terrorism had arrived in paradise.

During our last stay in Bali, Jiva and I had been discussing the September 11th event with our adopted brother and neighbour, Nyoman. I remarked to him that the *Kali Yuga* was truly unfolding.

He shook his head, "Not in Bali."

"No?" I asked, surprised.

"No," he replied. "Because the tourists come, everyone has enough rice." It was not my place to question the measure with which he assessed his reality. We sat together in the silence that followed, breathing in the soft tropical air. The Sun blazed relentlessly, highlighting the genius of creation all around us. A dazzling dragonfly lit weightlessly upon the luscious pink lip of the lotus blossom that rose royally from Nyoman's still, blue pond.

Now, with the event of the Bali bombing, the Balinese had been wrenched from their belief that their jewel of an island had somehow floated free of the perilous plight that gripped the rest of the world. They held the faith that the consummate and ceaseless devotion expressed through the daily rituals and offerings made in worship of their gods would ensure that Bali would be spared the punishment exacted upon countries and peoples who did not honour their spirituality. The lives of the intensely devout Balinese revolve around and are defined by their temples, rites and sacraments. Their religious ideology shapes and colours their art, music and dance, providing the cohesion of their culture.

THE SOURCE

That spring, as I walked through Ubud, the newspaper headlines blared the shameless propaganda of the western world-management team in their effort to incite the desire for war. Behind this thin veil lurked a transparent agenda to exploit the world's petroleum addiction. Sub-headlines spoke of the growing paedophile problem and the spread of AIDS and drug addiction in Indonesia. I felt raw and sensitive; it seemed to me that on every street corner the global insanity danced like a garish demon-marionette in the hands of a huge unstoppable force that pulled the strings with unmistakably malicious intent.

Over time, our humble haven in the rice fields just outside of Ubud in the hill country of south central Bali had become more and more over-run with houses. The organic bamboo and grass cottages that nestled into and complemented their surroundings were torn down and replaced with cement and tile monstrosities which overpowered and ignored the nuances of their environment. The sounds of hammering and chainsaws made our job of downloading and documenting information near impossible. Strip lighting polluted the night and obscured our view of the stars, so that we resorted to hanging thick blankets over our windows, which added to the newly-felt presentiment of oppression that hung over Bali. The mantle of grief across the country was consistent with the gravity of the information that we were receiving in conjunction with the Source circuitry, the periphery of which impinged upon our awareness with weight and solemnity, simultaneously holding at its heart a promise of deliverance.

We realized that it would take a clear and peaceful space in which to focus on this information that was to reach the very essence of the Human identity as a sentient instrument for the Benevolence of Creation. We decided to visit a newly discovered and somewhat secret water site; a sacred spring. Springs had long been for us a place for the retrieval of mysteries, for the illumination of the obscure.

A twenty-minute drive inland through the gradually climbing mountain brought us to a little-known piece of land that banked onto a river gulch. As we approached the long steep steps that led to the wide rushing Ayung River that is cradled by the gulch, we stopped to marvel at the distant yet clear colossal mountain of Singharaja, its peak exalted through a low-lying blanket of clouds. The vision of it restored to us, by its immutable presence, the true undefeatable strength and essence of the Bird Tribe sanctuary that is Bali.

We began our descent into the gulch. The steps led through a series of seven natural spring-fed pools. Halfway down to the river we found the enchanting and exquisite spring. Close to its mouth was a large livid-green and ancient-looking frog. Something in his countenance belied his mere frog-ness; he was a powerful guardian Deva in disguise. The obsidian domes of his eyes stared in timeless patience as the acknowledgment of our presence stirred in their depths. With delight, we saw ourselves mirrored in their brilliance, the clouds behind us passing over them, and felt our images captured for ever in his eyes and filed away in his memory as he is in ours.

We almost missed the small plaque that gave the name of the spring, as it was shrouded by the same moss that covered the stone surround and coalesced with the many vivacious green hues of the ferns and vines that coiled around, delicately framing the sacred spring. It was called 'The Source'. We reached for the surface of the spring's pool, our every move reflecting across the glassy blackness of the frog's eyes and cupped a jewel-like scoop of quicksilver water to our third eyes. The words of the Sacred Day Water Ceremony tumbled from my lips:

This sacred day
My communion with the element of water
honours my physical being as a chalice
overflowing with the purity of innocence.
Understanding brings forgiveness
cleansing my emotional body.
My mental body releases judgment
as I recognize the perfection in all creation.
Love is my protection.

The leaves and vines, the trees and exotic rainforest blooms whispered and wove a conspiracy of perfection around us. All my senses submerged into the elemental aroma of earth and the watery mantra of the spring falling melodiously into the sweet pool at our feet... falling, falling, falling...

I slipped into a dense magnetic trance, following the familiar path to the timeless space of unknowing, the blank canvas that would then be slowly filled with the vision I would then translate into language. As always, I came softly and silently upon the pregnant void, its emptiness full of undifferentiated potential. I waited patiently… and waited. I would have waited all day had I felt it was required of me - but it was not. It was the ever-expanding void itself I had come on this journey to witness, to embrace, to surrender to; to accept that there was no point of reference within my bio-computational awareness and its limited language for the understanding of what I sought. Now was not, could not be, the time for such a conception.

The knowledge and understanding of Source would open to me, within me, through the download of creative Intelligence delivered directly from Source. It could not be understood and named in the mind but would require the amalgamated comprehension that would arise from the resurrection of the holistic heart-body-mind system as it is re-embraced into the universal continuum… when I became both the answer and the question. With a sigh of surrender, I opened my eyes to see Jiva staring at me with intense expectancy.

"Did you reach it?" he asked me, at the same time realizing what my answer would be…had to be.

The reconnection was now upon us and together, at the mouth of the spring that flowed unbidden and ever-giving, we received the uninterpreted, energetic nature of the meaning of Source; delivered electromagnetically as circuits of never beginning nor ending spheres of consciousness merged into our fields of awareness. From that day forward, every sacred breath would be the solvent which dissolved the fiction to reveal the Benevolent Source of Creation.

We spent that night near the spring. It was May 1st, Beltane, Jiva's birthday. It was a night of deep and vigorous healing, difficult to integrate, as we did not have the full understanding of what we had initiated. We tried heartbreakingly hard to celebrate what we felt should have been a joyous occasion, going through all the motions of rejoicing, but we could not. We were overcome by the implications of the global disconnection from Source that had led to the endless suffering of Humanity. It all came crushing in on us and the evening ended in tears, the reason for which we did not completely understand.

We did not have the ceremony to assist the alchemical synthesis that would fully crystallize the event into time and space. The test points of the circuitry and the geometry were brought to light over the next ten days and it was not until we experienced the geometry in conjunction with the exquisite sonic code that the data delivered by the spontaneous reconnection of Source circuitry could be consciously reconciled and assimilated into our hearts and minds.

The healing from these circuits was an embrace that seemed to reach out from the beginning of time itself. Today, as I sit in another small bamboo home built above the same gulch and river that we visited to reconnect our Source circuitry, we feel ourselves released from the stealthy claw of deceit that holds this planet in its steely grip. Each day we marvel at the fact that it could ever have had such power over us. As the reconnection to Source nurtures, with each breath, our true identities, there is little to fear from the sound and fury that rages around us. We see it and feel it as images caught in time that cannot reach the well-spring of our divine immortal selves. We are unborn, eternal, everlasting… We are not only this…we are the Universe.

The positioning of the circuitry test points was very revealing. One of the Source circuits runs through both hands as they clasp together in the mode of prayer. With this circuit disconnected, the outflow of vital creative energy triggered spontaneously by this powerful mudra is non-reciprocal. Worship and communion are very different frequencies. The give-receive of communion is mutually beneficial: worship and prayer in the mode that it is experienced without circuitry reconnection is disempowering on an extremely deep and potent level.

The 'consciousness in form' which creates the alchemical resonance for the reconnection of the Source circuitry is the geometry of the creation mandala, popularly called the flower of life. After devoting some time to it, Jiva was finally able to design and have made a three-dimensional creation mandala constructed in glass. Holding it in my hands, I saw that the creation matrix spoke that which our language cannot. In this three-dimensional mandala the matrix reveals itself as a spherical covenant of spatial cognizance. In a flat creation mandala, one sees only one facet of the jewel, just as a rainbow is not simply an arc but a sphere that spans the sky and penetrates the Earth, precisely intercepted by the interference pattern of a myriad of other 'rain-spheres', as light plays with and teases water to reveal the intercourse of creation as an interconnecting interactive transmission of light-encoded spheres of Source Intelligence, each sphere a never-ending or beginning pod of monadic quintessence. The Source is everywhere.

As I meditated upon the three-dimensional glass mandala, I felt the grand Maha Gaia Tantra that emanates from the Heart of the Cosmos pulsing out in transiting waves of light flux to illuminate the journey of Prime Consciousness moving out from the monadic, omnipotent, omnipresent Source Awareness, geometrically morphing into the differentiation of manifest creation. I saw within the form the divine immortal continuum from which Earth and her people have been electromagnetically disassociated. I saw, within this superlatively inclusive sacred geometry, circuitry. The matrix is circuitry.

The 'matrix' is a concept now made known by the very successful films of that name, films that have raised profound questions about the true nature of reality and the visible and invisible prison created by this mutant paradigm. In the films, the matrix is shown to be a world generated by computer code, an illusion experienced in the minds of Human beings whilst their bodies are, in reality, being sustained in isolation and their vital energies harvested by the machines that built the matrix. The resolution of this situation occurs when Humanity unplugs from its machine-code dream and wakens to the world that exists beyond the isolated cells. The Template recognizes our world as an anomalous entropic paradigm, generated by the brain-wave frequency feedback of a genetically altered race. The inhabitants of this world reside in an isolated temporal zone that has been modified to enslave consciousness and deprive the individual being of its sentient sovereignty. As in the films, there is a need to unplug from this modified manufactured matrix. However, the deviant reality we now experience is, itself, the result of just such an unplugging. Electromagnetic disassociation from the modified matrix is necessary, but it will occur as a result of 'plugging in' to the true matrix as defined by the unadulterated translation of holistic life-force. In our present reality the systemic failure of self-regeneration, as a result of our disconnection from the holistic continuum, gives rise to the myriad of destructive ways in which we seek to support our existence, such as the splitting of the atom to generate nuclear power. No amount of 'green thinking' can reverse this predicament until a systemic reconnection is realized: the fault lies deep in the matrix.

The matrix is woven and spun by the collective unconscious. However, the units of circuitry whose brain chemistry contributes the frequency transmissions that stimulate and stabilize the matrix-reality have been genetically modified and so the manifest 'reality' created by the morphogenetic conspiracy of these transmissions is also modified. This 'reality' is a series of frequency transmissions and resonance-response patterns dictated by the stimulus-response mechanism of this dualistic paradigm. Due to our genetically modified system, our biochemical receptors, transducers and transmitters are not only in sympathy with this paradigm - they are creating it. The non-manipulated true matrix, in contrast, is built upon the vibratory infrastructure of a holistic mandate transmitted from the heart of the cosmic hologram; a matrix fashioned from the full spectrum of the geometric life-impulse. This manifests a reality which is in full resonance with creation, in which nothing that owes its existence to the subjugation of the male or female potencies can hold its molecular structure; a reality that is a stargate to every time and energy level in the universe.

Some who have been impressed by the films and have also glimpsed, via the ingestion of ayahuasca, the geometric light structures that birth manifestation, have concluded that nothing that happens in the matrix is 'real' and that everything is an illusion. Just because we have been back-stage at the continuum and seen how the sets are put together does not mean that manifest reality is an illusion! Form is the shape of consciousness; matter matters! Everything is real, nothing is an illusion, not even 'nothingness' itself, which is simply 'everything' at a different stage. To be repulsed by and retreat from the matrix is to return to the undifferentiated void of potential. We have been given the honour of sentient autonomy in order to make this journey of growth and discovery. Do we run home to the void because the bullies in the playground are making life uncomfortable and difficult? We go forward, not back, to resurrect, transform, transcend. What is required is an upgrade of dataflow from the heart of the universal hologram to explode the mutant paradigm with light.

In the Template, Source circuitry is concerned with our reconnection, without censorship or mediation, to the Benevolent Source of our Creation. This is realized through the translation of Source Intelligence introduced energetically via the five circuits reconnected in the Source Ceremony. The erroneous definition of God, instigated by archetypal inserts upheld as deities, is the most fundamental and powerful manipulation of consciousness in the history of the Human race. It is through religious structures that our most empowering connection, our direct communion with the Benevolent Source of Creation, has been short-circuited. This has been possible due to the disconnection of circuits of electromagnetic Source Intelligence that would otherwise draw us into the cosmic embrace. Through the reconnection of these circuits our innate knowledge of Source will unfold through the progressive revelation of our individual omniscience.

As a race, we have reached a point at which we can awaken to the truth of our origins and the predicament in which we find ourselves and let go of the fear, shame and guilt-based philosophies that have been imposed upon our definition of self and the Source of our Creation. We need to let go of the residual consequences of the religious indoctrination that has predominated in our history and which continues to infest the fear-based consensus field of reference upon which our core decision-making processes rely.

Seeing the erroneous structures of our present day orthodox

religions and our guilty resonance with the devastation perpetrated by the western world, we turn to ethnocentric models, not realizing that there is no corner of this reality that is free from the manipulation of consciousness. Were you to investigate a tribe deep in the jungles of the untouched world, you would find its social and spiritual structures dominated by fear and guilt-based patriarchal ideology. We cannot be sentimental about the behaviour-modifying archetypes that have been cast in the soap opera of our false history, nor can we leave behind those prescribed and regurgitated philosophies only to adopt another. Spiritually, it is time to mature into an autonomous relationship with the Benevolence of our Creation.

The ruling concepts of all religions have been dictated by the patriarchal ministry of the high priests whose philosophies have been structured to suppress Human passions and natural impulses, imposing the conviction of shame and guilt that manipulate and control our behaviour and ensure our co-operation with the patriarchal paradigm, a paradigm that continues to manifest in spiritual movements as various forms of thinly veiled hierarchical 'master' structures which continue to revere the gilded ghosts of dying religions.

The Source circuits connect into the heart of the electro-magnetic holography that is the foundation of the Human blueprint to form a quintessential identity platform on which to incorporate the magnitude of the body of omniscient knowledge inherent within the original Soul Covenant that is the Human matrix. Once connected, these circuits energetically dissolve the fear, shame and guilt-based construct of the predominant ideology, entrenched by the religious definition of Source that reigns supreme within the archetypal arena of the Human psyche and replaces these erroneous definitions with the energetic truth of creation, a truth encoded into the alchemical components of the natural world. It is the integration of the energetic nature of Source Consciousness, present within the male and female potencies of electromagnetism, delivered by circuitry reconnection, which downloads the creation mandate - pure information delivered straight from Source - bypassing the mediation of entities attempting to translate Source Intelligence through disconnected, genetically modified instruments that do not have the iconic reference points to do so. It is within the creation mandate made manifest as a Human entity that the Benevolent Source of Creation reveals itself as the eye that sees, the ear that hears, the hands that touch and the heart that feels. This mandate made manifest is the sacred template of the original Human blueprint.

At this time on Earth only a fractal of the true Human potential is represented in the Human race. In the entire manifestation of the original blueprint the Human is capable of experiencing any time or energy level in the universe. This transcendent Human governs itself autonomously, functions in complete harmony with all forms of life and in total symbiotic resonance with the evolutionary light code of its solar system, responding in full conscious communion to even the softest of whispers carried on the solar winds and with every photonic nuance held in a ray of light.

The original Human was created as an ambassador of Source to represent, within the grace and beauty of its physical form, the compassionate ability of its emotional range and the omniscient knowledge of its genius mind, a fractal image of its Creator. This potency still exists within the Soul Covenant; holographically present within DNA and in the memory matrix held within the cerebral cortex that is the temple of remembrance. In this way the Human body is the sacred chalice of the Source made manifest. You are your body. Your body is the physical matrix of your divine Intelligence.

We are in a transitional phase of awakening. In order to overcome the narcotic-like denial state that has led to our pathological obedience, we must look to our biochemical informational signals that set in motion the response patterns of our subconscious co-operation with the mortal consensus. The fear-based dualistic frequency field of the present paradigm continues to find a mirror resonance biochemically within the neuro-transmitters in the Human brain and the mutant state of the endocrine system that supports their manufacture. The vibrational frequency of shame and guilt and the deep sense of spiritual betrayal and abandonment instigated by the false definitions of Source that exist within all religious indoctrination, create their own body chemistry. The subjugation of the spirit experienced as a result of separation from creation creates a collection of bio-signalling components that together create the 'death hormone'.

One of the definitions found in any traditional English dictionary for 'religious' is 'God-fearing'. Religious archetypes instil primal reference points that not only dictate our mental belief systems and our emotional response patterns, but also determine the ratio of neuro-chemical transmitters that trigger the deterioration of the endocrine system and the superstructure it supports.

The impact of our disconnection from the holographic continuum via the disruption of our Source circuits manifests as a paranoid self-revulsion on a larger scale than the neurosis that forms within a child that blames itself for parental betrayal and abandonment, whether it be emotional, mental or physical. This predicament creates its own chemistry; a chemistry that responds to what we feel and think about ourselves, our world and the Source of our Creation; a chemistry that biologically entrains Humanity to accept, without reservation, a brief mortal span of life believing this to be the 'natural' state. Mortality is the result of a systemic failure brought on by genetic modification.

In the genesis of our spiritual belief systems, the definition of Source and the archetypal galvanization of that definition is the corner-stone of our enslavement to the dualistic paradigm and its mortal confinement. Physical death is the loss of the creation pulse emanating from the Heart of the Cosmos. This pulse is on a path of dissolution with every breath taken as our communion is not reciprocal with Source due to disconnection of Source circuitry.

Simple re-entry into the continuum via circuitry reconnection will initiate the never-ending spiral of conscious evolution that is our true inheritance.

Your heart-body-mind system is your personal instrument with which to function as an ambassador of light, an emissary of love, a conduit through which the Benevolence of Creation can infuse this reality, not only for your sake, but for the sake of those who, in countries across this globe, will feel the shift in the quality of time and light and know that portals of opportunity are opening, through which they can transcend the pain and suffering that being Human has come to mean to them.

22

LUNACY

ON OUR FIRST VISIT TO CALIFORNIA to introduce the completed Foundation Ceremony a massacre had just taken place at Columbine High School. Jerry Falwell, who is considered to be the 'Father of Christianity' by the American people, was being interviewed on the six o'clock news.

"Why did these children murder their classmates?" he was asked. His answer was short,

"Because Humans are inherently evil."

This monumental statement with its abysmal implications reached out to and reinforced the bedrock of guilt and shame that is the foundation of religiously propagated programs of disempowerment. The interview was aired every hour on the hour for days. The magnitude of its meaning oppressed the already despondent spirit of the people, its interpretation echoed in the hearts and minds of America's mothers and fathers as they put their children to bed and wondered with hopelessness at the seed of evil that, according to their prophet and spiritual mediator, lay behind the innocent faces of their progeny. If this last frontier of their love and faith could be so debased, what was left? Waves of depression washed across the continent and rose in swells of desolation to pulsate through the morphogenetic grid of the collective global consciousness.

This form of frequency modulation uses an 'Orwellian' dark alchemy of religion, politics and the established authority of mainstream media to reinforce the psycho-social consensus that entrenches the desired prejudices of those in power. This perfidious program of consciousness manipulation is very effective as the drip-feed of continuous catastrophe, privation and torment that ravages most of the world is conveniently home-delivered via the state sanctioned media.

The psycho-social, political, chemical, electromagnetic and religious manipulation of consciousness that bombards this Earth and her people every minute of every day is a monstrous, forceful and convincing contributor to the constant fuelling of the fear-based consensus that keeps the world hostage to the frequency transmissions of its own thoughts and feelings. However, it is not enough to control and contain the bio-computational complexity and genius that is the Human masterpiece. If these modes of consciousness control, as well as the manipulation of DNA and the disconnection of circuitry, were all that held us in this mutant time-space confinement we would soon break free from them. Our intrinsic resonance with our Sun, the celestial nuances of the planets in our solar system and the radiant song of the star-bejewelled night would inflame our spirits, infuse our Soul Covenant with light and awaken us from this sleep of dark ages. The Earth herself would throw off this irritation of pollution like a flea from her back and shake free her body from the tarmac and concrete confinement that insults her. The rivers, oceans and sea would cleanse themselves, as the poisons that now befoul them would simply shift a molecule here, an atom there, to come into alignment with the acceleration of light Intelligence breaking through the surface of Earth's waters.

But there is another factor to be reckoned with. There is a monumental presence of manipulation and control that dwarfs the interference of the parasites that plague our planet; a presence that disturbs and disorganizes the Intelligence encoded into the light of our Sun, disarranging our symbiosis with it, occluding its ability to nurture and advance our evolution. The presence of this monolithic watchdog that distorts the cosmic influences which would otherwise draw Earth into the holography of the eternal continuum became apparent to us on June 8th, 2004 during the Venus – Sun alignment.

We were in Bali at the time. We had an uninterrupted panoramic view of the Sun as it neared the clear horizon that cloud-free late afternoon. We lived in the district of Penestanan, the highest tract of land above Ubud and the outlying area. As it was higher than any of the many temples that surrounded it, the Balinese felt it was disrespectful to their gods to live there. To us, the elevation was its most positive aspect. As we sat on our tiny uncovered deck that rose above every other structure, we felt we were floating above the planet itself as we awaited the alignment. Venus moved slowly across the face of the Sun, the planet a minuscule dark dot backlit by the brilliance of the Sun.

It was not the visual aspect of the event that was so compelling; it was the confluence of communion between Earth, Venus and our Sun that jolted a distant memory within the cerebral cortex, wherein lay all the forgotten knowledge of our symbiotic kinship with the planets that orbit within the embrace of our central star. Geometric light-grids spin a web of shared coherence between these celestial bodies, an ever-present light-matrix that revealed itself at that moment, as the potency of the alignment blocked the interference from the otherwise constant hindrance of a monitoring satellite that routinely distorts the geometry of the light Intelligence which is the language of celestial communion between these planets and their galactic mediator...the Sun.

There was no immediate instant flash of realization regarding the relevance of this event to the stratum of circuitry which was soon to be made known to us. There was, however, a quickening in the core of our beings and we knew, without reservation, that we had witnessed an event coded to prompt our download of the Temple of Time ceremony, its geometry and sonic code. As the Temple of Time circuitry concerns the convergence of electromagnetic potentials creating patterns of manifestation in specific time-lines, this grand celestial event was a perfect catalyst to activate our recall.

A few days later, at full moon, we prepared ourselves for the download, fasting and avoiding all social input. We greeted the sunset in an open reflective state, sitting in the upstairs room that opened out, through glass sliding doors, to an uncovered deck which jutted over the garden and the rice fields that reached to the jungle horizon. The room opened on three sides from floor to ceiling to the giant ferns and palm trees that encircled the house. Elegant mauve blossoms dripped from the vines that had taken hold in the grass roof to dangle in tresses of green around the room. Nestled in the corner was an altar arranged around a large shallow stone basin filled with water. Miniature violet water lilies floated among the amethyst and tourmaline crystals and the delicate opal-hued seashells arranged around a silver Star of Immortality that rose from the centre of the basin. Tea lights under-lit the altar in soft amber, the whole array sheltered under an ornate Balinese parasol.

Around us, night fell fast, as it does in the tropics and, as the violet vista of the horizon that almost encircled us deepened into darkest indigo, we kept pace with the transitioning energies as we focused on our breath and allowed it to merge our consciousness with the mercurial lightshow. There was a marked absence of the tension and anxiety that usually accompanied a journey of such import and we found ourselves relaxing into and relishing the adventure. The zillion insects of the night intoned a trance-inducing cacophony that coalesced with the gamelan perpetually playing in one village or another. The night held the heady intoxicant of night-blooming jasmine. In the garden a candle created dancing shadows in the pagoda that sat in the frog-filled lotus pond. Although we were fully aware of our commission to advance our understanding of the next layer of circuitry, the night was so captivating that we spent several hours simply being, melting into the night with light bodies and easy breath.

By the time that the moon, full and buzzing, had reached mid-dome of the cathedral night, our bodies were thrumming with high oxygen energy. We moved away from the candlelit altar out to the uncovered deck that was awash in neon-bright full-moon light. As this curtain of brightness cascaded around us I felt suddenly conscious of a mild paranoia whose source I could not trace. We dropped into a sober state; it seemed the night itself chastised us for our joy.

We shared with each other our recognition of the altered ambience and wondered what had changed. Perhaps we were being asked to focus more intently upon the information we had set out to retrieve? On the bed we had made on the small deck, we lay flat on our backs to stare into the zenith of the night, the stars that were strewn across the sky now overcome by the moon. Steeping our bodies in deep rhythmic breath, we let the silence take us.

My eyelids became heavy: a dense magnetism pinned my

body to the bed. I closed my eyes and, in the darkness, felt an unpleasant opiate-like sedation overcome my limbs. The dragging of time marched through my mind in a mechanical syncopation. At some point the background of the insect orchestra was overridden by mental static that tuned in and out of differing channels of chatter, broken conversations of useless gossip and commercial jingles that polluted the airwaves. Playing in my mind's eye was a morphing cartoon-like video game, both comic and violent. I had wandered into a layer of thought frequency, a scum-like consciousness, oily, moronic and pointless, coating my mind with a sense of futility. My heart hurt. Opening my eyes to escape this astral-like realm my gaze was caught by the neon globe that stared down at us. With a ragged intake of breath, I uttered something we Humans are prone to exclaim when confronted by something unexpected:

" Oh my God!"

"What?" from Jiva, jolted out of his own state of half-dreaming.

"It's the moon", I said.

There have been many times in the progressive revelation of the Template body of knowledge when I felt overwhelmed by the information I received: never more so than now. My mouth seemed unacquainted with my mind as words ran from my lips like lemmings off a cliff. My mind was not the only faculty left out of this loop of understanding as my emotions bucked at the implications of these words that I spoke into the night. 'What heresy is this?' some part of me demanded: another part came into grateful resonance. In the light of the realization that washed over me, a parasite of deceit was plucked from my heart; its long sucking tentacles had penetrated and raided my every living day, as it held on for dear life.

What I shared with Jiva that night was not the refined understanding that still grows in us today, but even in its raw state it was enough; enough to know that what we believed to be our 'moon' is a frequency-modulating device that stabilizes the restraining field of the mutant mortal paradigm.

23

THE TEMPLE OF TIME

THE EMERGENCE OF A NEW PHYSICS that recognizes matter and spirit to be one energy in different stages of manifestation has altered the way in which we perceive ourselves and our reality. Intrinsic to the theoretical base of the higher physics of creation is the recognition of the holographic nature of all manifestation. Through this realization we can recognize that every nuance of celestial influence within our solar system has significance and we can appreciate, on a deeper level, the symbiotic resonance that defines us as individualized aspects of one unified body of Divine Consciousness.

It was not until I had 'downloaded' the sonic code of the Temple of Time Ceremony that Jiva and I received the reconnection of its five circuits. Jiva then realized the geometry that is resonant with its waveform. Each complex and nested piece is a component of the coded alchemical structure of symbiosis, created when the energetic awareness of the seven planets identified in the Temple of Time Ceremony interfaced with the awareness of the Human entity. Each piece represented the co-ordinate created at the fractal convergence where the Human meets the celestial influences of its solar design; each piece was both the conception and the actualization of the Human entity's place within the holography of evolution which was coded into the Human matrix and its solar system.

We understood that these circuits were intrinsic to the recalibration of our evolutionary symbiosis with the planetary ratios of influence within our solar system, which has been disrupted and scrambled by the introduction of the planetoid which Humanity accepts as its moon. The derailing of our symbiosis with the solar system is not solely due to the presence of this 'moon' - that which the Mayas called the 'un-tuning of the skies' had been perpetrated by other means – but the moon is the warden that oversees the dualistic prison that had already been created.

Jennifer, our administrator, had hired a large venue in Glastonbury and invitations had been sent out for the fifth ceremony, The Temple of Time, on 5th December 2004. Around a hundred people booked in. It had all been arranged before we even knew what this ceremony was about, where the circuits were or what geometry was involved, so it was with great relief that, by the time we were to leave Bali, we had realized enough about the Temple of Time to be confident that we could facilitate the reconnection.

Back in England, we headed straight to the home of Jennifer and Cosmos, our ambassadors, supporters and trusted friends. Along with Cosmos' sainted mother, Teresa, who was in charge of the computerization of the Template administration, we had dubbed ourselves the 'Kitchen Cabinet'. Since Jennifer had innocently volunteered herself and Teresa to assemble the mailing list, her kitchen had morphed into an office over the years and had become the centre of organization and stability, the hub that kept the wheels turning and all our heads above water.

Jiva and I were energised with our recent reconnection, bursting with the information we had discovered about the cataclysmic event in our solar system and the impact it was having on Humanity. Suzy, a friend and benefactor of the Template, joined us that evening and before dinner we decided to share our information with this small intimate group. Before I had even mentioned the part played by the moon, Cosmos had guessed it. He was personally well aware of the disturbing power of the moon, particularly when it was full, and had used the homeopathic remedy 'Lunar' for some years to alleviate its effects. Jennifer spoke of the malefic influences ascribed to the moon by Vedic and esoteric astrology; influences which it was the adept's test to transcend. We left the next day for Glastonbury feeling lighter for having shared the burden of such controversial information.

We had arranged a training session on the Activation and Integration of the 13th Circuit for the core ambassadors before the ceremonies were to take place. We met in Glastonbury, at the home of ambassadors Jeremy and Claudie, overlooking the Somerset levels. Nick, Rhian and Lynn travelled down from Wales and Jennifer came from London. Teresa and Cosmos would join us later for the ceremonies. This was a group of committed individuals who understood the significance of the Template model and its implications for the future. They had been immersed in the Template journey of discovery for some years and supported the work in every way they could. Even so, we were apprehensive as to how they would respond to the bombshell that was about to be dropped.

Everyone was excited about the Temple of Time and eager to know what it was about. Before long we revealed to them the information that we had about the moon and demonstrated the effects of it through kinesiological testing. Although their reaction was an extraordinary mixture of contradictory emotions, the registration of the knowledge surrounding the Temple of Time circuitry was a fairly easy process. We knew, however, that we could not use this as a measure for the workshop that was to be held a few days later.

It was now important that we understood, were prepared to discuss and, to some degree, answer questions regarding the modification of the Human race. The new 'ism', 'Interventionism', is not being brought to light and slowly leaked into the mainstream media just to provide another interesting series of documentaries, to supply another fascinating angle on our long-lost Human history. It is being revealed because it will substantiate and validate the controlling alien presence on Earth, defining and asserting the pre-eminence of the Annunaki as the 'benefactors' of life and Earth's ruling blood-lines as their rightful inheritors. The event of 9/11 was specifically designed and executed to upscale this chilling agenda.

In the material which identifies the Annunaki as the creators of the 'Adam', the Human, using genes from a hairy ape-like beast, an explanation is given as to how it was that this race and their home planet Nibiru, 'The Planet of the Crossing', entered our solar system. On the 'Genesis Revisited' program, Zecharia Sitchin informs us that 'the story of Earth's history began four billion years ago when our solar system was much younger, and our planet Earth did not yet exist'. When people see the DVD, this statement draws sounds of deep disagreement and the shaking of heads.

According to Sitchin's interpretation of the Sumerian 'Seven Tablets of Creation', Nibiru appeared out of deep space and was drawn into the centre of our solar system by the planetary 'pull' of Neptune, Uranus, Saturn and Jupiter, thus determining Nibiru's orbital path. Nibiru was now on a collision course with the seventh planet, called Tiamat by the Sumerians. One of Nibiru's main satellites crashed into Tiamat, splitting the planet, half of which fragmented as the 'Hammered Bracelet', the asteroid belt, the other half coalesced as 'Earth' and Tiamat's main satellite became Earth's moon. Nibiru was cast into a clockwise solar orbit, returning to Earth's neighbourhood every 3,600 years.

Sitchin goes on to say that in advance of the Annunaki arrival, they sent androids to scout planet Earth 445,000 years ago and that 150,000 years later they landed and created Humankind. 'Adam', the first Human prototype, was created in-vitro; the first test-tube baby!

This 'capture theory' cites the planetary pull of Neptune, Uranus, Saturn and Jupiter as the reason for the intrusion of Nibiru into our solar system and, consequently, the catastrophic destruction that then occurred removes any culpability for this occurrence from the Annunaki. This theory backs up their account that would have us believe they strayed into this situation through circumstances beyond their control.

Over the past few years, many books have been written by various authors on Nibiru and the Annunaki, several citing the capture theory as the reason for the Annunaki' s intervention in our genesis, as though they sought to make the best of the situation and so busied themselves upgrading the indigenous inhabitants of their 'host' planet, gifting them with the many advantages of a more evolved civilization by splicing their superior genes into those of this hairy ape-like primitive race. In these works, it is not mentioned that, with the advantage of these 'superior genes', a large proportion of the Human race has mutated into a deadly, murderous, butchering, genocidal people, bent on the destruction of their Mother planet.

According to the information that we have received, the 'planetoid' Nibiru invaded our solar system with deliberate intent, using a large satellite which was dragged behind in its wake to collide with Earth and push it off its original orbit of the Sun. The satellite used to displace our Earth was then left to orbit the planet, to function as a massive destabilizing magnetic field. That satellite is our 'moon'. Just as our brain chemistry can be changed and alternate realities perceived by the addition of a substance outside of its usual neuro-chemical composition, the introduction of a foreign celestial presence into the ratios of celestial influence within our solar system has the same effect on a gargantuan scale.

Among the scientific community there is no consensus regarding the origin of the moon. Scientists find its orbit and origin incomprehensible. The elemental content of the surface rocks makes it clear that it has not been a part of Earth and there are many anomalies. This satellite, that only shows us one face, does indeed have a dark side. The moon orbiting so close to the Earth shadows the Sun's influence, thus disturbing the informational transmission of light and our ability to translate and utilize it. So large, so massive is the moon in relation to the planet it circles that the scientist Isaac Asimov commented, 'By all cosmic laws she should not be circling the Earth.'

The collapse of the hypothesis that the moon was once a part of the Earth led to the growing popularity of the capture theory. This hypothesis has been refuted. For the moon to have approached the Earth at just the right angle and speed to be caught gravitationally and hooked into orbit in a permanent satellite union is near impossible, particularly as its orbit is circular rather than the elongated elliptical orbit that would have been produced by a gravitational capture. Two senior scientists, Mikhail Vasin and Alexander Shcherbakov, at the Soviet Academy of Sciences, proposed an alternative theory which was published in 'Sputnik' magazine in the mid-'70s.

"The moon is not a natural satellite of Earth, but a huge, hollowed-out planetoid fashioned by some highly advanced, technologically sophisticated civilization into an artificial "inside out" world which was steered into orbit around Earth eons ago. Abandoning the traditional paths of common sense, we have plunged into what may at first sight seem to be unbridled and irresponsible fantasy. But the more minutely we go into all the information gathered by man about the moon the more we are convinced that there is not a single fact to rule out our supposition. Not only that but many things so far considered to be lunar enigmas are explained in the light of this new hypothesis."

Yes, there was a capture; but the planet captured was Earth. From the time of Nibiru's invasion of our solar system, Earth was placed under a governing magnetic field that affected every natural function of every life-form within its ecosystem. Earth's deviant orbit of the Sun created by her collision with Nibiru's satellite disrupted the dynamics of her relationship with light itself. The sacred geometry of tantric molecular cohesion was altered for all life forms within Earth's embrace. Earth was not only knocked out of her solar orbit but was geometrically disassociated from the holography of the divine immortal continuum... death came to Earth.

The present mortal paradigm experienced by Humanity at

this time in this dimension is due to our deficient morphic resonance with the solar system and by our inability to translate light. The transmission of light information emanating from our Sun spells out the immortal mandate that is our Soul Covenant. In the natural state of our original creation, we experience a primordial soul resonance with the Sun's Consciousness. We are a solar race, locked in a lunar reality.

At this time, planet Earth is trapped in a frequency band of extreme oscillation of magnetic influence that is disturbing the natural solar equilibrium, the subconscious matrix of archetypal reference and our ability to embrace the full spectrum of Source Intelligence transmitted by the Sun. The Sun represents to our psyche the most comprehensive monadic configuration that is the resonant field of our geometric Soul Covenant. This lack of solar resonance is being stabilized by our planetoid satellite moon, a synthetic influence which is triggering a chemical imbalance in the Human brain, creating a narcotic dream-state in which we are experiencing continual disempowerment as we play out our fear, guilt and shame. The moon's magnetic field overshadows the immortal harmonic of the Sun's transmission. This creates a distortion of light that manifests as a chemical imbalance. In females this creates a hyper-menstrual condition that weakens libido and creative power, a condition that contributes to the perpetuation of patriarchal power.

Due to the mutant space-time continuum of the present frequency zone, Humanity is tied into a cycle of degeneration with the passing of each year as the Earth circles the Sun. The Sun, the giver of life, instead counts off these increments of 'time' that define our journey towards the grave. In this way the Sun has become the hourglass of death.

The collective challenge that is now upon us is to greet the coming portal of transformational opportunity, having fully resurrected our ability to translate and utilize the creation mandate of light, coming to fully understand that it is a system of light waves that communicate the subtle impulses of spirit into the causation of matter. Our total recall of the Intelligence encoded in light will manifest, through our collective conception, as the transubstantiation of matter, ushering in the Solar Age. As we acknowledge the Sun as the mediator of Prime Intelligence between us and Galactic Consciousness, we will appreciate this, our central star, as our most comprehensive archetypal reference point, the Primary Seed of Creation, the Monad. To meet this Human responsibility, the reconnection of bio-circuitry that renders the Human electromagnetic field resonant with the quantum electro-dynamic transmission emanating from our Sun, our galaxy and ultimately from the Benevolent Heart of Creation, is required.

In the Temple of Time ceremony, the seven circuits relating to Earth, Venus, Mercury, Mars, Jupiter and Saturn and our Sun star are reconnected and the electromagnetic dataflow of each celestial body is reinstated as an energetic coordinate within the incarnate Human presence. The living archetype of each celestial body that exists beyond erroneous historical accretion of data and lunar influence translates as a true astrological imprint within the Human psyche and our perception of space-time; a perception that will not only be intellectually understood, but tangibly transmitted through our upgraded electromagnetic presence as we become the map and the calendar. As the dataflow of the entire solar system is reinstated as an energetic conscious coordinate within our incarnate body-presence, the frequency of creation breaks the barriers set in place by the lunar influence, awakening us as omni-sentient cognizant entities, not only aware of our symbiosis within the embrace of earthly, solar and galactic holography, but also as portals of time and space through which the Benevolence of Creation may play upon us as instruments of light and love. As we upgrade our cosmic comprehension through the reconnection of vital bio-circuits, the collective and unified field of our altered electromagnetic transmissions will send out a signal, a call to cosmic order. We will be heard.

It felt appropriate to bring the Temple of Time Ceremony home to Glastonbury. This ceremony and its circuitry reached the inception of Humanity's seeding and subsequent genetic alterations. Given the all-encompassing implications of our discovery, it was exciting to be sharing the astonishing and subversive revelations that accompanied it with the participants, but it was also daunting. Even though our confidence in the information was so solid that we felt a degree of 'divine ambivalence' to the reaction we might get, we were expecting resistance. To bring this declaration regarding the moon to an international stronghold of goddess worship would be seen by many Glastonians as high treason. To then convene, in the very centre of the town, an intensely powerful ceremony to neutralize its influence upon Human electromagnetic fields would undoubtedly fall into the category of heresy.

The three days of ceremony prior to the Temple of Time were brilliant. The group, many of whom had already integrated the reconnection of twenty five circuits, was warm, receptive and supportive and it was a pleasure having seven core ambassadors present to hold the frequency, looking forward to the new ceremony, knowing the portent of its implications and anticipating liberation through the breaching of a monolithic wall of denial. The workshops were catered for with high-energy, clean-frequency organic vegan meals. Old friends were reunited and there was an air of festivity. Some of this group had been receiving ceremonies slowly over the years; some would experience the series for the first time over these days. The deep reconciliation with the truth of our history and ancestry reached out to us all from the Temple of Time.

The first three days of the workshops had generated a crescendo of empowerment. On that December morning the circle of faces that looked back at us were filled with barely subdued excitement and expectation. My heart swelled with love as I saw Zak sitting at the back of the hall with a couple of friends. We were aware that there were some people present who had invested a great deal in moon work and in its archetypal goddess icons. However, we were confident in their ability to open their minds to the message we carried, knowing that the authenticity of the information and its circuitry would support their process.

We were surprised to feel our lack of anxiety and felt with every moment a growing sense of trust that all would be well. The solid shadowless certainty that the ceremony we were gathered together to share would enrich us all beyond measure and endure forever in the lives of these good people, overrode all else. We knew their faith was well placed in us, in the Template, in that Hall of Assembly, that day under our Sun.

We led the group slowly and carefully through the understanding of the disturbed photo-symbiosis of our solar system that was generating a mutant paradigm.

"There is a catalytic body of influence in Earth's orbit that is creating and stabilizing her disassociation with the true holistic continuum," I said. There was a charged and pregnant pause. I steeled myself for the announcement that had to follow, feeling the strong grounding presence of Jiva and the ambassadors.

"That body is our moon."

The silence that followed was beautiful. Just as at the moment of birth when the infant is beheld, and the pain is forgotten, I felt all the years of struggle and not a little persecution dissolve into that silence.

The strongest sense of all that resonated among us was unity, as the great deception that somehow divided us was swept away. I could see the confluence of opposing thoughts and feelings passing across their faces as each one present searched through the memory banks of their computational awareness for some certainty that would allow them to refute this ridiculous and heretical piece of information. And yet the eyes, the windows to the soul, showed that the battle was useless, as an ancient knowledge welled up from every cell of their beings. There was a sense of mental grappling for a habitual point of reference, but the battle seemed mechanical, an automated reflex that soon petered out. A wave of comprehension rippled through their bodies as a long-awaited piece of the puzzle made sense of the bigger picture; nothing would be the same again. Tears were shed by many. There was a feeling of great sadness, just as when you discover that a lover has been deceiving you - you know you have always known - the truth that is a relief also brings grief.

At the break, several of the group found me or Jiva to tell personal stories of dreams and experiences that had clued them in, although they had not felt empowered to voice their realizations. 'Nothing would be the same again'. These were words repeated to us many times in the years that followed. Our anomalous moon was identified as a negative attractor that has maintained much of the deception which has burdened Humanity for eons.

The December evening settled around us, candles were lit, and we prepared for the Temple of Time Ceremony. A cave of light glowed in the centre of the old stone Assembly Rooms of Glastonbury whilst outside the wind and rain thrashed around in the cold winter Avalon twilight. Suspended above the sumptuously luminous altar was the geometry of the Sun that was resonant with the first incantation of the sonic code within the Temple of Time Ceremony. Lying dormant yet ever potent, within the Human Soul Covenant was the alchemical counterpart to this sacred geometry. Its presence within the Soul Covenant was a data pod that contained the directive for the light assimilation that leads to conscious symbiotic evolution within our solar system. The identical frequency waveform created by the geometry, the sound and the Covenant converged to resurrect the divine immortal code of creation that is the vibratory infrastructure of the Human masterpiece. Each Human unit of electromagnetic circuitry re-attuned their primordial soul resonance to the quintessence of the Sun's Consciousness, reinstating their energetic symbiosis with the light of the Sun. This attunement was repeated with each of the other six planets. The incandescence and resonance of the ceremony filled each one present, reverberating around the old stone walls, spilling out into the Avalon night, suffusing time and space without limit.

The resurrection of our circuitry will engender the rejuvenation of our endocrine systems, reactivate our full genetic blueprints, and reveal the true nature of our genetic ancestry and our celestial soul seeding, to re-birth the solar-encoded race that we were created to be. The original innocence of our root race embodied the love-frequency as its central cohesive power. In this sense we were and still are a more advanced race than our technologically skilled captors. Evolution is not measured by the advancement of ecocidal technology, but by our ability to comprehend, resonate and cooperate with the forces of creation. Our complete resonance with the frequency of creation allowed us an organic technology that manifested in living structures of light and good intent... homes built not for shelter or separation from the environment, but molecularly intelligent structures that were in harmony with it and rejuvenated body, mind and spirit.

Unlike the patriarchally dominated concrete empires installed by our captors in that time-space zone, nothing that owed its existence to the subjugation of the male or female potencies of creation could maintain its molecular structure. There was no farming, no agriculture, no animals kept in captivity awaiting the day of their slaughter and consumption, for our race lived on prana. The core whole-systems that generated and sustained the life-pulse were interactive with the holography of the immortal continuum. There was no question about survival as we played within the unified field, riding upon the waves of ascending currents of life-force that ebbed and flowed with the rising and setting of the Sun. We did not know need. Our very existence and our technology were based upon our ability to translate light to maintain the integrity of our primordial soul resonance with our Sun's Consciousness and thus, with the supreme organizing principle of the Galactic Core transmission, for which this star is the prime mediator.

By restoring the energetic pattern of electromagnetic celestial influence that forms the infrastructures of our evolutionary symbiosis with the creative directive, the truth of our origins tells its own story wordlessly, beyond the guile of false historic inserts and the manipulation of religious indoctrination. As fractals of a holonomic symbiosis that governs conscious evolution within this corner of the galaxy, our destiny – and the future of this, our Mother planet – is choreographed by the embrace of our Sun's geometric light pulsations. We are a solar race.

To reunify with the synchronomic force that governs the divine mechanisms of creation, we must regain the original orbit of our Sun and reinstate the true ratios of celestial influence coded into the pre-cataclysmic cosmogenesis of the solar system. The light Intelligence of this star is the emissary of the Benevolence of our Creation. We will enjoy the true meaning of Source through our ability to download and translate the light information from our Sun within the alembic crucible of our incarnate body presence. Through the consensus transmission of this divine Awareness we will awaken, through resonance, our planet Earth's memory of Her true dimensional nature held within Her crystalline heart. For this is what means to be Human.

We and the Earth are one.

24

THE MASK OF GOD IS SLIPPING

A WAVE OF INSUBORDINATE CONTEMPLATION with regard to monotheistic religions swelled in the mid-1950s, gathering strength and mass by the early '60s. These philosophical explorers turned from the rote answers to ready-made questions that constituted the non-negotiable infrastructure of preordained religious belief systems. In their search for self-discovery, they explored mystical, esoteric, Kabbalistic and magical alternatives. The dogma put forth by the establishment religions did not resonate with the divinity that they knew resided within them and many began to study the teachings of eastern philosophy.

These teachings included an understanding of the flow of energies and the expansion of consciousness via techniques such as yoga and meditation, practices which brought the focus to the body's energy systems and which could lead to transcendental experiences and profound metaphysical insights into the nature of reality. This engendered an expanded reverence for all the manifestations of creation and, together with responsible psychedelic therapy, generated a massive pattern-interrupt in the rigidity of the prevalent social structures and the dominant political ideology – a cultural revolution that led to the demand for civil rights, racial equality and respect for the ecology.

The alternative eastern spiritual paths practiced outside the ethnic political and social environment in which they incubated lack certain spectrums of their traditional construct. For most followers in the countries in which they are practiced, these religions are not entered into by choice but by birth; there is a strict system of indoctrination and, in some cases, a caste system that ensures individual cooperation. Those who make autonomous spiritual choices are severely ostracized by their community. Many religious doctrines are mutations adopted to accommodate the aberrant agendas of those in incontestable power. The translation of these philosophies into the western stream was tailored to the sensibilities of the western mind and became homogenized and romanticized to fit the utopian optimism of the 1960s and '70s.

Eventually, many who adopted these eastern teachings realized they had left one set of spiritual regulations only to adopt another system of exclusive belief that led to separation and stagnation. These imported modalities were themselves formulaic and constrictive, ultimately defining the supreme Godhead in nondebatable, patriarchal terms. Representations of these anthropomorphic deities, used to this day as ornaments for their nostalgic and exotic power to evoke selective aspects of the religions they represent, are immensely powerful. By objectifying a preordained definition of God, their proximity revokes an individual's ability to define this for themselves, through their own sentient faculties, as fractal emissaries of Divine Consciousness. Ironically, these artefacts are, literally, able to usurp the Human electromagnetic energy field's holonomic connection to Source Consciousness, thus removing its system of circuitry from the immortal continuum.

The exploration of self-realization led to a disenchantment with the self-serving agendas of spiritual gurus and organizations and to the tentative birth of a new spiritual movement, one that envisaged a decentralization of spiritual authority that empowered the individual to experience, without censorship or mediation, direct communion with the Benevolence of its own Creation. These various modalities come under the umbrella of the Human Potential Movement and the New Age.

The New Age, as it is popularly understood, has come to suggest a personalized spiritual path, a synthesis, fusion, or pick'n'mix of eastern techniques, neurological and psychological processes, nutrition and restorative body-work. Rather than icons or deities, crystals – fragments of Mother Earth herself – grace many an altar.

Say what you will about the crystal obsession of the New

Age movement, but it is significant to note that even the most cursory interaction with any crystal will automatically reconnect the Earth Circuit into the medulla oblongata, albeit temporarily. This circuit feeds the pituitary-hypothalamus-pineal complex and recalibrates the Human electromagnetic field with the pulse of Earth. The implications of this are intrinsic to Humanity's ability to transcend this mutant paradigm.

In the Foundation Ceremony, a crystal is used as an alchemical component to permanently reconnect the Earth Circuit. It is the frequency transmission of this element, braided together with its resonant sonic code, which reconnects the circuit. Soon after his training, one of our ambassadors held his first Foundation Ceremony and was dismayed to find that, upon testing the twelve circuits involved, the Earth Circuits of his group were still weak. He had used a large piece of moldavite in the ceremony and it then occurred to him that as moldavite is from a meteorite it does not hold the Earth resonance. He exchanged the moldavite for a quartz crystal and repeated the Earth Ceremony. Retesting the group's Earth Circuits, he found them to be strong.

The New Age enthusiasm for crystals is not a frivolous enchantment with shiny pretty objects, but an instinctually devotional response to a non-anthropomorphic representative of divinity, whose frequency transmissions stimulate a counter resonance in the cerebral cortex, the temple of remembrance. Through this resonant feedback the memory matrix of a pre-modified Human identity is resurrected, and another circuit of electromagnetic consciousness is reactivated and reinstated within the holistic continuum.

The re-empowerment through spiritual autonomy that rose out of the New Age movement may have spawned an embarrassment of wacky, ungrounded processes that are not overburdened by intelligence and spiritual movements that venerate reincarnations of megalomaniac prophets, but its break from the institutionalized forms of anthropomorphic worship was unprecedented. It was this new spiritual autonomy that activated points of creative reference in the morphogenetic field which supported the exploration of non-theistic ideas regarding the Prime Creative Force and helped to tear the mask from the faces of the God impersonators.

Another obsession that unified the myriad of spiritual modalities of the New Age is the very elemental influence which had instigated the initial move away from the fear, shame and guilt-based religions...light. In the mid-twentieth century, during the 13th baktun of this age of Ahau, the data density of light had begun to intensify as the activation beam of the Aquarian ray entered our neighbourhood, looking for worldbridgers.

The insurgency against established religions bred a cultural dissent that inescapably included a break from political and social control, as all institutions come under the same auspices of mass consciousness manipulation. This mutiny did not go unnoticed by those whose best interests were served by the 'spiritual' and cultural manipulation of consciousness; alternative movements came under surveillance and were soon infiltrated by counter-intelligence programs. As a result of this and of over-commercialization, the backbone of the body of alternative knowledge was eroded, leaving a soft and sticky ambiguous residue permeated with revamped Christian creeds and archetypes; quantum laws of physics denigrated into platitudes and 'secret' ways of making money and getting all the stuff you want; all the power of truth bled out, filtered and homogenized so as to fit the marketing strategies of a big business careful not to scare the punters with the thorny truth. Running along the track it was purported to have been created to dismantle, the movement was patrolled from within by the 'rainbow fascists' and the 'positive police'.

This homogenized New Age, easily and often ridiculed in film and print, became the popular version that dominated the public domain. However, there is a counter counter-culture: a swelling tide of individuals and groups who, sharing information with speed and ease through the internet, maverick radio programs and a very few magazines, has risen out of the synthesis of quantum physics and mysticism to embody the very best of the New Age.

These contemporary aboriginals have shunned the more indulgent pillowed and pampering paths, deciding that it is better to be sorry than safe. They seek for the truth of their origins by studying the new physics, hyper-space and parallel universes. The recognition of the universe as a holographic system has brought them to the understanding that they have been fashioned from the same causative ocean of indivisible numinous substance which conceives the spiraling galaxies. You can indeed 'hold infinity in the palm of your hand, and eternity in an hour'. [6]

The emerging synthesis of science and spirituality does not reveal God to be an automated, computerized, holographic mechanism that spews forth impersonal fluctuations into the quantum field. The laws of quantum physics do not point to a Godless, random universe. In fact, they barely scratch the surface of a genius beyond measure, a genius that will be neither named nor frozen in the comprehension of a moment in time. A definition of God is coalescing in the sacred holonomic crucible of the Human heart-body-mind as it downloads and decodes the divinity of light, a definition that beckons us through the threshold of perception which reveals the Human masterpiece to be a fractal instrument of that genius.

In the light of the hypocrisy of our spiritual counsellors, the fraudulence and treachery of our political leaders and the colossal collapse of the neo-Darwinian synthesis, we have learned to trust very little of what we are told. We are no longer looking to authority figures of the past or to the messianic impresarios and gurus of the present, but are looking upward, not to the promised reward of heaven, but to the stars. The grand crosses and alignments of celestial bodies now speak the truth of Humanity's symbiotic resonance with the evolutionary mandate of light that is

---

[6] William Blake "Auguries of Innocence I"

transmitted from the Galactic Core.

Within the sphere of those who study quantum physics, sacred geometry, advanced body healing, and super-nutrition, and of those who travel to Peru and Brazil to ingest ayahuasca, there is a new common denominator of attraction and resonance, the ancient cosmogenic calendrical system of the Maya. A large, well-informed and discerning group of individuals have set their sights upon an empirical prophecy of realigned cosmic potential elucidated by the conjunction of the Sun with the intersection of the ecliptic and the plane of the Milky Way, 13.0.0.0.0, 4 Ahau, December 21st, 2012.

The portal of 2012 is a celestial alignment that will create a concordance of opportunity, a 'holonomic convergence', as a confluence of diverse realities compete for dominance of the space-time continuum. As Earth enters the periphery of this portal, each unit of sentient consciousness will gravitate towards the paradigm that holds resonance with the integrity of Source Awareness in its electromagnetic field. Circuitry is the delivery system for the energetic nature of Source Awareness. We began to make the choices that dictate our dimensional resonance some time ago and the need to continue to reaffirm these choices will continue to grow exponentially as our planet draws closer to the portal.

The geometric template of the original Human blueprint, undisturbed by subsequent modification and alien genetic invasion, exists as memory in the cerebral cortex. The activation of this memory matrix and the resurrection of the superstructure it dictates are achievable through exposure to a replicate resonant field. The Template ceremonies generate this resonant field. As with the establishment of any field, critical mass is required. Individual transcendence is reliant upon the whole, just as collective transcendence is reliant upon the individual: such is the definition of a holonomic system. The reconnection of circuitry upgrades individual frequency through the accelerated synthesis of electromagnetic Source Intelligence by the Human energy field and the collective frequency through quantum fluctuations in the unified field of global awareness. This new global resonance will re-establish the already existing morphic field which supported our existence prior to our genetic modification. That dimensional field is the paradigm we entered on Green Mountain.

With this in mind, Jiva and I are continually aware of the need to disseminate the Template Ceremony information. Margo, our administrator in the USA, had heard from various sources of a professional promoter who was gaining a name for himself. His catalogue of clients included Masaru Imoto and Deepak Chopra. It was, however, difficult to get his attention and he was very expensive.

Margo sent him a promotion package and we waited. Several months later, impressed by the Template material, the promoter contacted her and agreed to take us on as clients. We all worked hard to raise his enormous fee, but, in the end, we could come up with only a fraction of it; a loan from Margo's mother. For this amount, instead of the six-month, four city tour, we would spend a few weeks in Seattle and Portland. We were to discover that, contrary to what he had told us and Margo, he had never worked with an 'unknown' before. Apparently, those on his books were already established.

I spent six months writing six articles and wrote the scripts for and recorded three Template CDs: 'Foundation', 'Activation & Integration' and 'Actualization'. It was a huge body of work to accomplish in such a small amount of time. For me, one of the most difficult aspects of this project was the censoring by the promoter of both the language and the content. I was being asked to dumb down the language and form it into commercial sound-bites that sounded more like an advertisement for cut-price sofas than a call to share information regarding the global Human predicament. The promoter seemed to feel that the public were more interested in what they could get for free than in any idea of freedom.

As it turned out, not one of my articles was used and the huge database we were promised was never accessed. At our first presentation evening in a well-known venue in Portland, the promoter stood at the back of the room. When I began to introduce him, he made frantic hand signals to deter me and refrained from joining me on the podium. He should have introduced me. That night it became clear to Jiva, Margo and me that he did not want to be associated with us. I was devastated and gave one of my worst ever presentations. That afternoon, he had interviewed me on his radio program and some days later, when I asked for a CD of the interview, he was extremely reluctant to send it. He did eventually send me a copy, but when we played the CD you could not hear his voice asking the questions. The interview was unusable.

A few years earlier, not long after the 9/11 atrocity, we had made a visit to America. Understandably, there was a pall of depression across the nation. Arriving in Los Angeles, we booked into a hotel and I turned on the television to an advert for a drug called 'Ambient'.

"I used to be worried," the woman on the TV informed us, "Now I take 'Ambient' once a day and I'm not worried anymore". In the next advert a woman related her difficulty in finding a painkiller that could be taken in conjunction with the five other medications she was on. She was very relieved that one had been manufactured which was compatible with her list of pharmaceutical treatments.

On the surface, it appeared that the majority of Americans were in shock: their most iconic symbols of political and economic power, along with thousands of their citizens, had been annihilated in a matter of minutes. On a deeper level, they inherently knew that the atrocity had been perpetrated by a certain deputation of their own government, though this fact was registered at varying levels of consciousness. Those who for many years had recognized the Orwellian manipulation of consciousness via media saturation regarding the threat of global terrorism, instantly recognized that the New World Order had taken a quantum leap. Others stayed in deep denial, unable to integrate this concept and remain part of their patriotic communities. The message to the pathologically obedient masses was designed to feed their programs of national and religious superiority, to seal their cooperation in the restricting of civil liberties and the inevitable war of vengeance. The most far-reaching and damaging aspect of this violation of the American people was psychological. On an arcane level, a heartless and lethal force had unequivocally asserted its menacing posture of world dominance. It was not the body count, which is surpassed on any given day by deaths from genocide and war, but the ruthless and deadly intent that was behind the act which defied evaluation in Human terms. On that tour, many participants at our workshops were using 'Prozac', emotionally overwhelmed and unable to deal with the overview of the global predicament. They wanted only to hear how their reconnected circuitry would help them out of their fear and pain.

However, this time, our groups were alert, aware and wanted to know everything. The shock of 9/11 had jolted them into realizing it was not enough to improve the day-to-day quality of their lives, that quality could no longer be measured in self-concerned, consumer-based concepts of abundance. Their main focus was on the part they could play in healing the global grief. The myriad of conspiracy theories that had once seemed delusional became plausible in the light of 9/11. They realized that there could be no fixing of this fear-based paradigm which was specifically designed to run along tracks of conflict. The systemic contamination was deeper than political, economic or cultural corruption. The roots of our deviation from the all-encompassing nurture of the Divine Benevolence, that places love and compassion as the cohesive force which inspires true evolution, was to be found in the modification of our DNA, the disturbance of our symbiotic relationship with light and the de-orchestration of the complex oscillating fields of Earth bio-systems. The answer was transcendence.

There was a new level of comprehension and a new appreciation of the Template material among the groups we worked with on that tour. The recognition and acceptance of the information regarding the moon was moving and inspirational. It seemed for many to mark a turning point in their ability to comprehend the magnitude of the agenda to control Human consciousness and the impact the reconnection of circuitry had on neutralizing its power over us. At one workshop held near Santa Cruz, a gentleman who had just experienced the first four ceremonies was reluctant to acknowledge the negative effect of the moon. He spoke for others in the group, in particular a woman who had for many years been part of a circle which ritually honoured the moon and its goddesses. As it was daytime, and the moon was not visible, Jiva used a symbol of the moon to test the circuitry of one of the ambassadors who had already connected the fifth ceremony circuits. She tested strong on all her circuits, thus showing that the moon was not affecting her electromagnetic field. He then tested the man's circuitry while he looked at the moon symbol. Although he was a strong fellow, he could not keep his arm up. Jiva tested him again after he experienced the fifth ceremony while he was looking at the moon symbol. He was then able to feel the irrefutable strength in his circuits which were no longer affected by the moon's influence.

On many occasions we experienced the spontaneous and openhearted generosity and hospitality that defines the American spirit. At an evening talk in Tacoma, a woman we had barely met offered her home to us while she was away. Another, at a workshop in Seattle, offered her holiday home. At every workshop, gifts and food were always offered and help with the running of the workshop was always donated. Three wonderful women in California, Dawn, Gabriella and Joie worked selflessly to send out emails and hand out flyers.

Before leaving England, I had mentioned to Jiva that someone in Hawaii was going to make a considerable donation. He reminded me that Hawaii was not on our itinerary. At the first ceremony in Seattle an attendee was disappointed because she was not able to attend the last two ceremonies, the fourth and fifth. We agreed that if she could put together a group, we would come to her where she lived, in Hawaii.

As we got off the plane on the island of Maui we were enveloped in the soft fragrant air that only Hawaii offers. So many memories reached us, carried on the steamy scented breeze. It had been seventeen years.

Janice, our event manager, was on the mainland for a few days and we knew no one on the island. We rented a car and headed for the small, funky, wood-fronted town of Paia for some lunch. Across from our café was a realtor's office. After lunch we paid them a visit and the lady behind the desk could not take her eyes from the star-tetrahedron pendant I was wearing. Within a short time, we were making our way to Haiku and a property on the side of Haliakula, Maui's volcanic mountain. On this stunning land were two structures made of bamboo. The house we were to occupy was circular with a wide deck and a view of the mountain. It was called Bali Hali ('hali' being Hawaiian for home). The manager was there to greet us and, seeing our geometric jewellery, showed us a flower-of-life tattooed on his back.

We spent the next two weeks posting flyers, holding several introductory evening presentations and I was interviewed on a couple of radio programs. A few days before our workshops were scheduled we held a final talk at a small acupuncture centre in Paia. As the group filed in and settled in their seats, both Jiva and I noticed a woman seated near the front. Her energy was intense and focused and during the presentation she asked clear, concise questions. At the end of the evening she signed up for the full five days of ceremony. Her appreciation of the Template model was heartfelt, and it was this lovely woman who generously donated the funds that I had foreseen which helped to sustain us while we wrote this book.

Our Maui group gathered in a beautiful venue on the side of Haliakala. It was a wonderful gathering of individuals, though the atmosphere in the workshops was powerfully intense and it was near impossible to harmonize the energies of the group. On reflection, it might have been the build-up of energies that was to culminate in the spontaneous event which would occur during one of the ceremonies, or it might have been due to the transmissions of the H.A.A.R.P. (High frequency Active Auroral Research Program) installation that we were to learn was on Haliakala. This weapon of mass harmonic disturbance manipulates the rhythmic pulse of Earth's heart, creating chaos in the ionosphere registered by the brain as mental and emotional agitation. Not only does this scrambling of the biopsychic orientation of Earth's sensorium derange the sonar of whales and dolphins, it also creates dissonant fluctuations in a myriad of sub-systems and eventually causes ecological devastation.

On the third day of the five-day workshop, we woke to a tremendous wind storm. The road to the ceremony venue was littered with fallen branches and even a small tree that Jiva had to lift out of the way in order for us to pass. It was fitting that it was the day of the Ceremony of Sacred Breath. The gale-force winds added to the agitation of the group. As we formed a circle around the stunning array of stellated geometry that is an alchemical component within the Sacred Breath Ceremony, the wind was still howling, and we could see the trees waving manically beyond the glass doors of the elegant pine room. This group was puckish; however, they truly relished the ceremonies and behaved with great respect and reverence during them.

A short way into the Sacred Breath Ceremony I knew that

half way through, the wind would cease. As we drew close to the midpoint, the already highly-charged elemental friction of the ambience shifted into another dimension. Suspended a foot or so above the dazzling altar, heavy with exotic tropical flowers, candles and crystals, was an Embryonic Solar Star holding the resonant field for that fractal of the Soul Covenant which defines the ability of the Human entity to decode and utilize the tantric language of light, its electromagnetic field positioned as a mediator between Earth and her star lover, the Sun. I became aware of the Earth as a sublimely sentient entity. I was not only registering the sum of her natural elemental attributes but also something I can only describe as her personality. As the star before me slowly rotated, downloading the dataflow of Source Consciousness encoded within its graceful form, it multiplied into many stars, as my eyes inexplicably swam with tears. In that one moment the wind dropped entirely. I drew a sudden deep breath that seemed to well up from the crystalline heart of Earth to flood my body with ecstasy. My 33rd circuit reconnected. I had to make a focused effort to concentrate on conducting the rest of the ceremony as my eyes were drawn to the vista beyond the glass doors of the room. Although the wind had dropped completely, the tropical landscape was seething with a supernatural animation; all the colours were extravagant and shone with a luminous blush that came from an inner incandescence. The transcendence of the landscape was more than visual; it thrummed with a powerful sovereignty and a devic vivacity that conjured memories of some other time. I looked over at Jiva and knew that he, too, had connected his 33rd Circuit. It would be another eleven months before we would realize, back in Bali, the full implications of what had occurred and its connection to Green Mountain.

It seemed fitting that we should reconnect our 33rd circuit in the same islands where we had reconnected the first three, as if this in itself created a circuit. A couple of days earlier we had learned that Makua had left his body. At the ceremony that day, we felt his presence and support and I no longer grieved for him. He was now an even more influential presence, guiding his beloved people on the islands he cherished.

After completing our workshops in Maui, we returned to the Big Island for the first time in seventeen years. Here Jiva and I had met, my mother had died, we had been arrested, incarcerated and married and we met beings who were not of this planet.

We spent a few days with the neighbour who had bailed us out of prison while we looked for a house in which to spend a couple of weeks with Zak and his girlfriend Anjuli, who had flown over on New Year's Eve. We found an old Hawaiian-style, wooden two-story house that sat at the edge of a major tide pool in Kapoho, our old neighbourhood. One end of the long deep pool opened out into the ocean and was home to a family of giant turtles. It was here that we began to integrate the mental, emotional and physical download of the 33rd Circuit, the sixth fractal of The Template reconnection.

Both Jiva and I felt hyper-sensitive and raw. When we had to leave Kapoho to pick up supplies, the world outside our sanctuary was garish, loud and jarring. Although I had long acknowledged that the disconnection of circuitry, the modification of the genetic blueprint and the splicing of Annunaki genes had rendered Humanity's features a caricature of its true countenance, the faces of the people wandering the streets and the stores were either etched with pain or glazed over with a numb acceptance.

There seemed to be an aggressive number of helicopters and the perpetual sense of being watched and monitored was acute: the sensation of being on a prison planet was greatly heightened. Uncharacteristically, I found myself spontaneously moved to tears. It was not as though we were unaware of the 'hostage' position of our planet and yet we seemed to be experiencing it more dynamically. Looking back and assessing the situation from the perspective of what we now know of the 33rd Circuit, I realize that it was our connection to a realm that was resonant with the full spectrum of our original blueprint that allowed us to realize and accept the full ramifications of this mutant prison paradigm and the presence that patrols it.

Before we left Maui, we were contacted by a woman whose partner was a well-known anthropologist among the island community and who had focused his study and research on the Nibiruans. This included an in-depth study of Sitchin's body of work. This couple, who I shall call Jane and David, had heard of our work through the Maui grapevine and wanted to call a group of people together to meet with us for an evening of discussion on the subject of Interventionism. We were, at the time, taken up by family matters and dealing with the integration of the dataflow created by our recent reconnection. We had spent the last three months in intense situations dealing with many groups of people and felt we needed space. Even though this couple seemed to be hospitable and sincere people with a real passion for their work, we declined the invitation. My conversations with them were distracted and jumbled as I had been trying to talk on my mobile phone on the road between engagements. However, I had gleaned enough to appreciate that some of the information Jiva and I had tapped into was contrary to their beliefs and we imagined that we would be in the hot-seat amongst a group of people who were aligned with a professional anthropologist. At this point, our overview of the predicament with regard to Humanity's true history was incubating and hatching new realizations by the hour. Before confronting a group such as this it would be advisable to coalesce and stabilize our overview.

Most of my conversations had been with Jane and it was she who contacted me in Kapoho on a landline for a longer talk. She had gone through a great many extraordinary experiences, not only to do with the Annunaki, but also with the 'shadow government' which was very active on the Islands. She had a lot of knowledge about secret experiments going on in Hawaii. Before we left Hawaii seventeen years earlier, we had been in contact with a man called Daniel Giamario, who had given us similar information with regard to these experiments. It was Daniel who had informed us that, in around ten years' time, there would be a huge catastrophe perpetrated in a major city – probably New York – which would introduce a new level of control and restrictions of Human liberties. He pointed out to us that the islands of Hawaii are the most isolated pieces of land on the globe. Because of its geography, Hawaii is ideal for the experimentation with and the manipulation of consciousness. Apparently, there were many experiments being conducted with the use of frequency bombardment and psychotronic mind control – especially on the 'hippie' community. I remember that when I lived in Kapoho, on several occasions I woke up to the dark shadow of a helicopter, flying dangerously low over our house, emitting an infrared search light. Naively, I had thought that they were scanning for marijuana cultivation.

I spoke with Jane for about an hour and, when I got off the phone, I was shaken and deeply drained. The most perturbing aspect of my conversation with her was that she was in sympathy with the concept of Enki as a 'good alien', benevolent and contrite, who had always had our best interests at heart. It was apparent from our conversation that she felt it to be in the interests of Humanity to recognize Enki's penitence and co-operate with him in the coming revelation of the alien presence on this planet. This, coming from such well-informed individuals, was disturbing. During my conversation with Jane she spoke of attending one of Sitchin's seminars in the south west of the mainland and that he had said he was now in telepathic communication with Enki. Sitchin's last book, 'The Lost Book of Enki', is neither 'lost', nor by Enki, but is a channelled rendition by Sitchin. Earlier on Maui, during a conference call between myself, Jane and David, I mentioned that Jiva and I felt very strongly that the hypothesis made in 'The Lost Book of Enki' and in all of Sitchin's and Gardner's books, that Humanity was fashioned and upgraded from a 'hairy apelike beast' was fraudulent. This did not go down well and elicited from David an emotional and aggressive reply.

It was at this time that we were sent a copy of Laurence Gardner's 'Genesis of the Grail Kings' and a couple of Sitchin's books we had not yet read. The time spent in Kapoho was meant to be a break for us before we resumed our tour, a time to relax and be with family. We had not expected to have our attention drawn so continually and adamantly to the Annunaki and yet it seemed vital that we give the subject our full focus. Our recent reconnection of the 33rd Circuit had brought our attention to the part the Annunaki played in its disconnection.

Gardner's Grail Kings book reads as a supremacist promotion of the superior bloodline of the descendants of the Annunaki race. According to him, the 'Grail' is the Annunaki bloodline and he includes Jesus as its main descendant. Within the extensively documented text is an underlying message of domination and intimations of the consequences of resistance against it.

It seems from his biography that he is in allegiance with the high echelons of power that are in control of the agenda to exert, over Earth and Humanity, an inherited and 'God-given' right to reign supreme in dominion over lesser mortals. In 'The Grail Kings', Gardner comments:

'In real terms, the bushmen are the true inheritors of

nature's own slow progression. It is we of the civilized races who have advanced far ahead of spontaneous evolution by way of our strategically applied wisdom. But this cannot have taken place by accident; we cannot invent wisdom, it has to be acquired and inherited.'

With this breath-taking statement Mr. Gardner passes judgment on the efficiency of 'nature's own slow progression', strongly suggesting that some form of outside 'strategically applied wisdom' is superior to the plodding, dawdling, wearisome advancement of nature. Nature... that tedious organic force of divine creation, conceived from the union of electricity and magnetism, birthing immaculate translations of impossible genius from spiraling galaxies to the minuscule forms of delicately winged entities. Nature is simply too slow and needs a leg-up!

'We of the civilized races have advanced far ahead of spontaneous evolution' Mr. Gardner informs us. Here he reveals the deep disregard held by those for whom he is a spokesperson and advocate, towards the omni-competent codification of symbiotic evolution. This comment shows the chilling mindset behind the subjugation of nature and the resultant destruction of the ecosystem that we now endure.

All forms of biological life on this and every planet in our solar system would have enjoyed a holistic exponential maturation into a fully realized transcendental state had the celestial influences of our solar system been left in their original configuration. We would have remained in alignment with the holonomic forces of creation instead of abusing them by splitting the atom and employing this mighty force to instantaneously kill 66,000 men, women and children of Hiroshima, a death toll that would eventually rise to 200,000. This atrocity is one of a vast catalogue committed by the 'civilized' races.

Even if it were true that our original root race, prior to the upgrade bestowed upon us by our evolutionary interceptors, were slowly progressing bushmen and women, this race would have been impeccably coded to respond symbiotically to the evolutionary mandate, projected as light; an ingenious full spectrum luminary wisdom, each refracted nuance of which was organically qualified, regulated and designed to empower concordant sentient development. Time, in this context, is relevant only in relation to the complex orchestration of a cosmic cadence that ensures a full spectrum of symbiotic evolution in harmony with the divine immortal continuum. The acceleration of the process would only become desirable in relation to the agenda of an outside influence that would be serving its own purposes. As it is, the dormant resources evident within the Human gene code and its covenant with light signifies a highly evolved race. Rather than being upgraded by 'applied wisdom' it has been systemically corrupted and degenerated by an 'acquired and inherited' genetic propensity that is alien to its divine design and purpose.

Earth's inhabitants have for eons been compliant to the whims of the 'Lords of Entropy' who hold dominion over the time-space zone in which we have been caught and trapped. If we examine the patterns of history we find them to run along common lines of invasions, conquests, destruction, pestilence, inquisitions, holocausts and genocide... war, war and more war. For some reason we accept these endless barbarities, sanctioned by the 'divine right of kings', as the natural course of cultural and political development.

Cosmologies, myths, religions and legends are fashioned to explain the anomalies created by the distortion of sequential continuity created by time-travel, genetic experimentation and the manipulation of our definition of God through the insertion of archetypes portrayed as supremely divine entities. The socially and culturally accepted psychosis that comes under the sacred auspices of religion has diverted Humanity from the scent of our true connection to the Benevolence of our Creation and has robbed us of our quintessential identity as a fractal aspect of that genius. Ancient civilizations seduce the disconnected, automated, over-civilized, twenty-first century techno 'humaton' with their impressive pantheons of colourful archetypes and icons, especially when compared with the corrupt and lackluster leaders of government and the paedophile infested leadership of major religions. If it happened long ago it must be authentic. If it is ethnic it must be real.

Many of the rich archetypal pantheons of these ancient civilizations contain the myths and legends passed down by the patriarchal priests of 'astral religions', whose monuments of glory are built by slave labour. The infrastructures of their philosophies are fashioned by the megalomania of racially prejudiced elitists who believe in their own 'God-given' supremacy and whose genetics have been invaded and dominated by the Annunaki. Their occult practices arise from the unconscious urge to integrate their mutant perceptions into a schematic through which they can synthesize and accommodate the invasion of a parasitic alien consciousness. These civilizations were afflicted by the same genetic modification, laboured under the same Sun, the light of which reached them from the same inconsonant orbit of today. Can we call this inventory of psychopathic behaviour our history? Or is it the documentation of a planet and a people deep in the insanity of a conflict-riddled mutant realm?

We had once been informed that the situation on Earth at this time was close to the hypothesis of reality put forward by the film 'Total Recall', a film in which reality is controlled by false memory inserts. What you believe is so important. Belief creates powerful brain chemistry that, collectively, dictates the dominant consensus. Those who control belief control reality. The dark alchemy of religions, politics and the mainstream media has created a pathologically obedient and mind-controlled society that serves the agenda of those in power. Many are vying for our allegiance to their philosophy. Where do we place our trust in the midst of the many and differing spins on our history and our true identity as Humans?

With the implementation of psychotronic brain-entrainment technology that can create impaired recollection of the experiences of five minutes ago, can you even trust your own mind? Perhaps not. However, you can trust your heart-body-mind system and the electromagnetic energy-flow by which it is animated and connected to the Source of Creation.

Just days ago, from a Template attendee, we received the following excerpt from David Talbott and Wallace Thornhill's book 'Thunderbolts of the Gods'

'From the smallest particle to the largest galactic formation, a web of electrical circuitry connects and unifies all of nature, organizing galaxies, energizing stars, giving birth to planets and, on our own world, controlling weather and animating biological organisms. There are no isolated islands in an electric universe'.

It is this fundamental understanding of the infrastructure of the energetic organization of creation that lies at the heart of the Template. Regardless of who did what, when and why, ultimately it is the resurrection of the original Human matrix that will set us free of this fear-based paradigm. With the reconnection of the 33rd Circuit, Jiva and I began to feel our disassociation from this anomalous paradigm accelerate. We were unplugging from the false and plugging into the real.

At its heart, the Template is solution-based. Regardless of your response to the information shared at the Template workshops, what you ultimately take with you, back into your lives, is reconnected circuitry. As all those who have experienced the Template ceremonies know, this transcendent model sweeps aside dogma, icons and indoctrination to offer only the uninterpreted, uncensored energetic truth of creation, delivered by the simple reconnection of electromagnetic energy back into the Human heart-body-mind temple, that truth may open to you, within you. It is an interactive model of transcendence, a model that recognizes that the liberation of Earth and Humanity from duality is intrinsic to the realization of an authentic space-time frequency zone, a frequency that is resonant with the divine immortal continuum, a paradigm that is but a quantum flux away...

25

THE 33ʳᵈ CIRCUIT

AFTER SPENDING TIME with family and old friends, recovering from the initial disorientation brought on by the 33rd Circuit, it was time to return to California for more ceremonies. During our time in Kapoho we had not returned to Green Mountain. The night before our departure we realized we could not leave without doing so. We were due to be at the airport at 11am the next morning. At 8am Jiva began making calls to postpone our flight for forty-eight hours. It was impossible, we were told. There were no available seats for five days, which would have meant cancelling our first two workshops. We were deeply disappointed and felt we had missed an important opportunity through our own inability to face the place in which we had experienced our greatest initiation. We were packing the trunk of our rental car when the phone rang; there had been a cancellation; we would be staying for another two days.

It is often the case that a place or event from the past is recalled with all the embellishment of an imagined memory. When we arrived on the Green Lake property this was not the case. It was even more exquisite than we remembered. At four that afternoon there was a fine layer of cloud obscuring the Sun as we passed the keep-out sign and squeezed through the gap in the chain-link fence. As we made our way along the overgrown path a fine drizzle began, but the air was soft and warm, and the rain did not bother us. My body was taut and buzzing; every nerve on guard, every twig that snapped, every rustle in the undergrowth sent my adrenalin pumping. I looked over at Jiva. He was grinning, partly with the pure joy of being here and partly at my obvious and comical fear as I picked my way along as though walking through landmines. His lack of concern relaxed me, and I began to loosen up and absorb the grace and loveliness around me. The fractal transmissions of the transcendent realm we had experienced were lingering within the charged ambience around us. The colours of the early evening held a psychedelic tinge of vibrancy, a pastel lavender hue washed across the velvet green valley that lay between lake and mountain. As the Sun filtered through the curtain of drizzle and mist, a radiant rainbow burst into the sky to span the property.

The energy of the place reminded us that this was a portal. Between the lake and the mountain, we were standing in the centre of a lush volcanic crater, all around us the sumptuous expression of the Earth in love. We made our way to the edge of the land that fell steeply down into the lake. With the shadow of the coming evening the water was sunless, secret and hidden, a deep and peaceful dark emerald green. The light rain brushed its surface. It had been here all these seventeen years, tranquil and steadfast under the rising and setting of the Sun, while we were rushing around the world. Here we were back again, and it seemed that all the past was but a blink of an eye. Time is a strange phenomenon. This place felt like our true home. In a sense it seemed that we had spiralled back to the beginning of our journey. Although it had begun specifically on the morning that I awoke to the gun pointed at my third eye, it was here on this portal in time and space that our quintessential identities and our reason for incarnating on Earth had been revealed to us.

The juxtaposition of our confrontation with malevolent extra-terrestrial entities with our experience of the transcendent realm from which we had originated and to which we would ultimately return, was purposefully and perfectly planned. We had witnessed the pendulum swing from the depth of the dark to the shadowless light and we had stood on the razor edge between the two. It had been a simple chant of light that had retracted us from the jaws of imminent abduction and catapulted us into a luminous paradigm. The memory of that realm has been the ballast for the many years of initiations, sacrifice, struggle, and occasionally ridicule, which has sustained our strength and determination since we last stood upon this land.

Aware, as we are, of secret technologies that can produce hallucinations and ecstatic states via frequency transmissions, Jiva and I have considered the Green Mountain event from every possible angle. It is not only the experience itself that has elicited our certitude of its authenticity as a transdimensional experience, but also the events of the years that followed. We have lived daily with the Collective Consciousness that set our feet upon that spiraling mountain path. The measure of their compassion, humour, gentleness and transcendent Intelligence manifests in a myriad of ways, each with a unique nuance beyond the contrivance of technology. The signature of this Consciousness cannot be counterfeited. Year upon year, through joy, sorrow, tragedy and comedy they have authenticated their integrity. Coming full circle, we stood that day on the edge of the lake as their emissaries.

The reptilian humanoids we met on the mountain were and are present upon this planet. One of the reasons for which our meeting with them was arranged was to provide us with a point of reference that would allow us to distinguish between what we had experienced and the disinformation with which we would come into contact. These beings were not figments of our imaginations and they were not projected holograms. We cannot live in denial of the influence they have upon our brothers and sisters across this globe and of the suffering they inflict upon them. Neither should we deny their genetic influence upon the behavioural propensities of a race that is quickly becoming not-so-Human.

Our confrontation with the reptilians was frightening,

terrifying in fact. They are obsessively tyrannical and yet they were, even with the help of technology, unable to overpower us. Think about that. We have no special power other than an awareness of our affiliation to the light, to love. It was this simple yet organic power that rose up, not against them, but to greet them. In the face of it, their power seemed hollow and somehow fragile. Jiva and I came away from that meeting in agreement that what these entities wanted most was healing… love. As frightening as the event was, it left no residual trauma, other than a healthy and realistic concern. The experience instead led to an overriding sense of empowerment, awareness and a degree of exultation.

At the workshop in Maui a question was asked that we had been expecting, although we had not prepared an answer for it. That answer came spontaneously as the question regarding the existence of the malefic alien presence was put:

"Why is such a dark consciousness allowed?" Because all must be allowed: because there is choice. Besides, who would police the Cosmos? Who would take it upon themselves to allow this and forbid that? Whoever we are, whoever we have been designed to evolve into, had we been left in peace to engage in our symbiotic evolutionary covenant with light in our solar system, when we triumph over this dark obstacle we will be so much more.

We are in no doubt that our reconnected circuitry has influenced our ability to integrate and synthesize the truth of the global Human predicament. All the circuits have played a part in this, as layer upon layer of electromagnetic life-force Intelligence informed us of who we were beyond the deceit of this dualistic dimension.

We had learned from the Temple of Time Ceremony and its circuitry the importance of our symbiotic relationship with the specific ratio of celestial influence transmitted within the heliocentric embrace of the Sun's light decree. We learned of the cataclysmic disturbance in our solar system that resulted in Earth's distorted orbit of the Sun, which removed Earth and her inhabitants from the holistic space-time continuum. We learned of the insertion of a massive magnetic field of frequency modification, the destructive quantum interference that had rendered us a stolen race on a stolen planet.

The reconnection of the seven circuits activated by the Temple of Time ceremony stirred profound and haunting memories buried in our cellular consciousness, in the labyrinth of the cerebral cortex. As these aspects came clear, other mysteries arose. When did this cataclysm take place? How many extra-terrestrial races were involved? Where did they come from? Who were we prior to this event? How did they usurp our consciousness? How many of the original planets of our solar system were inhabited at that time? From the phenomenon of the structures on Mars it is obvious there was a civilization there.

Is the ghostly devastation on Mars a result of the Annunaki's presence and determination to usurp this planet's place within the symbiotic holography of the solar system? Is it a spectre of our possible future?

The program of total domination on this planet has accelerated since 9/11 and there have been times when the mass apathy and pathological obedience of many of Earth's inhabitants has made us wonder if there is any real possibility of reclaiming our true path of evolution. Since the realization of the 33rd Circuit, our doubts have been reduced, but we are also urgently aware of the need for numbers, for a critical mass of reconnected units of circuitry acting as portals through which the frequencies of the holistic continuum can affect a quantum leap in consciousness.

Reluctantly leaving Hawaii, we flew back to Seattle and arrived in time for our workshops at the 'East West' venue and went on to hold more in Tacoma. In all, this took about four weeks which we spent in a 'Motel Six'. It rained, every day.

With the help of our friends in Arlington, we bought a twelve-year old van and headed over the mountains to California. It was early evening when we left Seattle and by nightfall we were well into the thick of the most mountainous region of the pass. It began to snow. Our old van, weighted down with masses of geometry, was struggling. It began to overheat and, finally, broke down. Miraculously, it had done so outside the only gift-shop and café in miles of wilderness. We sat huddled over cups of coffee pretending that the van just needed a rest and to cool down. Much to our surprise, an hour later the van started up again. Foolhardily, we took off into the freezing snowy night. Later, we learned that these treacherous roads often become snowbound at that time of year and people have been known to perish in their cars from hypothermia.

We spent the last few miles willing the van not to give in as it toiled up each steep mountain pass. We limped into the small town of Mount Shasta at around midnight. The mountain towered ghostly white with snow and moonlight over the silent sleeping town as we pulled into the motel parking lot. Every muscle rigid with cold and the tension of not knowing if our old van would make the grade, we luxuriated in the overheated room and fell swiftly into sleep. The morning Sun appeared in a deep crisp blue sky as we took the descending road out of Shasta, through the winding, thickly forested canyons and over the lapis lakes, a pair of eagles wheeling above us, the scent of pine wafting in the windows. This was America's beating heart.

We were fully revitalized by the journey as the van staggered into San Francisco and dragged itself up the steep mountain pass through the Santa Cruz mountains to the funky Sunny Cove Motel where we caught a few hours' sleep before getting up at five for a radio interview in Monterey. The next day we began our workshops at a mountain retreat in Los Gatos, after which we caught a plane back to Bali.

Since we had last been there, Bali had been hit by a second bomb attack. In many ways this had a more disastrous fall-out than the first. The Kuta bombing was considered to be an isolated incident and, devastating as it had been, the population, particularly those involved in tourism, felt optimistic about the future and busied themselves rebuilding and inventing new ways to attract travellers to their country. After the second attack it began to feel like a pattern. Several governments strongly advised their citizens not to visit Bali and the tourist trade took another hard blow from which it had not recovered. We saw on our return home to Penestanan that things had changed drastically. Even though most of the Balinese-owned holiday rentals sat empty, several huge new houses had been built by members of the expatriate community. The welcome we usually enjoyed from the locals was subdued.

In Bali, when the rice is a couple of weeks away from being ripe enough to harvest, scarecrows and various noisemakers are erected, and the farmer's extended family would fill the field at about 5.30am to yell at the birds who came to feast on the rice, a ritual in which Jiva and I would take part. Over the years, the colourful cotton banners and the bamboo rattlers were replaced by strings of tin cans full of dead batteries, large sheets of corrugated iron, tin or aluminium and bamboo poles with windmills fixed to them with huge rusty nails so as to produce a high-pitched whine. For a couple of weeks after harvest, piles of debris would be burned, and several hundred ducks would be let loose to defecate in the drowned rice fields and eat the eels that bred in them. All in all, it was a loud, chaotic and malodorous business; however, this was Bali and these fields were for rice, not for tourists. For the three to four weeks that spanned the harvest season, in the morning when I wrote, I would play CDs on my laptop to cover the noise and I would spend as much time as possible away from home.

On our return that year the rice was still very young and so we were surprised when the next day eight sheets of metal and four whining bamboo poles were erected around our house. After a few days Jiva approached the farmer and asked why all this noise was necessary when the rice was only a few inches tall and there were no birds. The farmer said he would take down the noise-makers for fifty thousand rupees, about $5. It seemed a small price to pay. A few days later the noise-makers were back; apparently, we needed to pay the farmer's brother...and then his other brother...and his cousin. This went on for some time and the cost of peace kept going up. Worse than that was the lack of mutual respect.

Our home was made of bamboo and thatch. The walls of the bedroom and living/writing area were made of a traditional Balinese material called badeg, woven strips of bamboo which is very thin and has many gaps in its weave. We felt very vulnerable, not only to the noise but also to the psychic bombardment of frustration, anger and resentment that the people, now faced with another level of poverty, were directing at those they saw as so much more fortunate than themselves. They did not understand why Australians and Americans were being warned away from their country when, after 9/11, people were encouraged to continue to give their support and patronage to New York. While their rental homes sat empty, the European homes equipped with swimming pools took the custom of the tourists. The loss of revenue from tourism did not simply engender a less affluent life style, but literally meant starvation for some.

Jiva spent some time creating long sparkling tendrils of kitchen foil and one night draped the rice field with this silent alternative way to deter the birds. One of the farmers was very impressed with these and apologized for the behaviour of his fellow farmers. The extortion continued, however, and we continued to pay up. Sometimes the noise-makers were put up at night or very early in the morning and the farmer could not be found until the next day to be paid to remove them. Even though we felt, for our own personal reasons, obliged to cooperate with the 'rice mafia', other tenants in the surrounding homes did not, either because they spent most days out sightseeing and did not work at home, or because they felt it was unhealthy to buy into such blatant blackmail. We did not resent the money spent, but the many disruptions and the overall bad vibes were making it impossible for me to enter the zones needed to access the information for this book. We had very tight deadlines in order to dovetail the completion of it with the end of our visas and our funds.

The situation was heart-breaking. The most overwhelming feeling was not of blame to be laid on the farmers or even the bombers who had instigated a new level of desperation in Bali, but of the sense of even more widespread global decay that was bleeding into every level of our existence. The situation reached its zenith as building began on a new house a few feet away from us. A tourist moved in nearby who was taking a three-month holiday in Penestanan during which time he would learn to play the saxophone. It was time to move. A friend who had also been suffering this situation had moved to another less populated district and we paid her a visit to see if perhaps we, too, should move to this new community, only to find that she had gone from frying pan to fire. Shortly after moving in, she was kept up all night by the desolate and demented wailing of an animal in distress. The owner of the cow had starved it and tied it up a few feet from her bedroom window. It cost her 400,000 rupees to have the cow fed and removed. A couple of weeks later the pitiful little cow was back again. For an entire week Nora had been kept up by music coming from her local Balinese temple, non-stop, day and night. Finally, it ended, then two hours later it began again and in desperation she went to find out what was going on. She walked through the main doors in the temple to find it was empty. A young man was sitting beside a loudspeaker that was hooked up to a tape player pumping out the music. He was chanting tunelessly on another loudspeaker system. Incensed, she demanded to know what was going on. He confessed that they were trying to get money for their village from the owners of a new mega-hotel that had just been built, by bombarding it with endless noise. Apparently, it had worked before.

This new way of getting money from tourists was rampant and it seemed that everywhere we looked for a new home there was similar problem. Finally, we were shown a tiny semi-derelict house on a small piece of land of about three hundred square feet with a dilapidated gazebo a few feet away. The property was perched at the top of a gulch that overlooked the Ayung River. The opposite bank was a thick lush coconut and banyan forest, the horizon defined by seven mountains. The location was breathtaking: it felt like we were floating above the world and away from all its ills. Due to the steep sides of the gulch it would be impossible to build more homes and, most importantly, there were no rice fields! As soon as possible we signed a five-year lease and began making the renovations that would make the space liveable.

We converted the main building into a big kitchen, tore down the rickety gazebo and, in its place, built a small bamboo bedroom/writing room. We left three sides of the room open to the elements, as we ran out of funds before the walls could be put in. Each bamboo frame edged the vista of the seven mountains that reclined majestically on the far horizon and the sound of the rushing Ayung River was ever-present.

For some years now, our home has been a cat rescue sanctuary. We have anything from eight to twelve kittens at any one time. Often, they will be merely days old and require hand feeding. Before leaving Penestanan a couple of tourists found a kitten on the busy streets of Kuta, one of the main cities on the coast. They had heard about us and brought her to our door. At the time we were in the process of moving and already had eight kittens. I was reluctant to take her as I was behind in my writing schedule and our new home was perched on the side of the gulch. This worried us, as the kitten was completely blind. For several days I tried to find someone in a better position to give her the amount of care I felt she needed. I could not find anyone, for which I am so grateful, as Puka turned out to be the most wondrous companion. Sighted cats are intensely perceptive, but Puka, being blind, was even more so. She relished all of life and seemed to be in a continual state of gratitude for even the smallest of pleasures. She would spend hours 'staring' out at the view of the gulch and mountains and as a bird or insect flew by she would follow it with her head, her large ears twitching. I named her Puka after an invisible friend of Zak's who had joined our family when he was two. It is only recently that we discovered that 'Puca' is Sanskrit for cat! She would sit with me as I wrote each morning and I felt her heightened inner sight somehow assisting in my own visionary process. Puka is gone now. Sensing our departure and knowing her job was done, just days before our departure she disappeared. She had told me that she would be gone soon, and I fully understand her decision, but I grieve still, more sharply for her than I have for any other friend.

Most of our twelve-month visa period in Bali was taken up with the 'Worldbridger' book and it was not until the last two months of our time there that we were able to focus on the 33rd Circuit. It began while Jiva was away in the USA holding ceremonies which would fund the last stretch of our stay. Before he left he designed a piece of geometry that was completed during his absence and delivered to 'Stargate', our geometry gallery in the centre of Ubud. I was so engrossed in my own work that I had not registered that Jiva had been designing a piece of hyper-geometry and I was surprised when it was placed in my hands by our manager, Kadek. I was unprepared, and my reaction was entirely spontaneous: I recognized it instantly as a 'Worldbridger'. I had never seen anything like this before. Jiva later informed me that it was a toroidal hypercube spheroid. It was the first piece of three that would reconnect the 33rd Circuit.

I have always had trouble following the linear explanation of multidimensional physics and parallel universes, but when I first held this amazing piece I resonated with a non-linguistic explanation of hyperspace. As form is the shape of consciousness, so this form expresses the inter-dimensional migration of consciousness. The complex of vortices illustrates the progress of Source Consciousness transiting from one temporal zone to another, bridging worlds. As I sat with this piece, I felt a synchronous vibration activated within the vaults of my genetic seeding. A resonant receptor for this configuration was a component of my prototypical blueprint and delineated the Human ability to experience any time or energy level in the universe.

On Jiva's return from America, we set a day aside to focus on this new piece of geometry. As we meditated on it, it quickly made evident the position of its resonant circuit. We refer to the 33rd Circuit and all the other thirty-two, as 'circuits': however, to be exact, in keeping with the holographic nature of manifestation, they are spheres. A sphere is a hyper-circuit. Several years prior to this, I understood that this final circuit in the Template Model would systemize and codify the holography of the Human complex of circuitry. The positioning of the 33rd Circuit, as it was revealed to us that morning, confirmed this. The 33rd spherical circuit not only encapsulates the entire circuitry network but also informs and calibrates its thirty-two master circuits. The confluence of each aspect of circuitry projects into its centre the holographic semblance of the Human masterpiece.

The 33rd Circuit is a highly charged resonant pathway of continual communication, a stream of Intelligence flowing to and from the conscious entity and its point of sentient sovereign conception. This spherical circuit delineates the brink of our consciousness as it distinguishes itself as a fractal aspect of the whole, of Source: it is the horizon upon which we, as individualized facets of one body of divine Consciousness, simultaneously coalesce and differentiate. This is the threshold at which the varying densities of electromagnetic Source Intelligence converge and substantiate into dimensional compositions. It is from this intersection that we can choose to experience any time or energy level in the universe, from which we may bridge the worlds. However, our ability to do so is dependent upon the frequency of our resonant field of awareness, a vibrational field whose coherence is influenced by the incoming data contained within the delivery system of circuitry. As we alter our vibration, we adjust our affinity to varying densities of dimension. When a critical mass of conscious entities makes this adjustment, a new resonant global field of accelerated collective coherence creates the quantum leap required for planetary transcendence.

The particular paradigm we now inhabit is a temporal-spatial conjunction that has been diverted from the true holistic continuum. It has been perpetrated by a cataclysmic disturbance of the planetary configuration of our solar system, a configuration whose specific arrangement was intrinsic to the symbiotic evolution of every living entity within the embrace of the Sun's transmissions. The deviation from the true continuum set in motion a de-evolutionary state that was cemented by the disconnection of circuitry, the modification of genetic propensities and, finally, the splicing of non-symbiotic genetic material.

When I began writing this book, Jiva and I were aware that when the information regarding the 33rd Circuit was recalled, it would provide a facet of perception that would elucidate some of the events that had taken place in the odyssey of our awakening. When Jiva brought through the other two pieces of hyper geometry that completed the geometric code which would reconnect the 33rd Circuit, we realized its connection with our experience on Green Mountain. As we were leaving the clearing at the top of the mountain that day, we became aware of an energetic sphere of active and numinous light surrounding us. We now realize that this was the illumination of the whole complex of circuitry encapsulated within the spherical 33rd circuit. It was this temporary reconnection that had allowed us to resonate with and enter an alternate paradigm. We had bridged the worlds. When our 33rd Circuit was permanently reconnected seventeen years later in Maui, a fractal of our sentiency was anchored in that transcendent realm. An electromagnetic connection was re-established within the confluence of its temporal-spatial continuum. Humans are not only worldbridgers, but also the bridge.

The propensity towards interdimensional cognizance is a natural Human function that lies dormant in the disconnected mass of genetic resources in the original Human blueprint. This inherent ability belies the Interventionist theory that we are upgraded from primitive, ape-like prototypes.

As I write this, we are a couple of weeks away from returning to Glastonbury to hold the first Worldbridger Ceremony, the reconnection of the 33rd Circuit. I hold within my electromagnetic field of awareness the potency of this circuit. Now aware that an electromagnetic fragment of my singularity is actively present in the transcendent realm to which I have yearned to return for the last eighteen years, my awareness of that continuum is becoming amplified with each day, with each conscious breath.

With the reconnection of the 33rd Circuit, not only is a fractal of our consciousness activated within that transcendent realm, that realm is being funnelled through our heart-body-mind instruments into this reality. Critical mass is required to stabilize this bridge between the worlds. The reconnection of the 33rd Circuit delivers a final fractal of the holonomic Human system and downloads the electromagnetic data of who we are, of the original masterpiece of Human design as it was prior to our capture and genetic modification. As the splendour of our original seeding manifests in our incarnate presence, the anomalies of our past will be reconciled - not that they will matter much anymore.

In the invitation sent out for the first Worldbridger

Ceremony it is listed as the final ceremony and the final circuit, but there is nothing final about it. It is not the end of the Template model, it is the beginning.

26

WORLDBRIDGER

WHEN NEXT YOU FIND YOURSELF staring into the night sky, consider the raw and elemental world of the ancient Mesoamerican shaman astrologers, those visionary calendar priests with their feet planted on an earth free of chemical pollution, gazing into a night sky free of the hindrance of air traffic and city lights. Their appreciation for the evolutionary relevance spelled out in the astronomical grand crosses and alignments that graced their skies drove them to transcend their personal needs and fears, to leave behind all that was safe and to leap empty-handed into the abyss of the unknown, to journey to the Centre of the Galaxy and retrieve the mysteries of time, explaining the implicit order of the Cosmos for the benefit not only of their own communities but of the Human race of the future.

Without the gift of their knowledge, passed down through artefacts and the integrity of their ancestral lineage to be translated by the shaman anthropologist of today, would we even be aware of the portal of opportunity that is now dilating in readiness for rebirth at the end of their calendars? As we look back in awe, so they looked forward, to this, our time; for we live in the time of prophecy, not a prophecy of salvation and atonement driven by guilt and fear, but one written in the empirical language of the stars and planets, that speaks of a coming synchronization of cosmic influences that will open the portals of time; a prophecy not of the end, but of the beginning.

The Mayan sky-watchers understood that, radiating from the Galactic Core, was the supreme organizing principle of creation, a light-encoded directive to be translated through the evolutionary symbiosis that is shared by all conscious entities within the embrace of our Sun's influence. Every day, every breath, every thought, is infused with an all-encompassing numinous Intelligence from the Sun, imprinting on our DNA, with every ray of light, a stream of Source Consciousness transmitted through the prism of the Sun's sentient body from the Benevolent Heart of Creation.

Those shaman astrologers understood that the challenge for Humanity was not merely to survive this time of transformation, but to birth its potential, through individual and collective bio-circuitry, into a manifestly new model of existence, a new paradigm. These sky-watchers ached to be present in these days of culmination, poised before the ultimate Human challenge of the total transformation of ourselves, our world and our solar system. To incarnate at such a time!

But did they know how hard it would be, how much courage it would take to awaken from the narcotic density which is being laid upon our world, creating the convincing illusion that renders us pathologically obedient to its insane political, religious and social structures? They may not have known the sophistication of consciousness manipulation that would evolve through time in this dimension, but they did know that we would succeed. Their shamans saw the future rise phoenix-like, as all the planets aligned with the solstice Sun and the Centre of the Galaxy to instigate the dismantling of the illusions of duality in one true moment of time and space; to calibrate, with the conscious co-operation of Human cosmic comprehension, a new measure of existence.

In the light of this prophesy, are we to betray our ancestors by concerning ourselves with shallow dreams of happiness, with a 'Hallmark' bells-and-smells spirituality that serves as a harbour of false calm in the sea of our present global insanity? Are we to passively accept the false time-space frequency that governs our deepest bio-informational programs, convincing us of a mortally defined parameter in which to organize our short existence? There are countless programs that have been instilled within the mass consciousness of Humanity through its archetypal belief systems, the manipulation of history and an erroneous definition of God. However, the entire memory of the true Human genesis is intact and exists in its entirety in the cerebral cortex, the temple of remembrance. We cannot be deceived forever, for we are the truth.

It is not enough to be informed of the false teaching of our history and ancestry. In order to override the deep indoctrination of this programming we must reinstall tangibly, within the body, the energetic circuit-board that will incorporate a synthesis of electromagnetic data, an omniscience that defines the true transcendental Human. As the Source circuits of the first fractal of the actualization phase put in place the data-feeding circuits of Prime Consciousness, which, through resonance, decode the memory matrix of the original Human blueprint, a deep healing occurs, as fear is diminished by the comfort of the cosmic embrace. It is in the second fractal of the holonomic actualization phase that the seven circuits of The Temple of Time restore resonance within the space-time co-ordinates of the incarnate body presence with the true living archetypes of our Earth, the Sun and five other planets within our solar system. The cataclysmic disturbance in our solar system and the subsequent deviation from our evolutionary relationship with the creative mandate transmitted by Galactic Centre will, ultimately, with the realization of a critical mass of reconnected units of circuitry, be countermanded.

The planetary alignment that zeniths on December Solstice 2012, 13.0.0.0.0, 4 Ahau, is the portal through which the core density of the galactic photon-wave will enter our neighbourhood searching for worldbridgers, for fully reconnected units of bio-circuitry, able to receive and transmit light. The magnetic cooperation of this planetary alignment is an opportunity to override the cosmic disorder within our solar system that is stabilizing the perverted spatial timing frequency of Earth's present dualistic dimension. The alignment of the solstice Sun of 2012 with the Centre of the Galaxy is the eye of a magnetic storm of realignment that will restore the symbiotic evolutionary order of our original solar system. Conscious Human co-operation is essential.

As Humans, our part in this grand realignment is to resurrect our ability to translate the creation mandate of light information and to embody the energetic nature of the true cosmic order. The fundamental requirement to achieve this is the reconnection of our circuitry. Thus, we express our Soul Covenant through our physical beings, becoming the template of light, love and life eternal. We must awaken to the totality of the Human predicament and the truth of what is now manifesting on our Earth. Our destiny and the future of our Mother planet depend on it.

In our present state of disconnection from holistic continuum there is no reference point within our psyche for the infinite. As we gaze into the starry night, we try to imagine eternity, our pulses quicken, we reach for a part of ourselves that might understand a holographic identity, the starlight evoking a distant memory of a world beyond the walls of our homes, the streets of our cities, beyond the pain of being Human. In the starry heavens we feel the possibility of deliverance from the brutality, the genocide, the suffering. In the celestial cathedral night, a fragment of ourselves, immersed in the reservoir of pleasure and causal desire, is free.

We must now breathe ourselves into this starry identity, spinning the wheels of light through our circuits that connect us to the stars, the planets, the rainbow spheres of light that are everywhere. The night will no longer hold the little death of sleep as, instead, we sink through the fiery gates of the setting Sun to explore the indigo depths of space in lucid states of deep communion, no longer looking up to the stars…we play among them.

The Human Soul Covenant contains a holonomic symbiotic code in which the Human design is the sensory organ for planetary ascension as Earth is the sensory organ for Human ascension. As this code is reactivated and integrated through the acceleration of electromagnetic input, via circuitry reconnection, the Human becomes light sensitive, able to join the galactic conversation as every celestial nuance is understood within the occipital receptor at the top of the spinal column, every stellar transmission embraced as the stars and planets recalibrate their intercourse with the Galactic Core. Concentric spheres of cosmic comprehension ripple through the heavens, registering in the shifting sands upon the shores of Human consciousness a holographic celebration of celestial evolution that murmurs…then whispers…then sings, throughout the universe. The awakening has begun…and it all begins with you.

EPILOGUE

My commission as a Mayan king was defined by my responsibility
to dynamically explore the symbiotic intercourse
between the stars that graced our heavens and
to know the prime orchestrating force
that composed their celestial dance.
I no longer dreaded these voyages;
the Navigator and I were one and the same consciousness.

Each voyage would expand the horizons of my visionary range,
imprinting new neural pathways
that allowed me to perceive more of the matrix of governing systems
that animated the holonomic harmony of creation.
Although each journey stretched the boundaries of my ability
to interpret the ever-growing scale of that
which I perceived into my language,
it was not until I shifted from observer to participant
that I was able to retrieve the future aspects of my self, which allowed me
to develop new points of cognitive comprehension and
to extend my memory bank.
I began to travel in time.

My first experience of transiting temporal zones occurred
when I had once again spent the night
in preparation for the shamanic journey
that would begin just before sunrise.
The night, once not long enough,
now stretched out slowly
as I awaited the melting into the light
that would set me free
to travel beyond the constraints of the possible.
As the geometrically coded molecular structure of the vision-medicine
entered the alembic crucible of
my pituitary-hypothalamus-pineal complex,

EPILOGUE

it reorganized the ratio of reality
that tyrannically governed my mind.
Passing through the bardos of my identity I broke free
of the isolated fragment of existence that separated
my conscious awareness from the holistic continuum
and dived into the circularity of true time.

Almost instantly, I found my awareness
on the periphery of the solar system,
observing the Sun's position
as it held the planets within its cocoon of light.
The entire solar system was an intricate interspatial holonomic weave
of co-creative, interactive spheres of light information,
sharing cognizance.
The source of the light data originated from the Galactic Core
and was funnelled into the portal of its hyperbolic centre
to be decoded into cascading matrices of geometric frequency
whose confluent fields of coherence converged
into ever denser and more complex patterns of nesting forms
that blossomed into apparent matter; a symphony of light.
Co-existing fields of varying harmonics
created parallel realities.
By regulating my breath and focus
I could zone into co-existing
and yet differentiated waves of time.
I became aware of my desire to know the future of my own world,
and set my attention on a wave of movement
that brought me hovering above the Earth.

Although I myself was still,
the blue-green planet beneath me
was in a state of rapid and continual metamorphosis,
a seething mandala of living and dying.
This journey I would not share with my people,
for the wonder and the terror of the future that I saw
would be beyond their comprehension.
They did not have the points of reference

to comprehend the inventive diversity of the Human suffering
that lay in the beckoning arms of our future.

From horizon to horizon,
Earth was swept by massive waves of potent light energy
pulsing and pounding down from the Sun,
broadcasting its undefined propensities as pure possibility,
flooding the matrix with light,
its potential never fully manifest,
as its mandate was translated
through the distorted prism of Earth's warped unified field,
astounding, wondrous marvels of creation
degenerating into corruption, depravity, decay.
As the false time-space frequency marched on,
its pollution rippled out into layers upon layers of contamination
as Earth was raped;
her body slowly dying of grief and abuse.
It all lay beneath me;
a feast crawling with vermin,
the pyramids and tower blocks,
the saints and the tyrants,
beggars and kings,
birth and the battlefield;
all the beauty and poetry crushed and broken
beneath the rubble of war.
And as the empires rose and fell
and rose again,
presiding patiently over all, seeing all,
was the Sun,
giving and giving without censorship
its cosmic instruction in the knowledge
that in one moment of true time and space
its waves of divine Intelligence
would turn back this butchering tide of history.
Its full light potential would be realized
as a co-ordinate of immortal divine Presence within each Human entity,
bursting forth as a wave of awareness to break the barriers of fear,
set in place and held there by that mortal emissary…the moon.

EPILOGUE

It was just a matter of time.

As this knowledge washed over me,
I saw, with my heart,
beneath the tragedy and comedy of the living,
the dying and the dead,
that which endured;
the Human spirit.
I saw the gift;
the jewel buried deep in the long dark age of its suffering;
the facets of strength, courage and ultimate invincibility
that, when all was said and done,
would, from the battlefield of its rotting history, rise.
This extraordinary race would not just survive
…it would triumph.
Time and all its many masks of passage upon this race
would be but the blink of an eye.
I felt within myself an expanded sense of identity
as ancestral fragments of one being converged and synthesized
as a multifaceted, inter-dimensional entity.
I saw my self then as a member of this transcendent race,
as a renewed morphic resonant mandala of the Sun's Consciousness,
able to receive its nurture
through my umbilical connection to its field of numinous awareness,
birthing ripples of divine immortal cognizance
spreading through the innumerable chambers of my cellular sentiency.

Too soon the vision escaped me
and merged into the running river of time.
As I sank weightily to my stony throne,
I saw that the Sun was setting...
the Sun that bridged the worlds.

CONTACTS

For more info and events visit:
www.thetemplate.org
Ceremony is a seed - plant it.

Made in the USA
Las Vegas, NV
25 August 2023

76603566R00216